CLOSING THE SHOP

CLOSING THE SHOP

INFORMATION CARTELS AND JAPAN'S MASS MEDIA

Laurie Anne Freeman

PRINCETON UNIVERSITY PRESS   PRINCETON, NEW JERSEY

Library of Congress Cataloging-in-Publication Data

Freeman, Laurie Anne, 1957–
Closing the shop : information cartels and Japan's mass media / by
Laurie Anne Freeman.
  p. cm.
  Includes bibliographical references and index.
  ISBN 0-691-05954-3 (cloth : alk. paper)
  1. Mass media—Political aspects—Japan. 2. Press and politics—
Japan. 3. Mass media—Censorship—Japan. I. Title.
P95.82.J3F74 2000
302.23'0952—dc21   99-31737   CIP

This book has been composed in Galliard

The paper used in this publication meets the minimum requirements
of ANSI/NISO Z39.48-1992 (R1997) (*Permanence of Paper*)

http://pup.princeton.edu

Printed in the United States of America

10 9 8 7 6 5 4 3 2 1

To My Parents

The hottest places in hell are reserved for those who, in time of great moral crisis, maintain their neutrality.

(Dante [1265–1321])

Contents

Tables and Figures

Tables

Figures

WHEN A RESEARCHER embarks on field research, perhaps no question looms larger than the theoretical significance of the project at hand. So it was when I began to study Japan's ubiquitous and institutionally distinctive press clubs (*kisha kurabu*).[1] Are these institutional anomalies of interest only because they are precisely that, anomalies, or do they play a larger role in the framing and presentation of important political and social issues and the way such issues are understood by society and elites in Japan? In short, are Japan's *kisha* clubs merely functional equivalents of newsgathering and news-dissemination routines found in other advanced industrial democracies, or do they have a substantively different impact on the way "reality" is socially constructed in Japan and the functioning of Japanese democracy?

Keeping these questions in the back of my mind, I felt that, as one of the first systematic attempts to analyze Japanese press institutions and the linkages among press, state, and society in Japan, the project was intrinsically an important one. I was pleased, nonetheless, when I was invited by *Asahi shimbun*, perhaps Japan's most prestigious newspaper, to observe the press clubs in the Liberal Democratic party (LDP) headquarters, the Diet, and the prime minister's office. My hope was to be able to gain a better understanding of the role the press clubs play in the flow of information from elites to society by observing them firsthand. I did not expect the experience to be the revelation it soon proved to be.

The way in which I gained access to the clubs was itself instructive, and it serves as a telling introductory example of the kinds of relationships that exist between journalists and politicians in Japan. While my sponsors at *Asahi* had gained permission from the members of a number of important political clubs for me to act as a participant observer, they found themselves in a bit of a dilemma when it came to gaining my entry to the prime minister's office, the Diet, and LDP headquarters, and therefore to the clubs housed inside these organizations. These institutions can only be accessed by presenting official identification cards or badges, but participant observership of a *kisha* club is not a category recognized by state bureaucrats in charge of issuing them. The solution the *Asahi* political journalists devised in order to get me past the guards and reception areas and into the clubs was as ingenious as it was illuminating. The process was actually quite simple, requiring only what the Japanese refer to as "*kone*," a term derived from the English word "connection," here a close, personal relationship.

In this case, one of my *Asahi* sponsors contacted a politician in the LDP with whom he had developed close relations earlier in his career, asking whether the Diet member would mind signing me on as one of his personal political secretaries. Since the Diet member in question had not yet filled his allotment and, as a freshman politician, was unlikely to do so, he agreed to the arrangement even though he benefited in no direct way, as I was to be his secretary in name only. Shortly after I was introduced to the Diet member I obtained the coveted identification badge allowing me free entry to and exit from the prime minister's official residence compound, the Japanese Diet, and LDP headquarters. Though I have always thought it curious that there appeared no other way to get me in, I was thankful to the journalist who had no doubt either cashed in on a debt the politician owed him or taken on a debt of his own in order to get me into the clubs.

Within a month of gaining entry, I was witness to an event that was even more significant in shaping my understanding of the relationship between media and political elites in Japan and the role the press clubs play in that relationship. The story of what happened in the spring of 1990 is worth telling here, albeit in brief.

In May 1990, several weeks before South Korean President Roh Tae Woo was to make an official visit to Japan, the Japanese press began to write a flurry of articles, the central focus of which was the possible wording of the speech (*okotoba*) that the emperor was to make during an official reception honoring the Korean president. Each news organization tried frantically to outscoop its competitors by being the first to publish the actual text of that speech. As the Ministry of Foreign Affairs, the Liberal Democratic party, and the Imperial Household Agency were themselves at odds over how Japan should respond, a considerable amount of "leaking" of what was purported to be the actual text of the speech went on, resulting in somewhat conflicting news reports.

Things came to a head on the morning of May 15, however, just ten days before Roh was to arrive in Japan. On that day, every major Japanese newspaper carried a front-page headline referring to the now famous *dogeza hatsugen* (prostration comment) that they uniformly attributed to "one of the heads of the Liberal Democratic party" (*jimintō shunō*). The media commonly use this phrase when they decide not directly to attribute a statement; the initiated know that it refers to one of only three individuals: the prime minister, the party secretary general, or the chief cabinet secretary. The remark read in part, "it is because we have reflected on the past that we cooperate with Korea economically. Is it really necessary to grovel on our hands and knees and prostrate ourselves any more than we already have?"

Although the Japanese media had neglected to attribute the story, the Korean media soon began to report that it had been Ozawa Ichiro, at that time the powerful secretary general of the LDP (and subsequently the main strategist behind Prime Minister Hosokawa, the first non-LDP prime minister in almost four decades), who had made the statement. The following day, during a meeting with top LDP and government officials, Ozawa apologized for having allowed the problem to escalate, and later that day he met with South Korean ambassador to Japan, Lee Won Kyung, to apologize directly. Japanese newspaper reports of these two meetings were written in such a way that it was never made clear whether Ozawa had apologized for a statement he himself had made, or one that was made by some other "head of the LDP" (this could only have been either the prime minister or the chief cabinet secretary).

On the evening of May 16, *Asahi* broke ranks with a front-page article in which the newspaper claimed that Ozawa had in fact made the *dogeza* (prostration) statement. By the following day, however, *Asahi* reverted to the phrase "one of the heads of the LDP" when referring to the incident, and in the weeks that followed, affiliated publications refrained from attributing the statement to any single individual. What had happened to make *Asahi* effectively retract its attribution?

By attributing the *dogeza hatsugen* to Ozawa, *Asahi* had broken a tacit understanding within the press club that statements made during certain types of briefings can be quoted but not attributed. *Asahi* claimed that once Ozawa had made the apology to the LDP heads and to the Korean ambassador on the 15th, such tacit understandings were no longer applicable. However, by attributing the quote *Asahi* had effectively scooped its competitors, and they were outraged. As a result, Ozawa refused to talk with *any* journalists in the club for several days—another reason why *Asahi*'s competitors were so angry.

As is common in such circumstances, *Asahi*'s competitors in the club called a general meeting of club members during which *Asahi* journalists were made to explain their actions. After they explained *Asahi*'s rationale, they were asked to leave the room. The other club members then came up with a list of "demands" (actually, punishments) that *Asahi* was to follow. The club members stated that while they would take a "wait-and-see" attitude with respect to measures to prohibit Diet attendance by *Asahi*, if similar problems arose in the future they would take such measures. In addition, they demanded that the appropriate person from the political desk at *Asahi* write an apology to the club, and that an *Asahi* representative apologize to Secretary General Ozawa in person. Finally, the club members stated that no *Asahi*-affiliated publications were to be permitted to refer to "Secretary General Ozawa's *dogeza hatsugen*."

Asahi and its affiliates abided by these demands, apologizing to the club and to Mr. Ozawa; several weeks later, the journalist who had been responsible for covering Mr. Ozawa and attending his briefings (a special category of generally neophyte political reporters known as *ban* journalists) was transferred to a club in the Labor Ministry. In fairness to the *Asahi*, however, the newspaper has claimed that this transfer had been in the works before the incident occurred.

The issue of Ozawa Ichiro's *dogeza hatsugen* provides an interesting illustration of the internal dynamics of the Japanese press clubs and the symbiotic relationships that develop between the media and their sources in Japan. These practices and relationships serve as mechanisms for institutionalized self-control; yet because of their informal nature, until now they have remained undetected and little studied.

I was reminded at the time of this incident of Chalmers Johnson's assertion that "the fascinating problem of the study of modern Japanese government (and a source of its considerable intellectual attraction) is the fact that the formal and overt aspects of its institutions *are* misleading as guides to how the society actually works."[2] The formal institutions of the Japanese media in many respects resemble those of other advanced industrialized democracies—many of them were imported from the West during the Meiji era (1868–1912). Japan has a free press, as that term is generally used in the West: there are few formal or legal constraints on press freedom. The events related to the attribution of Mr. Ozawa's statements took place under conditions of no formal control of the press; formal control would have been redundant.

The practice of press group self-censorship is one of the most noteworthy aspects of the Japanese press club system. Codified and institutionalized, the practice is made possible by the cartel-like conditions that form the basis of the club system itself. Confronted firsthand by the implications of these practices, it becomes increasingly difficult to view Japan's press clubs as functional equivalents of the general journalistic practices found in other countries to withhold certain information to protect sources.

My experience as a participant observer in the press clubs provided the "real-life" background within which I carried out the core theoretical and empirical portions of this study. In addition to obtaining participant-observer status in several key press clubs, I also established my own network of relations, both with journalists within the clubs and with those (mostly from news weeklies) who were excluded from club activities. I sought out information on corporate interlocks and ownership, much of which is confidential, and on the history and development of press institutions in Japan. I interviewed Japanese journalists, presidents of major news organizations, editors, foreign journalists, and scholars specializing in the media, and I gathered together a substantial library of materials—both critical and supportive—on the press clubs and the Japanese media in general. I also interviewed members of the Japan Newspaper Publishers' and Editors' Association (and its magazine counterpart, the Japan Magazine Publishers and Editors Association) and obtained detailed histories of this industry association. Finally, I obtained copies of official press club contracts and other press club documents, including the written memo describing the "punishment" that *Asahi* was to receive for breaking ranks in the Ozawa case.

Together, these various materials form the basis for the empirical portions of this book. The chapters themselves are organized as follows. The first chapter provides an overview of the theoretical and empirical arguments of the book. In addition to discussing the general importance of the media in political science, it also introduces the specific institutions through which the media are organized in Japan and the implications of these institutions for understanding state-press-society relations. Chapter 2 reviews the historical development of the Japanese press, beginning with the early Meiji period, when Western press institutions were first imported into Japan, and continuing through to press clubs renascence during the first decade after World War II. In contrast to studies of Japan that emphasize disjunctures in its political processes over the past century—for example, between the wartime and postwar periods—I argue for the importance of significant institutional continuity.

Chapters 3 and 4 develop theoretically and empirically the idea of "information cartels," a major leitmotif of the book. The main focus in these two chapters is a detailed analysis of Japan's press clubs. Now located in approximately seven hundred major business and state organizations, the contemporary clubs serve to control access to and presentation of news in ways suggested above. Within the club structure, sensitive information is limited to an exclusive group of news organizations and is governed by tacit rules of reporting. Reporters and their companies face expulsion if they break these rules regarding confidentiality and the divulgence of privileged information. The clubs are also in large part responsible for the uniformity of views apparent in the Japanese media and make investigative reporting by major newspapers virtually impossible.

Chapter 5 extends the discussion of information cartels by considering them in light of Japan's larger media industry. In addition to reviewing basic features of its industry structure, interfirm rivalry, and readership, I also consider two other institutional arrangements that have effectively extended the club structure—and its consequences—to the entire industry: the newspaper association (Shimbun Kyōkai) and intermedia business groups (*keiretsu*).

Chapter 6 brings the discussion full circle by setting Japan's distinctive press-state-society relations in a broader institutional and comparative context. Three specific issues are considered: (1) the substantive implications of information cartels for understanding the press-politics relationship in Japan, as well as Japanese studies more generally; (2) the extent to which these cartels are distinctive to Japan; and (3) the issue of change and reform in the role of the press in contemporary Japan.

This book could not have been written without the assistance of many individuals in Japan and the United States, some of whom must remain unnamed. My greatest indebtedness, however, must be to the two people who first took me to Japan as a child in 1963—my parents. Without their early intervention I might never have turned to Japan as a source of intellectual fascination or yearned to return there as an adult.

Academically, and in many other ways, I am especially indebted to two individuals who offered substantial intellectual support and guidance—Chalmers Johnson and Robert Scalapino. I can only hope that they feel in some way that their considerable guidance and efforts on my behalf were not wasted.

Several other individuals have been key supporters of my work and are deserving of special recognition. Thomas Gold made important suggestions that were incorporated into this work; Sheila Johnson read an early draft of the book and provided thoughtful comments and support along the way. Susan Pharr, who shares my interest in the Japanese media, invited me to spend an important and intellectually stimulating year as an Advanced Research Fellow in the Program on U.S.-Japan Relations at Harvard University during which a number of the chapters were first drafted. Two anonymous reviewers for Princeton University Press who offered numerous invaluable suggestions which I have incorporated into the book are also among those deserving thanks. My editor, Brigitta van Rheinberg, was also especially patient and supportive.

I received financial support for this project from a number of organizations. I am especially grateful to the Japan Foundation for its grant to carry out research in Japan during 1990–91, and to the Institute of International Studies at Berkeley for providing a Simpson Fellowship. I would also like to thank the Abe Fellowship Program of the Social Science Research Council for funding research in Japan during 1996–97 that allowed me to bring the work up to date.

In Japan, I owe a good deal to two professors at Hokkaido University who oversaw my studies at the Faculty of Law there—professors Hiroshi Kimura and Kenichi Nakamura. It was under their guidance that I first became interested in the Japanese press. I am extremely grateful to Professor Akio Komorida, who has served as my sponsor at Tokyo University on numerous occasions, and Professor Katsura Keiichi, formerly of Tokyo University. I am also indebted to the individuals at *Asahi shimbun* who opened doors for me and sponsored me as a participant observer in several key press clubs. Without their support, I could not have written this book.

Finally, a number of people—friends and journalists—have been truly dedicated supporters of my work. While many of them by necessity must remain anonymous, I would like to express gratitude to a few of those whom I consider close friends—Iwase Takatsugu, Gail Eisenstodt, Jocelyn Ford, Francis Loden, and Joe Loree.

One person's contribution, however, can neither be measured nor be repaid—that of my constant companion and closest friend, my best critic and most enthusiastic supporter, my partner in life, Michael Gerlach. Not only did Michael often take time out of his own busy schedule to talk over my ideas, encouraging me to pursue those that had merit and drop those that were clearly off the mark, he frequently went beyond the duty of friend or spouse, particularly when it came to offering invaluable suggestions for how I might improve the manuscript. Although we have had to endure numerous separations, we remain intellectually and spiritually connected. I can hope for no greater friendship.

As I conclude this book, my daughter, Mera Z., conceived and born while I was working to complete this project, is just beginning to look with awe at her surroundings. I hope to follow in the footsteps of my own parents, taking her to Japan and the rest of Asia and fostering in her a sense of curiosity about the world that will serve as the basis for her own lifelong adventures, literal as well as intellectual.

CLOSING THE SHOP

One

Bringing in the Media

A popular Government, without popular
information, or the means of acquiring it, is but
a Prologue to a Farce or a Tragedy; or perhaps
both. Knowledge will forever govern ignorance:
And a people who mean to be their own Governors, must arm themselves with the power which
knowledge gives.
   (*James Madison, 1822*)

Between consciousness and existence stand
communications, which influence such
consciousness as men have of their existence.
   (*C. Wright Mills, 1951*)

PERHAPS NO INSTITUTION in democratic society has the same Janus-faced
image as the media. On the one hand, they profess and are believed by
many to exist for the good of the public. Their job is to inform their
readers and audiences about important events and help them interpret
those events. They are also to guard against the unrestrained exercise of
power by vested interests—their famous role as the "fourth estate" in democratic society. On the other hand, in order to get the information that
would enable them to play this role, they must locate themselves within
the political and economic centers of state power. This position exposes
the media to possible cooptation by those same powers and affects their
ability to remain independent and objective.

Our normative image of journalism in a free society reflects the idea of
market competition—one of an intense rivalry for information and audiences, and of adversarial relations with sources and competitors. The idea
is that this competition is important to the development of "a vigorous
and diverse marketplace of ideas"—one that nurtures and sustains the social and political life of its citizenry.[1] This is an ideal type that is perhaps
nowhere fully accomplished. Yet the degree to which theory and reality
diverge varies substantially across countries, making this an important, if
underdeveloped, component in comparative political analysis.

This study challenges the applicability of this marketplace metaphor to
the press-politics relationship in Japan. Through arrangements such as

press clubs, industry associations, and intermedia business groups, the media in Japan are dominated by what I refer to as *information cartels*: institutionalized rules and relationships guiding press relations with their sources and with each other that serve to limit the types of news that get reported and the number and makeup of those who do the reporting. By reinforcing close ties with official sources while restricting competition among journalists, Japan's information cartels have redefined the relationship between political elites and news outlets. Instead of anticipating stories and shaping emerging news, the Japanese press primarily responds to an agenda of political discourse that has already been set.

Why should we care about this aspect of the press-politics relationship? Because the cartelization of information that results from the institutionalization of close relations between reporters and official news sources limits the ability of journalists and newspapers to carry out independent reporting and standardizes news reporting within the mainstream press. While these cartels have no doubt proven mutually beneficial for political and media elites in Japan—the first by controlling access to and the dissemination of information about political events, and the second by limiting rivalry among ostensible competitors—the consequences of cartelization for other groups inside and outside of Japan are more problematic.

Consider the following events that have occurred over the past decade, each of which saw the Japanese press play a role not as anti-establishment critic but as active participant:

- In the Recruit stock-for-favors scandal that broke in the summer of 1988, executives from three of Japan's major news organizations were implicated and later forced to resign.
- In the Itoman loans-for-favors scandal two years later, the Prosecutor's Office charged that a defendant in the case had paid a collaborator in the *Nihon keizai shimbun* (Japan's *Wall Street Journal*) and a lesser-known weekly magazine the equivalent of $75,000 to write favorable stories about the scandal-tainted company.

No doubt blatant abuses of media power such as these are relatively rare, yet their existence requires explanation. So too do instances where the press has failed to report stories of obvious importance.

- In January 1992, for example, when U.S. President George Bush collapsed at an official dinner in Tokyo, the American public was the first to see the video of the incident—the Japanese press having acquiesced in toto to a Japanese government demand that it not air the piece.
- A year later, in January 1993, it was again the American public who were the first to learn that Owada Masako, a career diplomat, would wed the Japanese crown prince—the Japanese press having agreed months earlier to an Imperial

Household Agency request that it impose a complete news embargo on the crown prince's search for a bride, a ban that lasted for close to a year.

• In a more alarming case, in 1995 a major Japanese national broadcasting station, TBS, shared with members of the Aum cult (responsible for gassing Tokyo subways) video footage of a critical interview with a lawyer representing families who had grievances against the cult. Several days later, the lawyer, his wife, and their infant son disappeared, never to be heard from again. But TBS never revealed to the police (or its viewing audience) its activities preceding the disappearance, though timely reporting might have saved lives.

Although at first glance these appear to be disparate events, they reveal both the strength of the symbiotic bond between Japanese news organizations and their sources and the peculiar relationship that has formed between ostensibly competitive news organizations in Japan. By looking at press clubs and other cartel-like arrangements, one comes to understand the process by which the flow of information in Japanese society is controlled and regulated. These arrangements also, at the theoretical level, point to limitations in received democratic theory more generally, especially regarding the function the press is presumed to have as the "fourth estate" in democratic societies.

While numerous studies of Japanese political economy have sought to explain the marked degree of state-society interpenetration in Japan, frequently labeling Japan a "strong state," few have sought to explain the role the media play in maintaining state strength. I argue that it is through the various institutional arrangements constituting Japan's media system that the Japanese state, its political leaders, and its bureaucracies are protected from intensive scrutiny. Mechanisms such as Japan's press clubs provide political (as well as economic and intellectual) elites with a convenient means of filtering news and information and socially constructing the worldview held by the public. At the same time, this influence is at least partially reciprocated, as the media provide an important prism through which elites obtain news and information. Indeed, it is in the interaction between the political and media worlds, organized within long-term and often intensive relationships among individuals and institutions, that fundamental features of Japanese state-society relations are evident.

Why the Media Matter

Although the press[2] has long been regarded as a key component of political and social life, its function, power, and effects are not well understood. One of the earliest social scientists to recognize the importance of the media was Max Weber, who in 1910 submitted a proposal to the Congress of German Sociologists to conduct an analysis of the press's role in modern society. Unfortunately, the plan was shelved when he became embroiled in a lawsuit. In the period that followed, scholarship on the media moved forward in fits and starts before finally taking a giant leap backward.[3]

During the interwar period, media scholars, recognizing the potential the mass media had to influence public opinion, turned their attention to the study of propaganda techniques and deception.[4] By 1940, however, and well into the 1960s, the field came under the influence of the work of Paul Lazarsfeld and other media scholars. These observers did media studies—and the fields of political science and sociology—a great disservice by concluding that the media had "minimal or no effects." In spite of considerable evidence to the contrary, Lazarsfeld's Columbia school maintained that the media are merely neutral conduits transmitting information and, therefore, of marginal significance.[5]

While it is difficult to understand how their arguments could have been so influential in the face of competing data, one thing is clear: they had a tremendous impact on the direction of the field.[6] The conclusions reached by Lazarsfeld and others influenced not only academics conducting sociological studies of the media, but also those interested in the press's role in the political process. The impact on political science was so profound that "for years many political studies scarcely bothered to consider the role of the mass media in the crystallization of votes or, more generally, in the formation of public opinion."[7] The media had been so thoroughly marginalized as an area of academic inquiry that even today, on the rare occasions when they are incorporated into studies of the political process, their impact on that process is frequently considered peripheral at best.

By the early 1960s, perhaps weakened by the advent of broadcast media and the dissemination of television, this minimalist view was overtaken by a contrasting idea that held that the media had the potential to exercise power in their relations with both state and societal actors. While vestiges of the minimal effects argument remain, this is the generally accepted view of the media today. It contains, however, two competing strains. On the one hand is the belief—based on a notion first espoused by Edmund Burke—that the media act as the fourth estate to the political process (i.e., as an autonomous force).[8] On the other is the notion of the press as a servant of the state (i.e., as a dependent entity).[9] In either case, the media are seen as playing an important role in the political process, whether as watchdog or government mouthpiece. And in that sense, a good case can be made for "bringing the media (back) in" to studies of contemporary politics.[10]

While each of these is satisfactory as an ideal type, such characterizations belie the complex relationship the media have with state and society.

Rather than assuming a priori that the media are neutral transmitters of facts, agents of the state, or pillars of democracy, a more heuristically useful approach, and the one used here, is to accept that the media play all of these roles at different times and in different contexts. In this *synthetic* view, the media are not only neutral conveyors of information; more importantly, they have multiple institutionalized linkages—patterns of relations with other actors in contemporary society and the state—that serve to limit, constrain, or, alternatively, amplify their role by influencing the messages they convey. By positing that the press's role and impact are variable, we are able to gain a more balanced understanding of their place in contemporary politics and society.[11]

If we accept that the media's role varies, what does this say about our understanding of press power? Ben Bagdikian has suggested that "media power is political power."[12] Political power it may be, but it is not power in the Weberian sense of "the probability that one actor within a social relationship will be in a position to carry out his own will despite resistance."[13] Nor is it power over the allocation of political (or monetary) resources (unless we consider knowledge a political resource), another common definition of power. The power of the media resides instead in their ability to channel information and ideas (both to and from elites, to and from society), to influence the setting and framing of political and social agendas, and to legitimize certain political, economic, or social groups and ideas as they delegitimize others.

The media are powerful because, as C. Wright Mills noted in the introductory quote, "they influence such consciousness as [people] have of their existence." To use more contemporary sociological vernacular, they are powerful because they play a central role in "the social construction of reality."[14] A precondition of organized social life, as McQuail has pointed out, is a degree of common perception of reality; the mass media contribute to this on a daily, continuous basis probably more than any other institution.[15] Gitlin begins his analysis of how the mass media "made and unmade" the New Left with the same basic premise:

> The media bring a manufactured public world into private space. From within their private crevices, people find themselves relying on the media for concepts, for images of their heroes, for guiding information, for emotional charges, for a recognition of public values, for symbols in general, even for language. Of all the institutions of daily life, the media specialize in orchestrating everyday consciousness—by virtue of their pervasiveness, their accessibility, their centralized symbolic capacity.[16]

In short, the media do not just transmit information, they provide us with an ongoing framework for interpreting that information and for defining our social world.

Deriving power from their messages, the media retain that power whether they serve state, societal, or their own interests. Consequently, when groups of nongovernmental elites are asked to situate themselves within a power hierarchy composed of other elites, they have tended to place the media at the apex of that hierarchy. In a comparative study of elites in Japan, Sweden, and the United States conducted by Sidney Verba and his colleagues, "established" elites (labor, business, and farm organizations, etc.), "challenging" elites (disadvantaged minority groups and feminist groups, etc.), and "mediating" elites (political parties, the media, intellectuals) consistently rated the media at the top of an influence hierarchy.[17] As illustrated in figure 1, in Japan all groups except the media (who put bureaucrats slightly ahead of themselves) chose the media as the most powerful elite actor in society—in some cases by a wide margin; in the United States, all groups except the media rated them among the top two; and in Sweden, all groups rated them among the top three. Verba's conclusion concerning the importance of the media is worth quoting in detail:

> That the media are viewed in the same way in three nations so diverse is an arresting finding. The debate about who governs has generated an enormous political science literature, but almost all of this literature, whether of the pluralist or "power elite" school, centers on the political influence of economic classes or of interest groups organized along (mostly) economic lines. Virtually none of this vast literature highlights the influence of the media—a group that makes no campaign contributions, controls no factors of production, and has few votes—much less suggests that the media might be the most influential elite group in society.[18]

The Media and the Political Process: A Relational Approach

In focusing on the linkages among state, media, and society, I adopt a *relational* approach. As that term has been used by Theda Skocpol, states are examined "*in relation to* particular kinds of socioeconomic and political environments populated by actors with given interests and resources."[19] When applied to studies of the state, the relational approach makes it possible to incorporate into the analysis the notion of state capacity, a necessary counterpart to discussions of state autonomy. By recognizing that the state operates within a larger environment composed of actors having their own interests and resources, we can develop explanations for why putatively autonomous states have been unable single-handedly to implement independent goals.

Contemporary comparativists have increasingly relied on a relational approach to explain state-society relations. In his *Between Power and*

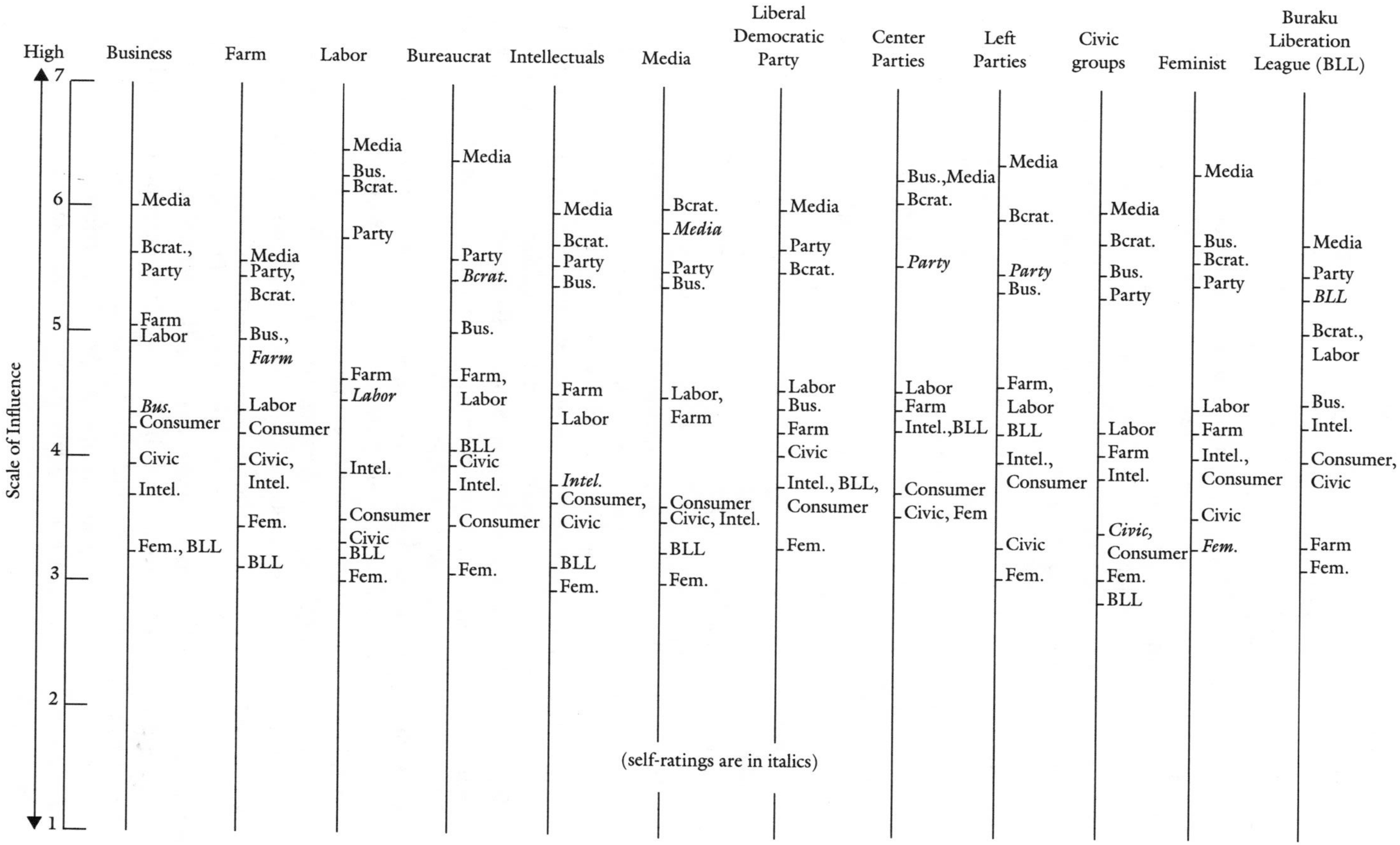

Figure 1. Perceptions of Influence: Mean Ratings of Target Groups by Respondent Groups in Japan.

Source: Sidney Verba, ed., *Elites and the Idea of Equality* (Cambridge: Harvard University Press, 1987), 162. Copyright © 1987 by the President and Fellows of Harvard College. Reprinted by permission of Harvard University Press.

(self-ratings are in italics)

Scale of Influence — High 7, 6, 5, 4, 3, 2, 1

Business
- Media
- Bcrat., Party
- Farm, Labor
- *Bus.*, Consumer
- Civic, Intel.
- Fem., BLL

Farm
- Media, Party, Bcrat.
- Bus., *Farm*
- Labor, Consumer
- Civic, Intel.
- Fem.
- BLL

Labor
- Media, Bus., Bcrat.
- Party
- Farm, *Labor*
- Intel.
- Consumer, Civic, BLL, Fem.

Bureaucrat
- Media
- Party, *Bcrat.*
- Bus.
- Farm, Labor
- BLL, Civic, Intel.
- Consumer
- Fem.

Intellectuals
- Media, Bcrat., Party, Bus.
- Farm, Labor
- *Intel.*, Consumer, Civic
- BLL, Fem.

Media
- Bcrat., *Media*, Party, Bus.
- Labor, Farm
- Consumer, Civic, Intel.
- BLL, Fem.

Liberal Democratic Party
- Media, Party, Bcrat.
- Labor, Bus., Farm, Civic
- Intel., BLL, Consumer
- Fem.

Center Parties
- Bus., Media, Bcrat.
- *Party*
- Labor, Farm, Intel., BLL, Consumer, Civic, Fem.

Left Parties
- Media, Bcrat., *Party*, Bus.
- Farm, Labor, BLL, Intel., Consumer
- Civic, Fem.

Civic groups
- Media, Bcrat., Bus., Party
- Labor, Farm, Intel.
- *Civic*, Consumer, Fem., BLL

Feminist
- Media, Bus., Bcrat., Party
- Labor, Farm, Intel., Consumer, Civic, *Fem.*

Buraku Liberation League (BLL)
- Media, Party, *BLL*, Bcrat., Labor, Bus., Intel., Consumer, Civic, Farm, Fem.

Plenty, for example, Peter Katzenstein uses the term "policy network" to describe the patterned relations that "link the public and private sector in the implementation of foreign policy."[20] Likewise, Stephen Krasner, who takes a more statist approach, recognizes that there are "internal constraints . . . imposed by the domestic society upon the state."[21] Finally, in his *Politics in Hard Times*, Peter Gourevitch examines policy choices in five countries in three time periods and concludes that, "In shaping policy, societal actors and the state interact; the one requires the other. . . . The state, that is to say, may be more active, more able to intervene, but it is not necessarily stronger or more autonomous from society. Indeed, its interventions frequently require the complicity of forces it seeks to regulate or direct."[22] A common thread weaving these studies together is the notion that there is a point where state and society, public and private interests, intersect and become more powerful than either would be alone. In Gourevitch's words, "State action is frequently corporatistic, in that state and groups borrow from each other the authority to do what they cannot do alone."[23]

The above views of state-society relations are not without their critics. Friedland and Alford suggest that in bringing the state back in, Skocpol and others confuse the *factors* explaining autonomous state action with the *aspects* of autonomous state action. Such theories, they argue, "tend to reduce the meaning of governance and political participation to interests in power or resources used by elites to elicit obedience and assent."[24] In short, these theories develop explanations of state autonomy "without resorting to any 'societal' factors to help explain state actions."[25] One of the problems with the way the state has been brought back in to the analysis, they argue, is that it runs the risk of tilting the scales too far, substituting for society-centric analyses those that are excessively state-centric.[26] Skocpol herself is aware of this possibility: "Bringing the state back in to a central place in analyses of policy making and social change . . . does not mean that old theoretical emphases should simply be turned on their heads: Studies of states alone are not to be substituted for concerns with classes or groups; nor are purely state-determinist arguments to be fashioned in the place of society-centered explanations."[27]

But providing this balance is more easily said than done. Even when studies mention such environmental attributes as public opinion or ideology in their empirical analyses, Friedland and Alford argue, they have not found a place for them at the theoretical level.[28] The movement to "bring the state back in" began as a reaction to studies that failed to consider the state as an actor in its own right. But without recognizing the symbolic-social aspects of state power, and the mechanisms by which state and society are connected in ongoing relationships that circumscribe the actions of each, the arguments run the risk of becoming what Skocpol seeks to avoid—state determinist. While the authors mentioned above—Katzenstein, Krasner, and Gourevitch—recognize the interaction between societal actors and the state and their mutual reliance upon one another, the practical application of this viewpoint remains a considerable theoretical and empirical challenge to political scientists.

The Media in Relational Perspective

A central thesis of this study is that the media offer a critical link connecting these two opposing theoretical frameworks. Located in the interstices between state and society, they provide the political scientist with an important component in the development of a fully relational theory—one that focuses on the concrete relationships between state and society and evaluates their impact on one another, and one that considers the ways in which "the institutional structure of society . . . shapes the rule[s] by which resources are accumulated, transformed into capacities for action, and made available as motives by which that action is made meaningful."[29] Embedded in society, the media reflect in many ways the organizational structures and social norms of other institutions in society. At the same time, in their close interaction with the institutions of the state and elite actors, they have a degree of access to information, organizations, and individuals in power that no other nonstate institution has. In short, the media straddle both arenas.

The state-media relationship is also one in which both sides "borrow from each other the authority to do what they cannot do alone," to return to Gourevitch's phraseology.[30] The media need the state to supply them with legitimate sources for their stories, to provide their raison d'être as it were; the state needs the media to bolster its capacity to implement its goals. In a sense, both are giving up an aspect of their autonomy in order to gain a degree of legitimacy vis-à-vis society.[31] The media trade their formal and legal right to more autonomous (though possibly meaningless) action in order to obtain access to information; the state gives up its potential for total control over information in order to become a shareholder in the exercise of media power.

While each of the authors discussed above uses a relational approach to examine the state in relation to nonstate actors, the explanatory value of this approach extends as well to the media and their relation to their own environment. Skocpol's comment about the state applies equally well to the media: they "matter because their organizational configurations, along with their overall patterns of activity, affect political culture, encourage some kinds of group formation and collective political actions (but not others), and make possible the raising of certain political issues (but not others)."[32] The media, like the state, have an independent institutional reality that must be accounted for in examinations of political and social systems, processes, and change. Their intermediate position between state and society thus makes them an important tool for bridging the gap between competing interpretations. For this reason, they need to be brought back in to political analysis.

Japan's Relational Society

Another central argument of this study is that the notion of "relationships" incorporated here has special applicability to the study of Japan, including its press-politics relationship. An emergent view within the Japan field is that Japan represents a strong form of "network society" dependent on informal, long-term relationships within and between key organizations. In contrast, social organization in other Western countries, particularly the United States, is viewed as more fragmented and transactional (i.e., based on shorter-term linkages).[33]

The idea of relational interaction among partially autonomous groupings discussed here is frequently incorporated into the political science literature on Japan. It is implicit, for example, in Samuels' idea of "reciprocal consent" between political and business elites in Japan, which he defines as "the mutual accommodation of state and market."[34] Johnson's study of the Ministry of International Trade and Industry (MITI), which focuses on the high degree of autonomy enjoyed by the Japanese bureaucracy, also discusses the ways in which two practices—"descent from heaven" (*amakudari*) and "administrative guidance"—serve to weaken the boundaries between state and business in certain circumstances. These connections, he asserts, result in a "cozy relationship between officials and entrepreneurs."[35] Okimoto makes these interactions a centerpiece in his own study of MITI, arguing that "Instead of labeling Japan a 'strong' state, . . . perhaps it would be more accurate to call it a 'societal,' 'relational,' or 'network' state, one whose strength is derived from the convergence of public and private interests and the extensive network of ties binding the two sectors together."[36]

One virtue in applying a relational approach to Japan is that it helps to explain the blurring of the distinction between public and private realms that studies have shown is particularly marked in Japan (though certainly not absent from other liberal capitalist democracies).[37] This blurring is no doubt beneficial in some respects. Johnson notes, for example, how "the Japanese have unquestionably profited from the elimination of legal middlemen and the avoidance of an adversary relationship in public-private dealings."[38] Similarly, Katzenstein argues that "The lack of differentiation between state and society is [a] feature of the Japanese situation which facilitates policy implementation."[39] But it is also not without its costs. In the economic world, critics of Japan's trade practices have pointed to ways that public-private blurring reduces access to foreign products and companies, especially where such practices are reinforced by industrial cartels.[40] Garon's recent work on "social management" in Japan extends these costs to social policy. He argues that key "intermediary activists" (including lower-middle-class community leaders, middle-class professionals, organized women, and social democrats) have, in joining together with the state, effectively precluded the formation of alternative social policies in Japan. According to Garon, "their active collaboration more often than not strengthened the state's capacity to regulate society to a greater degree than if a small cadre of bureaucrats had simply imposed its will from above."[41]

Criticisms of economic cartels and social management in Japan are especially relevant to the study of the process of information cartelization by the media. Cartels, after all, involve reciprocal relationships among designated parties, but they also result in the exclusion of outsiders. In so doing, they come to be dominated by the institutionalized interests of a set of privileged elites and impose costs on others in society. And when these elites are the leaders in the social management process itself—members of the ruling party or state bureaucracy, members of the mainstream press— the "outsiders" in the process become the public as a whole, and the costs come in the form of the public's right to know.

Fourth Estate or for the State? Critical Institutions of Press Control in Japan

The relational approach taken here suggests that where the media stand in relation to state and society is a direct function of the specific institutional arrangements that have developed over time for gathering, interpreting, and selling the news. While the media have considerable potential power and a widely recognized influence over politics and society, they are also subject to a number of forces that limit their autonomy and shape the ways their influence is utilized. I focus on three institutions in the cartelization process, termed here the "three K's": *kisha* (press) clubs; the newspaper *kyōkai* (industry association); and media *keiretsu* (business groups). The interrelationships among these three K's is represented schematically in figure 2.

As depicted in the figure, each institutional arrangement represents a distinct level of analysis: The *kisha* clubs focus on relationships that exist between official news sources and the reporters that cover them as well as

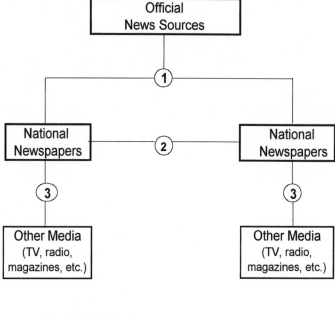

(1) = Kisha Clubs

(2) = Kyokai

(3) = Keiretsu

Figure 2. Key Connections within Japan's Media Networks.

relations among journalists from competing firms; the Newspaper Association organizes relations at the industry level among news agencies themselves; and the business groups link the critical print media with other sources of news available to the public. Each also has a distinct impact on the content or flow of information in Japan, and therefore on the state-media-society relationship.

First, and by far the most important, are the institutionalized linkages journalists have with their news sources—bureaucrats, politicians, business leaders, the police, interest and consumer groups—and each other. These influence the impact, content, and slant of the media's messages. While such linkages may be constant and enduring, their effect varies across time, space, and issue area. The task in trying to understand the media's function in the political process, then, is to determine the conditions under which they play one role rather than another by demarcating the boundaries and strengths of these institutional ties and by describing the rules and practices that govern their behavior. Here we must answer such questions as: What actors have access to the media and on what terms? Whose view of the world ("reality") and events is presented? What news stories are ignored or underreported?

In the case of Japan, these linkages are organized through a well-established network of press clubs. These clubs are located in most of the major business, state, and political organizations, and serve to control access to and presentation of news. Although their exact number is not known, it is estimated that there are more than one hundred clubs in Tokyo alone, and anywhere from seven hundred to one thousand nationwide.

The clubs are fundamental to the cartelization of information in Japan. As chapters 3 and 4 discuss, they share with other cartels three defining features: First, membership is limited to an exclusive group of news organizations (including major newspapers, broadcast stations, and wire services) that hold a virtual monopoly over news sources. Second, there are strict rules governing the activities of members, which prohibit much of the kind of independent and investigative reporting one finds in less cartelized systems. And third, there are strong sanctions against violators of these rules and effective means of enforcing them.

In considering the second institution in the news cartelization process—the newspaper association—it is important to note that successful cartels anywhere typically require the intermediation of an industry trade association (in Japanese, *gyōkai* or *kyōkai*). In the case of the Japanese press, this role is played by the Nihon Shimbun Kyōkai (Japan Newspaper Publishers and Editors Association). The Newspaper Association, discussed in greater detail in chapter 5, monitors the management of the clubs, has the ultimate authority to make judgments regarding their role in the gathering of news, and arbitrates disputes arising from the club system. As such, it acts as the legitimating and adjudicating overseer of the press clubs. Only those companies that are members of the association can gain admittance to the clubs. This means that weekly and newsmagazines, freelancers, industry newspapers, party and religious organs, and (until recently) foreigners are excluded.

Interestingly, the Newspaper Association has on numerous occasions during the postwar period been unwilling to make unambiguous rulings about the clubs' proper function, vacillating between arguing that the clubs are nothing but collegial organizations for member journalists to gather together to socialize and recognizing their important role in the newsgathering process. One of the association's major policy concerns has been to prevent the clubs from becoming autonomous organizations outside of its control. It has been less concerned with the reality that the club system itself has, if not by design then by actual practice, placed journalists in a position whereby the news they report and the agenda that gets presented are primarily those of their official sources.

The third category of ties requiring attention are the direct relations among the different media. Although Japanese newspapers are influenced by the existence of other sources of news, in many cases this influence has been managed by intermedia control through ownership, financing, and personnel ties. In extreme cases, these may take the form of media conglomerates—what Bagdikian refers to as "the media monopoly."[42] Such linkages are common to all advanced industrialized democracies, but the histories of their development, extent, and impact vary considerably. The shape these take, I argue, reflects broader patterns of social organization and is national in origin.

Better known in their industrial context, Japan's *keiretsu*, or business networks, are pervasive as well in the nation's media businesses. Most newspapers, television stations, and weekly magazines are organized within diversified media groupings interlocked through complex networks of news dissemination, ownership, and control. Japan's most powerful and prestigious newspapers form the apex of extended groups that typically include television and radio networks, a family of weekly magazines, and a variety of nonmedia firms. These dominant newspapers, of course, are themselves part of the press clubs and the Newspaper Association and therefore must keep an eye not only on the news they report, but on the news reported by their family enterprises as well.

National Newspapers and Japan's Media Industry

These three institutions—*kisha* clubs, Shimbun Kyōkai, and media *keiretsu*—provide the underpinnings for Japan's information cartels. Before analyzing them in detail, however, it is worth reviewing several overall features of Japan's media industry. While it is true that the Japan of today is a complex, multimedia environment, it is also evident that newspapers, and especially the national dailies, remain by far the most important media outlet in the news-making process. This central role as conduit for serious news is reinforced by the high levels of concentration in the media industry and the lack of an independent, mainstream alternative.

In considering the main players in Japan's media industry, one must first turn to the newspaper press, which enjoys one of the highest per capita readership rates in the world, with an average dissemination rate in 1993 of 580 papers per 1,000 people, behind only Norway (610 per 1,000) and Switzerland (592 per 1,000). The average Japanese household receives 1.2 newspapers per day, about 1.4 times that in Great Britain and 2.2 times that in the United States.[43]

Japan's core print media include five national papers: *Yomiuri, Asahi, Mainichi, Nikkei,* and *Sankei.* These five dailies are each among the world's ten largest newspapers, as measured by readership, with individual circulations ranging from three to fourteen million. In addition, Japan has four "bloc," or regional, papers (*Hokkaido, Tokyo, Chunichi,* and *Nishi Nihon*), as well as ninety-eight local papers that, for historical reasons, are based in local prefectures.[44] While many households in Japan subscribe to more than one paper, it is the five national newspapers that dominate the industry overall, constituting more than half of the total newspaper market share in Japan. When the four bloc papers are added, this number surpasses 60 percent.[45]

Magazines represent another popular print medium, and one that was the main alternative source of information to newspapers before the advent of television. In 1992 there were 2,341 monthly magazines (with estimated monthly circulations of 2.8 million) and 83 weekly magazines (with estimated weekly circulations of 1.9 million). There are also various comic magazines (many intended for adults) and magazine-book hybrids known as "mooks" (magazine-like books).[46] About half of these magazines are published by companies tied by financial relationships to one of the big five national newspapers.[47] Many of the remaining magazines are produced by large publishing houses. The latter are often more willing to pursue independent reporting than are their *keiretsu* counterparts but also tend to be sensationalist in tone, and the information carried in them is often less reliable due to their lack of direct access to key elite sources. Among the most highly regarded is *Bungei shunju,* which gained considerable fame in 1974 after it published an exposé on then Prime Minister Tanaka Kakuei.[48]

In the field of broadcast media, Japan has one national public service television station (NHK) and 123 commercial stations scattered around the country. It also has 47 ground-based AM radio stations, 43 ground-based FM stations, and 11 companies operating channels through satellite broadcasting.[49] Although TV is now pervasive in Japan, with an estimated forty million Japanese households owning seventy million TV sets, its role in news reporting has until recent years been limited.[50] For nearly thirty-five years after television was introduced to Japan in 1953, NHK was the only station to carry a regular news program. Its monopoly assured, NHK news programs were generally bland and boring, their newscasters' lackluster performances enough to make even the most diehard watcher want to change the channel (had there been an alternative, that is). In the most thorough English-language discussion of Japanese television news, Ellis Krauss describes the NHK's evening news broadcast as follows:

The anchors . . . are generally conservatively dressed, with the unsmiling male anchor looking particularly stolid in his round-rimmed glasses, having the look and demeanor of a serious businessman. The female anchor smiles more often, but would pass unnoticed among younger middle-aged mothers at a PTA meeting in Japan. . . . Neither infuses the program with much personality, and neither uses a trademark sign-off—no "that's the way it is" or "courage."[51]

Adding to the monotony is the content of NHK's news coverage, which reports primarily from official news sources, often in settings such as formal conferences, and rarely adds editorial insight or perspective to the proceedings. As a result, Krauss is rightly skeptical of the watchdog view of NHK: "If this view has any validity for television, one would expect to find patterns of television news that emphasize the conflicts of government, opposition parties and protest movements, and the failure of policy. But this is not the case."[52]

Surely the banality of NHK broadcast news was one of the reasons the Japanese public relied more heavily on their newspapers for important news for much of the postwar era. An important turning point occurred in 1986, however, with the airing of the first commercial TV news program, Asahi Terebi's "News Station." Since its introduction, Asahi and its four competitors have begun to produce regular news programs and to compete with both NHK and their parent organizations—the newspapers—in providing news about politics, economics, and so forth to the Japanese public. But Krauss is as skeptical of these new competitors as he was previously of the NHK: "If News Station injects a somewhat healthy attitude of cynicism toward both bureaucrats and politicians . . . it does not, however, provide either a marked alternative viewpoint or true investigative journalism."[53]

On the surface, then, there appear to be a number of mainstream alternatives in Japan to the newspaper press. But the existence of media sources other than newspapers does not mean that they serve as effective substitutes. When examined more closely, as we see later, it becomes apparent that these alternatives are not as substantial, independent, or diversified as might first appear. Not only do local newspapers and many magazines maintain close financial and information ties to the dominant national dailies, so too do Japan's five national commercial television networks: Nippon Television Network with *Yomiuri*, Asahi National Broadcasting with *Asahi*, Tokyo Broadcasting System with *Mainichi*, Television Tokyo with *Nikkei*, and Fuji Television Network with *Sankei*. These ties extend to regional broadcasting stations as well, nearly all of which are also part of these five media *keiretsu*. Among the major broadcasters, only the "gargantuan semiautonomous public entity" of NHK retains financial independence from this industry structure.[54]

Given the importance of the national dailies in the Japanese news reporting process, it is worth considering their basic features in more detail.

One of the striking things about Japan's nationals is that, despite having circulations in the millions, they represent "quality" rather than "popular" (or "mass") newspapers. In other countries where national papers play a central role, there is a tendency to differentiate papers based on the style of reporting and the nature of readership. National newspapers in Britain, for example, are targeted either for elites, intellectuals, and professionals (e.g., *The Times, The Guardian, The Independent, The Daily Telegraph*) or toward an even larger audience of middle- and working-class readers with a considerably more sensationalist outlook (e.g., *The Sun, The Daily Mirror*, and *The Daily Mail*).[55] A similar pattern can be found in Germany, France, and Italy, where the largest-selling newspapers again tend to be popular, as opposed to quality, papers.[56]

In Japan, however, the core print media represent a hybrid—they are both "quality-oriented" (as opposed to sensationalist) and "mass" (in terms of their readership levels). This combination has important virtues in terms of producing serious but widely read news. The national dailies produce a paper that is consistently sober-minded rather than sensational. But as we see in later chapters, the very size of their readership has had the perverse consequence of preventing Japan's major dailies from writing about controversial news subjects that might alienate their readers. They have largely avoided independent pursuit of scandals involving the elite of Japanese society and have also refrained editorially from taking partisan political stances.[57] These efforts to maintain high circulation levels by appealing to a very broad-based readership have resulted in a "neutrality" in their dealings with news sources, but this neutrality is that of the closely linked insider who rarely challenges the status quo, rather than that of the independent outsider.

There are also several less important differences. To begin with, unlike many Western papers, where stories are broken up to be continued on another page, each article can be found in its entirety on a single page, with related articles generally close by. This practice is made possible through a format known as *mendate*, where pages of the newspaper are reserved for a certain category of news—either general, political, economic, international, social, or sports.[58] While this makes the Japanese newspaper more reader-friendly, articles tend to be shorter than their Western counterparts.

More substantial distinctions appear when one examines the employment and labor practices of Japanese newspapers and the impact these have on the structure, style, and organization of the newspaper. As is the case in many industries and businesses in Japan, newspapers have adopted the practices of "lifetime" employment, seniority wages, and enterprise unions, the "three pillars" of Japanese management. These practices have had a fairly predictable impact on journalists' career patterns, on the norms and behavior for newsgathering and writing, and thus on the printed page. Two outcomes at least partially driven by these practices are the lack of bylines and a related "groupism" among Japanese journalists. Until quite recently, the only Japanese journalists to have bylines have been those living abroad as foreign correspondents. As a result, most of the well-known journalists in Japan (and there are relatively few) are broadcast, not newspaper, journalists. In a survey conducted in 1995, when a group of university students was asked to list the journalists whose names they knew, not a single newspaper journalist was among those listed. Those most frequently mentioned—Kume Hiroshi, Tahara Soichiro, Chikushi Tetsuya, and others—were all TV personalities. And at least one of them— Kume Hiroshi—considers himself an "entertainer," not a journalist.[59]

With wages and promotion determined by seniority, and articles often written by groups of journalists rather than individuals, there have been relatively few incentives for journalists to establish name familiarity with their readers by practicing aggressive, investigative journalism. This situation is exacerbated by the fact that most Japanese journalists are on a career track for promotion to management, frequently moving to management positions by the time they are in their mid-forties and leaving Japanese news organizations without a sufficient number of veteran or specialist reporters on the beat. Another, and perhaps more important, consequence of the "corporate" nature of the news profession in Japan is that many journalists are increasingly dissatisfied with the profession, seeing their work "not as a calling but as 'just another job.'"[60]

These differences in the reporting function are also reflected more generally in what is perhaps the single most striking feature of Japanese newspapers to a Western observer—their high degree of uniformity, homogeneity, and standardization. Comparing random issues of the three major national newspapers, one student of the Japanese press found that there was an "extraordinary uniformity or similarity in the angles employed and the degree of emphasis allocated to particular news items," and that "the expressions used in headlines and subheads as well as the items chosen for major treatments are remarkably similar."[61] Yamamoto Taketoshi, a sociologist and historian of the Japanese press, has also commented that "Rare indeed is the capitalist nation that has print and broadcast media that carry such uniform news as Japan. If you were to hide the masthead, it would be virtually impossible to tell from the contents which newspaper you were reading."[62] Even a recent report published by the Newspaper Association, admitted that a large number of newspaper editors queried were concerned about the lack of an "independent front page" (*koseiteki na shimen*) in news reporting.[63]

In sum, Japan's daily papers are characterized by their high quality, large and broad-based readerships, lack of political affiliation, and considerable

homogeneity. A highly educated professional elite—graduates of the nation's most prestigious universities—Japan's journalists share an educational background similar to that of the political and bureaucratic elites
who are the major sources for many of their stories.[64] At the same time,
the Japanese not only are among the most prolific newspaper readers in
the world, they have been particularly loyal to their newspapers for most
of the postwar era. A Newspaper Association survey conducted in 1993
found that "70% of the people 18 or older said that they trusted their
newspapers, 74% said they read the newspaper every day and the average
time spent reading the newspaper was 41 minutes per day."[65] These are
numbers that newspapers in most other countries would covet.

What Role for the Japanese Press?

The study of the Japanese media helps us fill in a critical but underdeveloped component concerning the nature of state-society relations in Japan.
Is Japan a "strong state," as some have suggested? Or is it a pluralist system
where interests get mediated in relatively distinctive, yet nonetheless real,
ways? Alternatively, as another observer has suggested provocatively, is
Japan a "stateless" society, made up of numerous semiautonomous entities
with no ultimate arbiter of power at the top?[66] A study of Japanese press
institutions contributes to this debate by identifying a key intermediary
in state-society relations that plays a part in determining state capacity. If,
for example, the state is a more powerful force in the economic, political,
and social life of Japan than it is in most other advanced industrialized
countries, then this should be facilitated by the media institutions that
shape opinion within each arena.

I argue that the reality of the mainstream media in Japan is different
from the various roles sometimes ascribed to it. While it rarely plays the
role of independent "watchdog" of the state, the alternative images of the
media as "servant" of the state or as neutral "spectator" do not quite capture their role either.[67] Neither image is sufficiently attentive to the independent interests of the mainstream media itself or to the tangible benefits
they have received as members of information cartels in promoting their
interests against the outsider media. Rather than merely serving the state,
or observing it from afar, they have been active collaborators with the
state in a system of mutual convenience. Their role is closer to that of
coconspirator in the cartelization of the news in Japan: benefiting from
close ties with official news sources; collaborating with each other to exclude outsiders from the same benefits; and, very occasionally, breaking
cartel agreements when they believe it is to their advantage.[68]

It is clear that the press has a critical role to play in the Japanese political process. Yet it is also clear that the extent to which it has been able to effectively carry out this role, and the precise mechanisms used, must be addressed in a systematic, empirical way. How successfully has the Japanese press been able to monitor powerful political and bureaucratic actors, and how has this changed over time? Which specific institutions serve to strengthen or hinder the media's ability to challenge differing interests, and which serve to represent the media's own interests? Finally, what distinguishes these institutions from those of other liberal democracies? These are the issues to which we now turn.

Two

Press, Politics, and the Public in Historical Perspective

Let them serve you, but keep them ignorant.
  (*Anonymous*)

Show me a man who thinks he's objective, and
I'll show you a man who's deceiving himself.
  (*Henry Luce*)

THE PRINTED press in Japan differs from that of Europe and the United States in its origins, the timing of its introduction, and the very different political and social milieu in which it was nurtured. The two most important developments in the history of the Japanese press are the rapid rise during the late Meiji (1868–1911) and early Taishō (1912–1926) periods of a dominant organizational form with a distinctive editorial and management "philosophy" (*fuhen futō*) and the concomitant establishment of the cartel-like newsgathering associations known as *kisha* clubs. These developments served to solidify the relationship between the press and the state in profound ways, circumscribed the press's fourth estate and agenda-setting functions, and had serious implications for the development of a democratic polity in prewar and postwar Japan.

Antecedents

Although newspapers first appeared in England during the seventeenth century and Americans were using the medium to publish dissent as early as 1721, the first Japanese-language newspaper was not published until 1862. By that time, the presses of Europe and the United States had already achieved prominent positions in political and social life. By the middle of the nineteenth century, when the Japanese first began to learn of this Western "invention," the British press was already referring to itself as " 'the Press,' with a capital letter. . . . Eager and seemingly equipped to exercise a decisive influence on the course of national—and, by extension, international—affairs, these custodians of the printed word arrogated to themselves the designation of the Fourth Estate."[1]

Having delegated to themselves the roles of government watchdogs and spokespersons for the public, the European and American press had played an important and relatively independent part in the maturation of politics and the increasing sophistication of society. Their growth coincided with the transition from subject to citizen, defined in part by the gradual attainment of one important and inalienable right: the right to carry on a frequently vociferous and public discourse about the affairs of government. Not only had newspapers been "both agent and expression" of an important social change in the West—the rise of civil society—they had played a critical role in the establishment of a legitimate locus for the public's voice in public policy, the creation of what Habermas has called the "public sphere."[2]

But the situation in Japan could not have differed more substantially. While the West underwent important social and political transitions, Japan remained feudal in its political institutions and economy. Its inhabitants were subjects, not citizens. For two and a half centuries, the nation had lived under a peace imposed and administered by the leaders of the feudal Tokugawa *bakufu* (1603–1868). Fearful of Western intrusion and wary of the impact of Western ideas and religion on the nation's subjects, the *bakufu*'s rulers had closed off the country to all but a modicum of contact with the West. Desiring total control over their subjects, they pursued an obscurantist communication policy best summarized by the phrase "let them serve you but keep them ignorant," enacting draconian regulations on the dissemination of information.[3]

The "closed door" (*sakoku*) policy administered by this coterie of elitist samurai-bureaucrats was an early and extremely successful experiment in information control, one whose legacy remains today. Still, although Tokugawa rulers sought to restrict the flow of information and ideas to their subjects, they had not completely isolated themselves from the outside world. In exchange for permission to conduct a limited commerce, Dutch and Chinese traders residing on a small island in Nagasaki known as Deshima provided the shogun with an annual summary of the state of the Western world.[4] These tidbits of information were considered state secrets: only the members of the shogun's Council of Elders (Rōju) and other important members of the cabinet were allowed to read them.[5] Access to information—whether about affairs of state or the state of the world—was understood to be a privilege, not a right, granted to only a few.

Restrictions on the dissemination of information meant that the newspaper was unable to evolve independently as an organizational form in Japan. So effective were these controls that almost no one in late Tokugawa or early Meiji Japan knew precisely what a newspaper was or what purposes it might serve. Indeed, in 1866 the well-known, beloved educator and introducer of things foreign, Meiji Japan's most prominent citizen

Fukuzawa Yukichi, found it necessary to include a chapter on newspapers in his best-seller describing Western institutions, *Seiyō jijō* (Conditions in the West).[6] But Fukuzawa chose to ignore the medium's more politically sensitive role as Fourth Estate watchdog. Focusing instead on the newspaper's educational and entertainment potential, Fukuzawa explained to his readers that "apart from the great personal pleasure to be derived from reading newspapers . . . they [are] unequaled *as a tool of education* and as a means of getting on in the world."[7]

Confronted by domestic forces for change such as "the impoverishment of the samurai, the growth of a market economy, and the emergence of new social classes," on the one hand, and the external push to open up the nation to trade, on the other, Tokugawa elites realized that they would have to implement changes if the nation was to maintain its independence and sovereignty.[8] The *bakufu*'s inability to do so quickly enough, however, led to its ultimate downfall. Thus, although the Tokugawa government published the first Japanese-language newspaper, the *Kanban batavia shimbun*, in 1862, the regime's Meiji successors made the first real attempt to use the new medium as a tool to gain support for the government's modernizing aims.[9]

The printed press became one of numerous Western institutions imported in the waning years of the Tokugawa era and the early part of the Meiji period to aid in the rapid modernization of the country, the establishment of a modern state, and the "civilization and enlightenment" of the public. In contrast to the West, where the rise of the press had been inextricably bound up with the development of politics and the creation of *society* (what Hannah Arendt has described as "that curiously hybrid realm where private interests assume public significance"[10]), "the Japanese press came into being almost simultaneously with the modern Japanese *state*."[11] Like the Meiji Restoration itself—often referred to as an "aristocratic revolution" or a "revolution from above"—the press had been introduced by and for elites; citizenship was neither a prerequisite nor a motive force.[12] This aspect of Japanese press history—its introduction by the state—would have a profound impact on the medium's development.

Establishing the Press-State Nexus

Once the Meiji leaders gained control, they found themselves in a tenuous position: not only was their power base a fragile one, they knew that in order to avoid the fate that had befallen China and to renegotiate the unequal treaties the Tokugawa government had signed with the Western powers, they had to quickly build Japan into a modern nation-state, one capable of competing with the West.[13] Dedicating themselves to the at-

tainment of a "rich country and strong army" (*fukoku kyōhei*), the leaders
of this emerging developmental state introduced state capitalism, working
to gain a consensus for modernization through the civilization and enlightenment of the masses. Naturally, the Meiji leaders were aware of the
potential of the new newspaper medium as a tool in reaching these goals.
Indeed, as one historian of the early Japanese press pointed out, they
promptly set out to "[use] the young press as an adjunct of government
. . . , [a] channel through which to transmit information about the government's policies and accomplishments, and as an instrument for convincing
and persuading the population to accept the new national framework in
which its life was now set."[14]

Eager to use this new vehicle for the dissemination of information about
their modernizing aims, the Meiji leadership quickly set out to nurture its
development.[15] At the same time, they sought to establish and maintain
close ties between themselves and the editors and journalists. In short,
while they aimed to make the inchoate newspaper press financially stable,
they also wanted to make sure that it was politically malleable.

The Meiji oligarchs relied on a variety of mechanisms to accomplish
their dual aims of development and control, but three stand out as particularly noteworthy. First, they provided direct and indirect financial support
and subsidies to the fledgling newspaper industry, much as they did for
other developing industries. Second, they employed legal constraints and
extralegal and informal incentives to keep opposing viewpoints at bay and
delimit the legitimate role of the press in society. Finally, relying on the
shared understanding of duty and service to nation found among Japan's
Confucian-educated elites, they worked to cultivate close ties with the
press, establishing networks of relations between themselves and the editors and journalists of key papers. Because subsequent governments
throughout the prewar period used each of these mechanisms to control
and mold the press in ways beneficial to the state, they are worth considering in some detail here.

Providing for Financial Stability

All of the most influential early newspapers—including the *Yokohama
mainichi shimbun* (1870), *Shimbun zasshi* (1871), *Nisshin shinjishi* (1872),
Tokyo nichi nichi shimbun (1872), and *Yūbin hōchi shimbun* (1872)—were
subsidized or sponsored by prominent officials and/or the government
itself.[16] Even newspapers published by foreigners residing in Japan received
financial favors from the Meiji government. The *Nisshin shinjishi*, for example, was published in Japanese by the Englishman John Reddie Black
and was known to have had government sponsorship through the close ties

Black's partner, F. da Roza, had with government officials.[17] Additionally, according to Huffman, the English-language *Tokio Times* "existed only because of a secret financial arrangement between Finance Minister Okuma and its editor Edward H. House."[18]

A second method employed by the Japanese government to bolster the financial standing of the infant press was to require prefectural and local governments to buy newspaper subscriptions. Based on this arrangement, "the finance ministry purchased 3 copies of every issue for each of the 72 prefectures and three *fu*," setting aside additional funding for local governments to purchase their own subscriptions.[19] Not only did the government's purchasing policy popularize these papers, it gave them a considerable financial edge. One author notes that "Official purchase, in addition to lending prestige, greatly benefitted newspapers by guaranteeing a sale of about 175 copies per paper per issue. This was crucial in early days, when official purchase probably accounted for over twenty percent of sales."[20] Additionally, the government played an important role in the establishment of prefectural reading rooms where individuals could read papers themselves, or, in some cases, have them read to them and their contents explained by local officials.[21] They also proffered discounted postal rates[22] and provided assistance for the development of modern metal-type printing presses, which they offered to individual newspapers in exchange for their continued loyalty to the state.[23]

Two of the most effective methods of cementing the early press-state relationship were the covert placement of journalists and editors on government payrolls and the payment of subsidies to individual papers. Because early newspapers were inherently unstable and journalists' salaries notoriously low, these methods proved to be extremely effective means of co-optation and were employed with considerable frequency, both with lower-level information gatherers and with newspaper management. The journalist Tokutomi Sohō, for example, well known for his close relationships with Yamagata Aritomo and Katsura Tarō, was among those who were "amply repaid for marching in step with the oligarchs."[24] The state rewarded Sohō with "the psychological satisfaction in being close to the powerful, as well as receipt of inside information, political favors, and *outright payments of cash*."[25]

Evidence indicates that the Meiji government made covert payments to a number of newspapers, including an initial investment of 100,000 yen in the *Tokyo nichi nichi* and subsequent monthly subsidies of about 1,000 yen.[26] In 1882, a year after the *Nichi nichi* reorganization, a dummy company was established to supply covert subsidies and capital to the *Osaka asahi shimbun* (1879), the paper that would eventually become the industry standard.[27] Itō and Akita have concluded that there is "ample precedent for this exchange (e.g., cash for loyalty) in government-press relations in Japan" throughout the prewar period.[28] In 1927 Wildes commented that "As long ago as 1876, the *Japan Mail* suspected that the *Nichi nichi* men were being carried on official payrolls. Forty years thereafter, two editors, Kuroiwa of *Yorodzu* and Matsui of *Yamato*, charged that papers 'carefully cooked their news to please the influential moneyed patrons.' "[29]

At the time Wildes was writing, the state was not the only entity trying to influence the press. Prominent politicians and members of the *zaikai*, or financial world, also understood the value of having a press "on their side." Lower-level journalists in the press clubs were offered gifts, cash, and even stock in the companies they were covering in return for favorable stories.[30] In 1915 the newspaper *Nihonjin* claimed that the Marquis Okuma had bought off journalists in eight newspapers in Tokyo, and in 1921, when the Tokyo Gas Company was embroiled in a scandal, investigators discovered that the company had "paid out ¥88,000 for bribing journalists, including a sum of ¥40,000 for 'influencing favorable editorials.' "[31] The practice of bribing journalists for favorable treatment by bureaucrats, politicians, and businessmen was firmly in place by the end of the Meiji period, facilitated by the rise of the press clubs and the establishment of close relationships between newspaper managers and editors and prominent political and business figures.[32]

Legal and Extralegal Means of Controlling the Press

To mold the early press the Meiji state used legal regulations and extralegal, informal practices to elicit compliance. The Meiji leadership had firsthand experience with the adversarial potential of the newspaper press, as both the recipients and the creators of antigovernment propaganda. When the *bakufu* collapsed and civil war began in January 1868, there was a loosening of the strict censorship and control over speech that had existed since the Tokugawa government placed its first ban on printed materials in 1630 when it prohibited the publication of books on Christianity.[33] Both pro- and antigovernment editors took advantage of this hiatus, and for a brief period debate about the future of the nation flourished in the incipient printed press. Some of the earliest Japanese-language newspapers, including the *Chūgai shimbun* published by Yanagawa Shunzan and the *Kōko shimbun* published by Fukuchi Genichirō (later the editor of the *Tokyo nichi nichi shimbun*) carried articles that were both political in nature and critical of the individuals who would soon take over the government.[34]

The new Meiji leadership was troubled that the attacks on them did not abate once they came to power. A number of Tokyo editors maintained close ties to the former shogunate, and many of the articles in their papers were critical of the new leadership. To remedy this situation, the Meiji leaders published a paper of their own—the *Dajōkan nisshi* (Council of state journal)—which they intended to act as a counter to the antigovernment press.[35] This strategy served only to spur on the pro-*bakufu* press, which published even more articles critical of the Meiji state. Consequently, on April 28, 1868, only a short while after their rise to power, the Meiji leadership announced a draconian press law prohibiting the publication of *all* newspapers, both pro- and antigovernment alike.[36] Not a single newspaper was published in Tokyo for almost ten months.

With this temporary ban in place, the Meiji leadership moved to further control the press, announcing in February 1869 the establishment of a new newspaper publication ordinance (*shimbunshi inkō jōrei*), a publication licensing system (*hakkō kyoka-sei*), and a postpublication censorship system (*jigo kenetsu-sei*).[37] In summing up these regulations, one author notes that "there was very little in them that a Tokugawa publisher would have found unusual."[38] The licensing system alone was enough to halt the publication of papers critical of the government since "only tractable editors were granted publication privileges."[39] At the same time, the new regulations represented a recognition by the government that the printed press had an important function to serve, not as a government watchdog, but as a tool of the state.

Once the Meiji government instituted the new regulations, a number of papers began to publish again, but few touched on political events, and almost all were working in the service of the state, publishing government documents as "patronage papers."[40] By regulating the Japanese press when it did, the Meiji government deprived it of an important opportunity to transform itself into a medium for political debate and effectively denied it the possibility to play a critical, adversarial role. As a consequence, the traditional form of top-down communication between state and subject that had been extant since the Tokugawa era was maintained.[41]

In October 1873 an ordinance was enacted that prohibited journalists from attacking the government, discussing its laws, "appending uncalled-for remarks to the laws when published in the newspapers," or casting "obstacles in the way of working on the national institutions by persistent advocacy of foreign ideas."[42] In 1875 the "Newspaper Ordinance" sought "to counter seditious criticism from the reactionary press."[43] But this law had a considerable loophole: while it included provisions allowing the authorities to prosecute editors, it did not permit them to shut down papers that violated the law. As a result, the press began to hire so-called editors, whose main purpose was to serve the jail sentences handed down when their papers were caught having published offending articles.[44] Later laws, in 1876 and the 1880s, sought to close this loophole.

In addition to these legal regulations issued by the Meiji government, the authorities also controlled the press through the administrative discretion they had as ministerial bureaucrats. Exercising what the Supreme Court had determined was an "inherent right in the government" to stop publications, state bureaucrats interpreted press laws with wide discretion.[45] They also utilized other extralegal, informal mechanisms to encourage self-censorship among publishers and journalists. Among these were such practices as "consultations," "administrative guidance," "advice," "warnings," and "threats."[46]

One of these extralegal mechanisms was the "banning an article" system, designed to prevent publication on topics that had been banned.[47] "By 1920 the 'banning an article order system' had three categories of orders: (1) instruction (*shitatsu*)—an order, sent to most publishers that contained the threat that if anything was published on a specific subject it would be prohibited; (2) warning (*keikoku*)—a threat of probable prohibition; and (3) consultation (*kondan*). While periodicals were expected to follow the third order, they might escape censure if they did not."[48] Government censors used this system in the period before and during the Pacific War. Immediately after the China Incident of 1937, for example, the army and navy drew up warnings that were conveyed by the police "in polite 'consultations' (*kondan*) with media people, employing 'unofficial announcements' (*naishi*) to 'positively guide' (*sekkyokuteki ni shidō*) newspapers and leading magazines."[49] Even after the war, certain aspects of this system were left in place. As outlined in chapter 4, the third category of orders—consultation—remains an important part of the newsgathering routine of journalists in the press clubs today.

Informal, extralegal methods such as these were honed and perfected throughout the Meiji period and proved extremely effective during wartime. Several months before the Russo-Japanese War (1905–1906), for example, "twenty-eight Tokyo editors were called into the war office to be reminded that caution was desirable in printing news concerning Japanese maneuvers." Later, several editors who had taken part in these conferences agreed that their purpose was "to receive our orders as to what we may not print."[50]

In the decade before the Pacific War, these methods formed a system of unofficial control.[51] Particularly noteworthy is the consultation system, or, "ongoing direct contact between officials and subjects, initiated by the former to extend state control. It involved telephone calls, individual interviews, and group meetings arranged in conference halls or private restaurant rooms" and resembled the postwar practice of "administrative guidance." Government bureaucrats used this system to control the mass media, the economy, religion, art, and education when they had no legal means to do so. According to Kasza, it is "key to understanding state power in late imperial Japan."[52]

One author writing in the 1920s described just how effective were the two systems of control outlined here—the informal and formal: "The older methods of suppression are no longer needed. The more recalcitrant newspapers, such as the *Chōya* and the *Akebono*, have been cut off by past press laws, or persecuted into uniformity, or acquired by interests more friendly to the ruling cliques. By interpretation of embargo power, the whole press of Japan has been reduced . . . to a virtually semi-official status." The advantages to the government of these informal mechanisms were clear. They were efficient and, because they were behind the scenes, could easily be denied. But as one author notes, "the methods utilized possess all the greater danger because they may be indirectly exercised under cover of a 'warning,' a 'suggestion,' or 'advice.' 'Advice' has become a vital factor in the extension of press restrictions, particularly when it can be exercised by such methods as will not definitely commit the government to any specific embargo on the news."[53]

As a result of these repressive regulations, news editors adopted self-censorship, hoping to avoid the heavy hand of the state and the financial ruin that publication bans often brought. An early method of self-censorship involved replacing " 'dangerous' words or sentences that might draw official criticism [with] meaningless symbols like x-es, or circles, or squares or triangles," a practice known as *fuseji*. In addition, journalists and editors wrote only stories that they knew would make it past the censors' blue pencils, avoiding editorial comments altogether. In one instance in 1927, the magazine press even requested government officials to reinstate pre-publication censorship so that it would not have to face the possibility of a financial loss for publishing articles the authorities ultimately chose to ban.[54]

The Meiji government, seeking to use the press as an effective educational tool in support of its policies, had to limit its adversarial potential. At first the government used strict regulations to control the press, but later it devised and perfected more informal, extralegal means of control, while the press began to adopt self-censorship. By the Taishō period, these methods had become as important as the formal legal regulations, and formal censorship by the government began to be employed "only when the extensive array of informal methods failed to elicit compliance."[55]

The Shared Beliefs and Goals of Japan's "Public Men"

The Meiji state did not have to rely solely on monetary, legal, or extralegal mechanisms to coax loyalty out of the infant press. Elites in Meiji Japan had a shared ideology as a result of their common Confucian training and educational backgrounds. These elites, whom Barshay called the nation's "public men," shared two important attributes: a nationalist mentality and the belief that they should act as the enlighteners of the masses.[56] These characteristics explain much of the attitudes and behavior of the Japanese press during the Meiji era and subsequent periods, including its support of the Sino-Japanese (1894–1895) and Russo-Japanese (1905–1906) wars, its criticism of the concessions made by the government at Portsmouth, and its backing of the war in the Pacific. They also explain the press's lack of response to the rise of fascism in the 1930s, and the fact that no underground press arose to challenge the actions and activities of an increasingly fascist state.

Japan's early editors and journalists shared not only the national goals of the leaders of the Meiji state, but also their feelings about the role of the press in achieving those goals. Many of the founders of the earliest newspapers were former samurai, and the editors and journalists of these papers often "ran for public office, moved back and forth between the bureaucracy and the press, helped establish and run the stock exchange, formed their own political parties and founded educational institutions."[57] Because they were frequently a part of the ruling elite, early journalists generally had little interest in the more confrontational and adversarial aspects of the Western press.

Traditionally, "opposition had been equated with disloyalty and those who formed factions outside the government were thought to be acting in pursuit of selfish ends rather than the public good."[58] One consequence of this was that journalists did not emphasize the notion of an independent "watchdog" press.[59] For them, the value of the medium lay in its ability to serve as an effective tool to educate the ignorant masses in the interest of the state. It was not a means of informing the state about society's needs, nor was it an instrument for challenging the state's policies as was its Western counterpart. The reading public shared this evaluation of the media's role in society. Yamamoto writes that in the early part of Meiji, "readers assumed that the newspaper was but one arm of a governmental communication system having at its core the civilization and enlightenment of the masses."[60]

Because of common backgrounds and shared goals among Japan's elites, an extremely fluid boundary between press and state developed early on. Strong personal and institutional ties quickly developed between the editors and publishers of influential papers and prominent government and business figures. Later, with the establishment of the press clubs, similar linkages also formed among bureaucrats, politicians, businessmen, and beat journalists. The close relationship between Tokutomi Sohō, who turned his influential *Kokumin shimbun* into a government mouthpiece, and two Meiji oligarchs—Yamagata Aritomo and Katsura Tarō—has been the subject of numerous scholarly works.[61] A relationship also existed between members of the ruling oligarchy and Fukuchi Genichirō, a former Ministry of Finance bureaucrat who became the editor of the *Tokyo nichi nichi shimbun*. Fukuchi eventually joined with other progovernment journalists in 1882 to establish a progovernment political party, the Rikken Teiseitō.[62] Even Yukichi Fukuzawa, the founder of several influential newspapers and a "liberal" intellectual, had close ties to government officials, eventually agreeing to publish a progovernment newspaper.[63]

The lack of a firm border between press and state was not an aberration of the formative Meiji period. Relational webs remained an important aspect of press-state relations throughout the prewar era and were active even when the press was at its "liberal" peak during the period of Taishō democracy.[64] Wildes describes the considerable interlock between press and state in Taishō, with regard to newspaper editorship and ownership patterns. He suggests that the relationship between a given paper and prominent officials was maintained even as individual editors and owners resigned, retired, or passed away, and even the most liberal of them was allied with the government.[65] These relational ties proved extremely useful to the state in the 1930s and 1940s as it sought to use the press to mold public opinion in support of the imperial system.

The state also encouraged and fostered the development of institutional linkages such as the establishment in 1893 of government deliberations councils (*shingikai*) whose members included bureaucrats as well as journalists.[66] Like the press clubs described below, these councils still exist today, and prominent journalists are frequently invited to participate in them. At the same time, the government also began to aid in the establishment of press clubs in important ministries and government agencies. These clubs added an extra dimension to the press-state network, bringing together lower-level bureaucrats, politicians, and businessmen with journalists "on the beat." Additionally, in 1909, Prime Minister Katsura advocated the establishment of the International Newspaper Publishers and Editors Association (Kokusai Shimbun Kyōkai), ostensibly as a forum for Japanese and foreign journalists to meet. According to Yamamoto, however, Katsura's real aim was to "promote 'exchanges' between the government and the executives of the newspaper companies."[67] Pro-Katsura bureaucrats also encouraged the formation of what became known as the Shunjū-kai (Spring and Autumn Association), which held regular meetings in the spring and fall attended by the owners and editors of prominent newspapers, magazines, and wire services; powerful government and party officials; and the chiefs of the Police Bureau and Tokyo Metropolitan Police.[68] The association also played a critical mediating role on at least one occasion when disputes arose between lower-level beat journalists and their handlers in the *kisha* clubs.

The government sought to foster the growth of a financially stable, politically loyal press by providing overt and covert financial subsidies and incentives, employing restrictive laws and extralegal inducements, and utilizing the shared ideology and educational background found among elites to develop and strengthen personal and institutional linkages. The efficacy of each of these tools, as well as their mix, varied throughout the prewar period depending on the political climate. Early on, the Meiji oligarchs relied on the more informal of them; later, when they felt that informal mechanisms were insufficient, the government resorted to repressive legislation and outright censorship. Eventually, the state and the newspaper industry arrived at a relatively stable ideological consensus about the role of the press in society and its relationship with the state, though legal means would still be used when necessary to keep the press in line.

A Summary of Press-State Relations: 1868–1890

Establishment of the "Patronage Press"

During the press's formative years, the Meiji state was particularly adept in its use of the mechanisms described above. In fact, any paper that did not fall within the state's purview during this early period perished, while survivors became known as "patronage papers" (*goyō shimbun*) for the close relationships they had with the state.[69] These papers, the first of four types of newspapers to emerge in Japan, were marked by their educative mission, their proximity and obsequious loyalty to the state, and the distinctive way they distanced themselves from politics. As Figdor notes, "As a *quid pro quo* for their favorable treatment, these newspapers generally sympathized with the government and willingly supported the *bunmei kaika* policy. They dutifully printed official government statements and decrees and presented other newsworthy occurrences in a straightforward factual manner. Their articles did not have a great deal of political coloration and remained for the most part within the bounds of government expectations."[70]

The papers that survived expressed viewpoints consonant with those of the Meiji state. This resulted in newspapers that lacked "political coloration," to use Figdor's term. They comprised journalists who were ardent supporters of the state and the status quo, priding themselves on their proximity to the government and the important role they were playing in conveying government information to the masses. In this respect at least, the early Japanese press differed little from the early American press of a century earlier, as described by Leonard in his history of American political reporting: "The early press is best defined by the political information it did not offer and the questions it had not yet learned to ask."[71]

The Rise and Fall of the "Political" Press

The Meiji government was able to maintain its absolute control over the press only as long as it remained internally cohesive. Once divisions appeared, the honeymoon between the early patronage press and the state came to an end, and a second type of newspaper known as the "papers of political discussion" (*seiron shimbun*) came to the fore.[72] These papers challenged the "apolitical" patronage press by taking an openly partisan perspective, and many of them eventually became the organs of Japan's first political parties. However, although the papers of political discussion played an important role in providing a forum for debating the establishment of a national assembly, most of them lasted less than a decade.[73]

The event that served as the catalyst for the rise of a political press in Meiji Japan was the split within the ruling coalition in 1873 over two issues, financial reform and relations with Korea.[74] Disagreements over how to resolve these issues split the ruling coalition into several groups: those who supported the government, those who hoped to bring it down by force, and those who wanted to change it peacefully through the introduction of reforms. On January 17, 1874, the members of the latter group presented the Privy Council with a petition for a popularly elected assembly.[75] By the following day, their demands were leaked to the press and published in Black's *Nisshin shinjishi*.[76]

This action marked the beginning of the movement for popular rights (*jiyū minken undō*) and brought about a temporary shift in the newspaper world toward a more issue-oriented, politicized front page. It also resulted in a de facto split within the newspaper industry and the creation of two broad categories of newspapers, the *ōshimbun* and the *koshimbun*. The *ōshimbun*, or "large papers," were so labeled because of their size. These papers focused on political issues and were read by elites. They included the patronage press, the papers of political discussion, and, later, the party organs (*seitō kikanshi*) and the "independent" newspapers (*dokuritsu shimbun*). In contrast, the newly developing *koshimbun*, or "small papers," were named for the smaller size of paper on which they were printed and included the "apolitical" and frequently sensational, mass-oriented entertainment press and later the large-scale commercial papers that came to dominate the industry in the late Meiji and early Taishō periods.

By 1875 most of the patronage papers in the Tokyo-Yokohama area had become papers of political discussion.[77] Not all of these papers were antigovernment, however. While some of them aligned themselves with the government faction (*kanken-ha*), which was calling for the gradual (as opposed to immediate) introduction of an elected parliament, the greater share affiliated with the antigovernment or popular faction (*minken-ha*) supporting the movement for popular rights.[78]

Unlike most of the other patronage papers, the *Tokyo nichi nichi shimbun*, edited by former Finance Ministry bureaucrat Fukuchi Genichirō, held fast to its position as a patronage paper, taking the extra step of obtaining official designation of that status in 1875, a move that resulted in a dramatic increase in its circulation.[79] This paper was the only one from which the government did not withdraw its overt financial support (e.g., its purchase and distribution of select papers) as part of a larger effort to put down papers that challenged its views.[80] The *Nichi nichi* would amply (if not directly) repay the government for its benevolence.

In July 1876 the *Nichi nichi* became the first of a series of newspapers to adopt a distinctive editorial and management philosophy based on the notion of *fuhen futō*. Translated literally as "impartiality and nonpartisanship," the term "connoted a nonpartisan neutrality . . . [and] reinforce[d] the contention that any overt pursuit of partisan interests was of questionable moral value."[81] On the surface, *fuhen futō* appeared relatively harmless; it merely suggested that newspapers aim for impartiality and neutrality, and it would have been readily recognizable to members of the Western press. But the *Nichi nichi* was not seeking to introduce notions of objectivity to press reporting when it adopted this editorial policy. Quite the contrary, its aims were purely Machiavellian. In adopting a policy espousing impartiality and nonparty affiliation, the progovernment *Nichi nichi* was able to continue to avoid the heavy hand of the state, increase its circulation, and, most importantly, gain an ideological vantage point from which to challenge the antigovernment newspapers that had recently aligned themselves with the popular rights movement. It thereby supported the state in its suppression of those opposition papers. Clearly, the issue here was one neither of neutrality nor of partisanship, but of how to suppress a vocal antigovernment opposition through indirect and surreptitious means. Paradoxically, five years after the paper adopted its editorial stance, its editor, Fukuchi Genichirō, spearheaded the formation of the first progovernment party in Japan, the Rikken Teiseitō.

In a country where factions were despised and denigrated by a dominant Confucian ideology, and political parties had not yet been recognized by the government, partisanship was seen as a direct challenge to the legitimacy of the state. Consequently, in June 1875 the government enacted a strict press ordinance (*shimbunshi jōrei*), followed in September by the issuance of a revised publication ordinance (*shuppan jōrei*) and, later, the enactment of a libel law (*zanboritsu*). These laws made newspaper editors responsible for the content of their papers and proved a powerful tool in controlling the newly politicized press. Suehiro Tetcho, who had the honor of being the first editor punished under the new law, was imprisoned for two months and fined 20 yen, while papers such as Fukuzawa's *Meiroku zasshi* chose to fold in protest.[82] From 1875 to 1880 approximately two hundred papers were punished under the new laws.[83]

This was only the beginning of the government's effort to denature politics and strengthen imperial rule. In October 1881 the emperor issued an imperial ordinance promising the enactment of a constitution and the establishment of a national assembly by 1890. Included in the imperial edict was "a warning that 'those who may advocate sudden and violent changes . . . disturbing the peace of the realm' would fall under imperial displeasure."[84] The government was not making an idle threat. More newspapers were punished *after* the imperial promise for the establishment of an assembly than before. In 1882, 70 newspapers were suspended compared with 16 in 1880.[85] Moreover, in the period from 1883 to 1887, "174 periodicals were suspended from publication for varying periods, and another 4 banned altogether, while 198 journalists served time in prison."[86]

Although the antigovernment papers had played an important role in the movement to demand the constitution and a representative assembly, in making this announcement the emperor removed the raison d'être of most of them.[87] With the establishment of Japan's first political parties shortly thereafter, however, some of the papers of political discussion were able to survive by transforming themselves into party organs.[88] But in 1882 and 1883, the government once again countered the political press and the parties by revising the law of assembly (*shūkai jōrei*), promulgating even harsher press laws (the *kaisei shimbun jōrei* and *hakkō hoshōkin seido*), and strengthening the mechanisms for enforcing sanctions against violators.[89] As a result, some of the papers of political discussion failed altogether, while others dissolved their relations with the parties, adopting policies to simplify their articles and make them more appealing to a broader audience.[90] Most of the remaining papers either perished before the Diet's establishment in 1890 or survived only to see their circulations fall dramatically.[91]

While the political papers had not really spoken for the masses, they had provided an important forum for the discussion of alternatives to the more conservative policies of the clique (*hanbatsu*) government.[92] For a brief period it had even seemed as though the Japanese press might move away from its role as conveyor of government information and educator on behalf of the state and adopt a more nuanced and critical stance, one that might open the way for the rise of a vibrant, dynamic, and discoursive civil society. In the end, however, these papers functioned only as long as they were needed. Once the constitution was promulgated, the first elections held, and the Diet opened, the goals of the popular rights movement had been fulfilled, and papers affiliated with the movement were no longer necessary.[93]

So complete was the demise of the political press that eventually a number of the journalists who had written for the antigovernment papers became government officials themselves, or began to act as "torch bearers" (*chōchin*), writing articles in support of the government's policies.[94] By 1890, newspapers "presented politicians in a light that was only slightly less unfavorable than the harsh beam directed by the government on the allegedly self-interested factionalism of the parties."[95] However unintentionally, the press was already becoming part of the apparatus that would destroy the constitutional politics it had earlier sought so hard to establish.[96] This "antipolitical" or "apolitical" (*hiseijiteki*) characteristic of the Japanese press remained long after politics were subsumed under the rule of an imperialist government. With the across-the-board adoption of notions of "impartiality and nonpartisanship" beginning in the 1880s and the standardization of newsgathering practices with the establishment of the press clubs in the 1890s, this feature became an institutionalized part of Japanese journalism, prevailing even after the imperialist state had been demolished and democratic institutions set in place in the postwar period.

Yamamoto conjectures that, "had the party organs been able to maintain an antigovernment posture during the latter part of the Meiji period and been able to increase their circulation over that of the newspapers that were adopting policies of 'impartiality and nonpartisanship,' they might have been able to serve as an important check on the oppressive policies of the government. However, that kind of paper dies in the latter part of Meiji."[97] The failure of the political papers to survive this critical juncture in Japanese political history had long-lived consequences for the growth of democracy, the establishment of representative government, and the evolution of the printed press in prewar Japan.

The Birth of an "Independent" Press

The adoption of repressive laws in the early 1880s, coupled with the concerted effort by the government to devalue politics in the period before and after the promulgation of the constitution, functioned as a double-edged sword.[98] Not only did these actions suppress the opposition and the political press, they also sent an important message to individuals wishing to establish new papers and to the editors of existing papers—both *ōshim-*

bun and *koshimbun* alike. That message was that it was best to divorce oneself from politically divisive issues if one wanted to survive. As a consequence, many papers intentionally distanced themselves from the parties and politics altogether, adopting policies of impartiality and nonpartisanship closely resembling that adopted by the *Nichi nichi* a number of years earlier. The papers that prospered in this period—the elite-oriented "independent papers" and the mass-oriented commercial press—did so by deliberately removing themselves from the partisan political debate. However, as they distanced themselves from politics, they began to publish an "informational product" that was both appealing to a broader audience and less objectionable to the state either because it supported the state's own goals or because the major source of the news contained within it was increasingly the state itself.

One group of papers adopting these neutral editorial policies were *ō-shimbun* seeking to identify themselves as a distinctive third type of "independent" newspaper (*dokuritsu shimbun*), one aimed at an intellectual, elite audience. The independent papers included the *Jiji shimpō*, founded in 1882 by Fukuzawa Yukichi; the *Nihon*, founded in 1889 and edited by Kuga Katsunan; and the *Kokumin shimbun*, founded a year later by Tokutomi Sohō. These papers lacked overt party ties and discussed political issues only as they related to national strength and unity, not partisan politics. They also tried to provide their readers with information about a broad range of topics, though frequently the nationalistic views of their editors colored the news they reported. In designating the *Nihon* as an "independent newspaper," for example, its editor Kuga Katsunan proclaimed that he intended to use the paper to espouse his own uniform ideology, "nationalism" (*kokuminshugi*).[99]

When Fukuzawa established the first independent paper, the *Jiji shimpō*, in 1882, he stated in the paper's first editorial that he wanted to create an "independent and free" (*dokuritsu fuki*) newspaper, one that "differed from the twelve newspapers the political organizations have to express their views and from the commercial entertainment press."[100] Aiming to distance the *Jiji* from the blatant partisanship of the party organs and the vulgarity and commercialism of the entertainment press, Fukuzawa hoped to substitute one-sided editorials and sensationalism with information about a wide range of topics, including government, the parties, the financial world, and academia, all while remaining independent of them.[101] In short, he wanted to provide his readers with "news."

While Fukuzawa's aim was noble and, unlike the *Nichi nichi*, genuine, his goal was not easy to achieve. From its inception the paper was closely linked to the Mitsubishi *zaibatsu*, and some even thought of it as an organ of the progressive party, the *Kaishintō*.[102] Moreover, the *Jiji* had been able to establish a censorship-free niche in the newspaper industry and remain relatively financially successful because its editor had close ties to political and financial elites, and because Fukuzawa had chosen to focus on a relatively safe category of news—financial news.[103]

The editors and owners of the other two independent newspapers—the *Nihon* and *Kokumin shimbun*—also had extremely close ties with a number of the Meiji oligarchs. Sohō, it will be remembered, was furnished with privileged information and cash in exchange for favorable treatment, and his paper, the *Kokumin shimbun*, eventually became an unabashed government mouthpiece. By 1905 the *Kokumin* "was defending the issuing of press laws whereby the freedom of press was almost completely ended." In much the same way, by 1906 the "independent" *Nihon* had been "transformed into a banking journal representing the views of the official Bank of Japan."[104]

Still, given an environment in which politics and partisanship were increasingly viewed as self-serving and vile, the establishment of papers professing independence was a brilliant move. Because the *Jiji* and other independent papers like it were for the most part managed and edited independent of the parties, they were able to avoid government censorship with relative ease (the *Jiji* was punished only once during this period).[105] These papers were also able to increase their circulations substantially. In contrast to the openly political papers (including the progovernment *Nichi nichi*), whose circulations dropped on average 30 percent from 1882 to 1883, the "independent and less political" *Jiji* was able to triple its circulation during the same time period.[106]

In their abdication of any kind of adversarial or oppositional function for the press, these papers were demonstrating their support for the fundamental belief the press had held since its introduction in the early Meiji period—namely, that the role of the press was chiefly to act as a supporter of the nation and educator of the public. Although these papers professed their independence, they were still operating within a journalistic framework supportive of the status quo, the state, and the nation. Their editorials as well as their articles (particularly those of the *Nihon* and the *Kokumin shimbun*) were heavily infused with the personal and nationalist ideologies of their founders, ideologies generally acceptable to the imperialist Japanese state.[107]

How different is the Japanese experience described here from the historical role played by the early American press? In the United States, the press aroused Americans' interest in politics by showing them not only what to think, but how. "The birth of political reporting," Leonard writes, "is part of the creation of those values that made politics, as America knows it, legitimate: the notions that competing points of view benefit a community and that the press exists to offer varied perspectives."[108] In marked contrast, the adoption of *fuhen futō*, first by the independent papers and later by the commercial press, served to further delegitimize politics and reinforced the state's position that competing points of view functioned only to promote social disharmony and unrest.

In sum, the state's enactment of repressive laws, coupled with its effort to devalue democratic politics and raise a patriotic mass consciousness in support of the emperor, resulted in the adoption of "impartial and non-partisan" editorial policies by the Japanese press. Because the state was itself vehemently antiparty, the adoption of these policies bolstered the government in its bid to suppress the parties and the party organs and thereby accelerated their decline.[109] In embracing neutrality, then, these papers had unintentionally supported the government in its "considerable effort to [deny] politics as a practice acceptable among those who would count themselves as patriotic countrymen."[110]

The Rise of a Dominant Organizational Form

The independent papers ultimately were unable to compete with a fourth type of newspaper that began to gain power in the 1880s, the commercial *koshimbun* led by the *Osaka asahi shimbun*.[111] These papers modeled their editorial policies after those of the independent papers, adopting neutrality in order to avoid state suppression and broaden their readership base. But they gradually diverged from the independent press in several important respects: their superior economic organization and management excellence, their mass appeal, and the degree to which they included neutral information or "news" (as opposed to opinion and editorials) in their pages. These differences made it possible for the *Asahi shimbun*, and papers modeled after it, rapidly to gain a hegemonic position in the Japanese newspaper industry, eventually dominating the industry by the beginning of the Taishō period.

As early as the late 1870s, during the peak of the popular rights movement, a subtle shift was already discernible within the newspaper industry as the mass-based *koshimbun* began slowly to gain ground over the political, elite-oriented *ōshimbun*.[112] This shift was made possible by the publication of the first mass-oriented entertainment paper, the *Yomiuri shimbun*, in 1874, and propelled by the government's reaction against the papers of political discussion, adoption of repressive laws, and denunciation of partisan politics.

The *Yomiuri* and similar papers (including the *Kanayomi shimbun*, *Tokyo eiiri shimbun*, and *Sakigake shimbun*) differed from the other papers available at that time in several important respects. First, they were written in the vernacular and had phonetic syllabary attached to all difficult *kanji* (Chinese ideographs) making them easier to read than the more formalistic political press. This meant that newspapers were no longer the exclusive information medium of educated elites. Second, these early *koshimbun* did not contain editorials. Instead, they included the kinds of news stories that would appeal to their readers: stories that were less politically oriented and more easily connected to the common citizen, including local news, gossip and social news, stories about crime, and other scandalous and sensational news items. They also contained other forms of mass entertainment, including serialized novels and other kinds of literature that was popular with the masses.

Within a year of its establishment, the *Yomiuri*'s circulation had climbed to about 10,000 copies; by 1878 the paper had a circulation of 33,000 and was the largest circulating paper in the country.[113] But just as the *Yomiuri* was beginning to gain ground in the political capital, another paper—the *Osaka asahi shimbun*—was establishing itself in the nation's commercial capital, Osaka. Borrowing the mass orientation of newspapers such as the *Yomiuri* and the editorial policies of the elite independent press, the *Osaka asahi shimbun* eventually overtook the *Yomiuri* and came to serve as the dominant organizational model for the rest of the industry. It is probably not mere coincidence, either, that this paper was established not in the political capital, but in the nation's business capital by two Osaka-based businessmen lacking in journalistic experience, Murayama Ryōhei and Ueno Riichi.

During the first few years after its founding, the *Osaka asahi* was not particularly profitable. Consequently, in 1882 when the paper's editors were offered covert subsidies and infusions of capital from the government, they accepted, concealing this fact by establishing a dummy company.[114] The Meiji state had learned by this time that the papers that were the most candid in their support of the government only incited the antigovernment press further. Their aim in supplying covert funding to the *Osaka asahi* was to have it subtly support the state at the same time that it was professing "nonpartisanship and impartiality."[115] For the government, having a paper to rival the political papers under the guise of "neutrality" was "desirable even if the paper did not directly act as the spokesperson for the government."[116]

Yamamoto notes that "although the image of the *Asahi* in the newspaper world was that of a moderate supporter of the popular rights movement, it was actually acting behind the scenes as a "camouflaged patronage paper" (*kakure goyō shimbun*).[117] The paper also benefited from this arrangement. One scholar of the Japanese press suggests that as a result of this inflow of cash from the government, the *Osaka asahi* was able to dominate the newspaper industry in the *kansai* (Osaka) area in a relatively short period of time.[118] By 1883, one year after government subsidies were provided, the paper had a circulation rate that was greater than that of all of its competitors in Osaka combined.[119]

Perhaps due to the paper's financial reliance on the government, the *Osaka asahi shimbun* "developed a symbiotic relationship with official censors, pioneering techniques of self-censorship," and adopted a strict self-censorship.[120] In the period immediately after Murayama became editor in March 1882, the paper was twice suspended for publishing articles the authorities found offensive. Eager to avoid further confrontations with the state and the financial losses they entailed, Murayama declared in an editorial that he had decided to adopt an editorial policy based on "prudence." Mitchell notes that "With this policy in mind, [Murayama] came each day to the editorial department and, red pen in hand, he 'strictly censored' (*kenetsu o genjū ni shita*) all manuscripts based on the following criteria: (1) will this material have a bad influence on society? (2) will this material offend the authorities? (3) will this material damage the newspaper's reputation?" Later, after the government instituted more restrictive press laws in 1882 and 1883, Murayama moved his chair to the center of the editorial department and personally "read with 'extreme care' all articles on politics, diplomacy, political parties and other sensitive material which might draw official wrath."[121] He also examined all editorials of a sensitive nature before they were published.[122]

Although the government had begun to escalate its suppression of the political press and force a number of the papers of political discussion to fold, the *Osaka asahi* was able to continue to expand its circulation.[123] By 1888 the paper became so successful in the Osaka region that it was able to move to the political capital and establish a sister paper, the *Tokyo asahi shimbun*. It purchased a failing organ of the Liberal party, the *Mezamashi*, and transformed it into a commercial paper modeled after the *Osaka asahi*. Ariyama suggests that the *Osaka asahi* most likely received some degree of assistance from the government in setting up its sister paper in the capital, noting that "the secret relationship between the government and the *Asahi shimbun* continued unabated after the paper moved to Tokyo."[124]

Indirectly, at least, the state played a role in the *Asahi*'s purchase of the *Mezamashi*. In 1887 the government promulgated a new press law —the Newspaper Ordinance—that inflicted considerable damage on the popular rights movement and the papers affiliated with it. One of the individuals caught up in the enforcement of this new law was the editor of the *Mezamashi*, Hoshi Tōru. Exiled from Tokyo, Hoshi decided to sell his paper, thus making it available for Murayama to purchase. Mitchell notes that the government was doubtless pleased with this turn of events, particularly the "switching [of] prickly Hoshi for a tractable Murayama."[125]

Once Murayama established the *Tokyo asahi shimbun*, he began a circulation war with the other Tokyo newspapers, which he eventually won.[126] Employing a sales strategy in which he provided free papers and gifts to potential readers, Murayama also offered half-price subscriptions to individuals who agreed to buy the paper for a minimum of six months. Two years after the paper's arrival in Tokyo, Murayama also introduced the first high-technology printing press in Japan, the Marinori roller. This new production method had ten times the capacity of preexisting presses, and because it reduced substantially the price of publishing the paper, it made the *Asahi* an even tougher competitor.[127] Other management strategies utilized by the *Asahi* included the increasing reliance on advertisements for revenue and the development of a novel method for distributing the paper through sales agents.[128]

During the same year that the *Asahi* moved to Tokyo, the paper that ultimately became its main rival—the *Osaka mainichi shimbun*—was established by a group of influential businessmen in Osaka who had also purchased one of the political organs of the Liberal party.[129] One of those businessmen was Hikoichi Motoyama, general manager of the Fujita Gumi, a large mining company with close official connections.[130] This paper adopted the editorial policies and management practices of the *Asahi*, and the two papers quickly gained prominent positions in the newspaper industry, having been given a substantial boost by the Sino-Japanese (1894) and Russo-Japanese (1905–1906) wars.

Although the government limited the number of journalists each paper could send to the front to cover the Sino-Japanese War, both the *Osaka Asahi* and the *Osaka mainichi* with the government's secret complicity, borrowed the names of friendly newspapers and increased the number of journalists they sent to cover the war.[131] When the Russo-Japanese War broke out in 1905, these papers had sufficient financial leverage to send large numbers of correspondents to follow that war. Naturally, neither paper wrote stories critical of the war effort, though later they would criticize the government for concessions it made during negotiations for a peace settlement at Portsmouth. Even this action was fully in line with the press's tendency to support national interests above all others.

The two Osaka-based papers were given an additional boost by the great Kanto earthquake of 1923. While most of the papers in the Tokyo area were badly damaged by the earthquake and had to scramble to gain funding to rebuild, both of the Osaka papers were able to continue publishing.[132] Within a year of the earthquake, these two papers joined together to form a monopolistic price and sales agreement in order to destroy the influence of the remaining Tokyo papers. This strategy was remarkably successful: before the sales war began there had been five major papers in Tokyo—the *Kokumin shimbun, Yūbin hōchi shimbun,*[133] *Jiji shimpō, Tokyo asahi shimbun*, and *Tokyo mainichi shimbun*. By the time this battle was over, only the latter two remained.[134]

The only other paper that was ever able to compete with the *Asahi* and the *Mainichi* was the *Yomiuri*, the first entertainment paper to be published in Japan. Like the other two papers, the *Yomiuri* also had close ties with Japanese officials.[135] Wildes notes that the paper's owner's son was in the diplomatic service and had been an envoy to France and Russia and that, in spite of its reputation as a liberal paper, the owner's "sympathies were enlisted on the side of the conservatives." But the earthquake had also dealt a heavy blow to this paper. Because the paper's editor, Matsuyama Chujiro, had irritated a number of his financial sponsors, "one of whom he had accused of complicity in a railway scandal," they refused to provide funding to rebuild as long as he remained editor.[136] When he resigned in 1924, however, the paper was purchased by Shoriki Matsutaro, a former policy agency bureaucrat and the son-in-law of the metropolitan police chief.[137]

In sum, while the two wars of the late Meiji period and the earthquake of 1923 were a great boon to the *Asahi* and the *Mainichi*, they had a correspondingly negative impact on many of the political papers and other types of Japanese newspapers. After the Russo-Japanese War, for example, papers such as the *Nihon*, *Tokyo nichi nichi shimbun*, *Mainichi shimbun* (related to the *Tokyo Yokohama mainichi shimbun*, not the Osaka paper), and other political papers experienced management difficulties.[138] But as these papers were pushed further onto the periphery, the "impartial and nonpartisan" *Asahi* and papers modeled after it continued to gain strength in the industry, achieving a hegemonic position nationwide by the beginning of the Taishō period.

The political climate extant at the time the *Asahi* and *Asahi*-type papers were beginning substantially to increase their power within the newspaper industry is significant. Only a year after the *Asahi* arrived in Tokyo, the emperor handed down the constitution as an imperial gift to the nation, and, as promised, he allowed the Diet to convene the following year. At the exact time when the oligarchs first permitted the establishment of a representative assembly, they also began to use the term first adopted by the progovernment newspaper press in 1876 to attack the party organs—*fuhen futō* or "nonpartisanship and impartiality"—in an effort to prevent the new parliament from acting as a rival to state power.[139]

By introducing the concept of *fuhen futō* at this time, the government was seeking to equate it with two interrelated political aims: the repudiation of the political parties (*seitō hinin*) and the establishment of "transcendentalism" (*chōzenshugi*).[140] Gluck downplays the practical (though not the ideological) implications of the adoption of this notion and the introduction of transcendentalism by the state at this time, noting that "in political practice the principle would be eroded over the next several decades by an evolving accommodation, however uneven, between bureaucratic and party politics."[141] However much the state and the parties accommodated one another in the late Meiji and early Taishō periods, by the 1930s the parties were rapidly losing ground in their battle with the Japanese state, acknowledging defeat in that battle in 1940 by voluntarily disbanding.

The press also made an accommodation with the state by adopting the notion of "impartiality and nonpartisanship" as its standard editorial policy. Ironically, however, in contrast to that of the parties, the press's accommodation with the state had considerable benefits for those papers that chose to make it.

One scholar suggests that *fuhen futō* functioned as both an editorial and a management philosophy, giving editors a logical basis for distancing themselves from partisan politics and providing management with the rationale for expanding circulation by acquiring readers with broad party affiliations.[142] But the concept was really much more than that. In adopting a policy of *fuhen futō*, the press was making a powerful statement about what a newspaper's role in society and its relationship with the state should be. Unfortunately, however, this definition of the press's role was of considerably greater benefit to the state (and the press) than to society, just as it was of little value to the parties and party politics.[143] The papers were able to minimize their political role, avoid state censorship, and maximize their economic position, all at the same time. What more could a commercial newspaper possibly ask for? But as the commercial press began self-consciously to remove itself from the political debate and adopt neutral editorial policies, it inadvertently acted to preserve and strengthen the existing imperialist power structure.[144]

Summary

As it became the dominant organizational form and model for the newspaper industry, the *Asahi* (and papers like it) played a pivotal role in defining and delimiting the function of the press in Japanese society, ironically by emphasizing straight facts or "news" over editorial opinion and political debate. As these papers deliberately began to substitute news for the partisan political debates of their predecessors, they relied more heavily on government bureaucrats and other elites as the major sources for the information contained in their news stories, strengthening their ties to state and other elites in the process. The establishment of press clubs in official agencies beginning in the 1890s and the gradual standardization of the newsgathering practices associated with them served to fuse the government-press relationship even further, making the expression and dissemination of alternative points of view increasingly difficult. While there would be important instances—particularly in the early part of the Taishō period—in which the Japanese press, led by the *Asahi shimbun* or its rival the *Mainichi shimbun*, would challenge government policies, by 1918, with its failure in the White Rainbow Incident, the *Asahi shimbun* would be forced to capitulate in its battle with the state and eventually come to support it in the critical period before and during the Pacific War.[145]

The gradual disappearance of the papers of political discussion, the party organs, and even the independent press was the result of a confluence of factors that acted as a centripetal force, simultaneously drawing the press closer to the state as it pushed it further away from political issues. As these newspapers moved away from partisan politics and adopted neutral editorial policies, they also began to place greater emphasis on the informational (as opposed to editorial) potential of the medium, gradually relying more heavily on state and other elite sources for news.

While the promulgation of the constitution, the introduction of draconian laws, and the press's adoption of editorial policies deemphasizing politics were primary factors in this development, the movement toward a "nonpartisan," "neutral," and news-oriented press was also facilitated by the establishment and rapid dissemination of press clubs in important government and business organizations beginning in 1890. Over time, the institutionalization of newsgathering practices within these clubs, including the establishment of rules and sanctions and the gradual development of close ties with sources, led to the "cartelization" of information, and eventually to the monopolization of sources by an exclusive group of elite papers.

The Emergent Information Cartel: From Meiji to Defeat

The First Official Press clubs

Although Japanese journalists had obtained a degree of access to official sources by the late 1870s (in special "waiting rooms" [*tomarijo*] set up by the government), reporters did not begin to gain widespread access to government agencies until after the establishment of the Diet, and with it the founding of the first official *kisha* club.[146]

In the fall of 1890, in anticipation of the opening of the Diet, a number of journalists from powerful Tokyo newspapers formed an association to push for access to the Diet called the Group of Journalists for Diet Access (Gikai Deiri Kishadan).[147] The movement for reportorial access quickly spread nationwide, and journalists from local and regional papers soon joined their Tokyo colleagues to form a new association, the Newspaper Journalists' Club (Kyōdō Shimbun Kisha Kurabu), to coordinate efforts to demand access to the Diet.[148]

Government officials eventually acceded to the creation of a special room within the Diet where journalists could gather to receive official news, and it is this room that is generally recognized as Japan's first official press club. In allowing the establishment of a club for journalists, they insisted on two rules as a quid pro quo for access. First, they demanded that only those national daily papers and news agencies licensed by the government that had published continuously for at least two years would be allowed access to Diet proceedings. Second, they announced that the government would issue only twenty gallery tickets per Diet session.[149]

In insisting on the first rule, the government was able to guarantee that new newspapers—those whose political leanings it did not yet know or like—and newspapers that had been banned or suspended during the previous two years were excluded from the Diet. The second rule, limiting access to twenty tickets, forced the members of the Newspaper Journalists' Club to decide among themselves which journalists and newspapers would have access. Consequently, club members sought to aid the more powerful papers in Tokyo by excluding the regional and smaller papers. The establishment of the first press club resulted in the first attempt by a group of powerful, Tokyo-based newspapers to prohibit rivals from having access to information and sources and thereby sowed the seeds for the establishment of Japan's "information cartels."

During the two decades following the establishment of the press club in the Diet, clubs were organized in a number of other organizations, including various government agencies, party and police headquarters, and the Imperial Household Agency.[150] These clubs began to formulate rules and sanctions to regulate club members and their elite sources. They also developed sanctions for enforcing these rules. Eventually, this rule-based exclusivity became an institutionalized part of newsgathering in Japan, and the press clubs served as important mechanisms for promoting the monopolization of sources and the news market by a select group of powerful newspapers. They also began to function as an important tool for government control of the news media.

The establishment of the press clubs was a mutually beneficial arrangement. The journalists got stories, and the government got its version of the news out. Before 1910 many of the early clubs were not highly regarded by the bureaucrats in the agencies with which they were affiliated. That year there was a rather sudden increase in the number of clubs and a dramatic change in the government's attitude toward them. Relying on a series of articles published in April and June 1911 in *Shin-kōron*, an influential magazine, Yamamoto Taketoshi, professor of sociology at Hitotsubashi

University, postulates that the rapid and spectacular increase in the number of press clubs resulted from a policy introduced by then Prime Minister Katsura Tarō actively to manipulate the press.[151]

Katsura had experienced firsthand the unrestrained power of the press. A series of newspaper articles critical of the treaty he signed at Portsmouth at the end of the Russo-Japanese War resulted in a riot, the destruction of the building housing the progovernment newspaper *Kōko shimbun* (which had supported the treaty), and, the collapse of his first cabinet.[152] By the time Katsura established his second cabinet, he recognized the opportunity the press clubs offered for controlling what news was reported, who reported it, and how. Consequently, government agencies under his administration began a coordinated effort to embrace journalists, helping them organize press clubs and supplying them with the necessary perquisites of their trade: rooms, tables, chairs—even chess and other popular Japanese board games. They also provided staff assistants who worked exclusively for the clubs at public expense. Soon, in addition to being supplied with information, journalists were also furnished with "money, liquor, and women," in what Yamamoto calls a policy of "emasculation through entertainment."[153]

Katsura's well-orchestrated attempt to manufacture the news and emasculate the press was an apparent success. Gradually, the Japanese press began to print fewer articles openly critical of the government, and newspapers began to look more and more alike. Although a number of factors accounted for the uniformity of the press at this time, including the adoption of standardized editorial policies by the commercial and independent press described earlier, the press clubs themselves also played an important role in the homogenization process. Indeed, by 1911 critics of the clubs were noting reasons for a considerable uniformity of views in the printed press. One critic lamented, for example, that

> All the "journalistic vassals" attached to any one ministry are given exactly the same news materials, which makes it impossible for one reporter to scoop another. Now any idiot can join a press club, and if he shows up every day, he'll get exactly the same news as the smartest veteran in the bunch. In fact, if a reporter decides to take the day off, it doesn't inconvenience his paper in the least. It will still get the news from a news agency and have a perfectly respectable article for its readers. Everybody can take it easy these days.[154]

By the time this article in *Shin-kōron* was written, a number of the defining characteristics of the modern press clubs were already in place: (1) they had exclusive rules. (By the end of Taishō, most of them had introduced membership fees, regulations, and sanctions.)[155] (2) Members made agreements with each other and with their sources about what to publish and when to publish it, practicing self-censorship or group self-censorship when necessary. (3) Smaller and provincial papers and magazines were excluded. (4) The clubs had spread to locations outside of the Tokyo area, particularly to government offices in provincial areas. And (5) they had begun to operate independently of their companies, yet increasingly in cooperation with their official sources.

By 1925 the press clubs had become an integral part of newsgathering in Japan. That year, there were twenty-seven clubs in Tokyo and many more in the prefectures. By 1931 the number in Tokyo had risen to fifty-one, soaring to eighty-four by 1939.[156] As one postwar writer on the Japanese press notes, by the end of the prewar period not only had the press clubs become "undemocratic" institutions that "maintained exclusive rights to the news," they were also a key part of a governmental system of information control. Coughlin notes that in the prewar period, "if a reporter uncovered an unfavorable story, the official concerned had only to go to the Reporters' Club to have the story killed and the newsman reprimanded. In return, officials lavished favors and gifts on the members."[157]

The Battle for Control: The Companies, the Clubs, and the Sources

As the clubs began to serve as the major focal point for the newsgathering activities of exclusive groups of journalists from competing firms, they began to develop into complex social organizations with rules and dues. As they developed, a curious "pathology" arose that was particularly troubling to the newspaper companies. Two problems existed: one was related to club journalists' relationships with newspaper management, and the other concerned club members' relations with their sources.

Club journalists began to challenge the employment practices of the newspaper companies, acting as a kind of labor union representing journalists against management. In 1931, for example, after a journalist from the *Miyako shimbun* in the Unemekai (the club in the Ministry of Commerce and Industry) was fired for violating company policy, club members appealed to the company to reinstate him. When the newspaper refused, they retaliated by prohibiting *all* journalists from that paper from having access to the club.[158] A similar incident in the Hibiya club from the Police Agency resulted in the expulsion of the Denpō Tsūshinsha (a wire service).[159]

A second concern of newspaper management involved the fear that club journalists were forming excessively friendly relationships with their sources, and that, as a result, sources were frequently able to bribe journalists in the clubs with cash or gifts as a quid pro quo for favorable news stories or the withholding of information damaging to the source. Because

club journalists spent most of their time in the clubs and not in the newspaper offices, sources frequently had more control over them than company headquarters. Although club members argued that, as a group, the
clubs were able to force sources to divulge information, the historical evidence suggests otherwise: the relationship between club journalists and
their sources was more often than not either a subordinate or a cooperative
one.[160]

At times sources stepped in to mediate a dispute between clubs and
newspaper management. In 1936, after the *Kokumin shimbun* and its sister
newspaper the *Shin aichi* laid off forty-five employees, the organization
representing all of the clubs—the Newspaper and Wire Journalists' Press
Club League (Shimbun Tsūshin Kisha Kurabu Sorenmei)—on behalf of
these journalists expelled both the *Kokumin* and the *Shin aichi* from all
of the clubs until the companies reinstated the fired employees. Eventually, Prime Minister Koki Hirota was called in to mediate, and the journalists were given back their jobs.[161]

The newspaper companies first became concerned about the kinds of
relations journalists were developing with sources and with management
after the Russo-Japanese War, and in the decade after that war they tried
to introduce reforms to strengthen their control over journalists in the
clubs. Despite these efforts, the newspaper companies were still concerned
about the considerable independence of action of the clubs and club journalists two decades later.[162]

In 1931, the organization representing the managerial and editorial
divisions of the fifteen most powerful newspapers and wire services in
Tokyo—the Twenty-first Day Club or, Nijūichinichi-kai (presumably so
named because it met on the 21st of every month)—carried out an investigation of the press clubs in the hope of developing some useful ways to
bring them under its control.[163] The investigation concluded that the only
way to create a reporters' organization responsible to newspaper management and not to sources was to dissolve the press clubs altogether and
to replace them with an entirely different kind of newsgathering system.
Recognizing that this would be extremely difficult to carry out, the fifteen
members of the Twenty-first Day Club agreed that they would begin to
reform the press club system by limiting the number of clubs to one per
government agency (many agencies had more than one club by this time),
and by refusing to recognize any of the "intraclub agreements" commonly
made among club members or between club members and their sources,
unless the club had obtained the prior approval of newspaper management.

In response to this attempt, the thirty-nine press clubs in Tokyo formed
the umbrella organization mentioned earlier—the Tokyo Newspaper and
Wire Journalists' League."[164] Ultimately, the league was successful in

thwarting the initial attempt by the companies to limit the press clubs' autonomy. However, within a decade the newspaper companies would achieve their objective of limiting the operational autonomy of the clubs. They did this by cooperating with the state in establishing a structural reform of the newspaper industry and instigating wartime press controls that included a complete overhaul of the press club system. Eventually, newspaper management had to share control over the clubs with the Japanese state, remaining in a subordinate position throughout the wartime period.

The Press Clubs under Militarism

With the rise of militarism in the early 1930s, the government established formal measures to strengthen its control over the press and the press clubs. In September 1932 representatives from a number of key government ministries—including the Ministry of Foreign Affairs, Army Ministry, Navy Ministry, Ministry of Education, Home Affairs Ministry, and Communications Ministry—met and established an "information committee" (*jōhō iinkai*) to coordinate the release of government information to the press. Originally an informal, extralegal organization, the committee relied on a variety of informal mechanisms, including "administrative guidance" and "consultations" (*kondan*), to keep unfavorable news out of print and to influence the reporting of important stories. In July 1936, the committee was placed under the control of the prime minister's office and renamed the Cabinet Information Committee (Naikaku Jōhō Iinkai), then becoming the Cabinet Information Bureau (CIB) a year before the outbreak of the Pacific War. The CIB quickly became an important source for official reports on the war, serving as a key point of contact among newspaper management, the press clubs, and the Japanese state.

Once the war in the Pacific began, the government introduced a series of measures to control the press, making the clubs an important part of the wartime propaganda machine. But the government did not act alone in drawing up and implementing press reforms—it had important allies in several key national, daily newspapers who wanted to reduce the number of competitors in the industry and limit the autonomy of the press clubs. In 1941 the managers and editors of the major national newspapers in Japan formed the Japan Newspaper Union (Nihon Shimbun Renmei) to work with government officials to overhaul the newspaper industry and bring the press clubs under their joint control.[165] Headed by the vice-president of the *Asahi*, the organization stated in its bylines that its overarching goal was to "pursue the national mission of the newspaper industry."[166]

The Newspaper Union carried out this "national mission" by cooperating with the state in forcing the merger of its competitors in the prefectures. This task was accomplished by enlisting the aid of prefectural governors and special police (*tokubetsu kōtō keisatsu*) who helped enforce a "one paper per prefecture rule." The goal of this policy was to limit to one the number of competing papers in all of the prefectures and administrative units except Tokyo, Osaka, and Fukuoka. By 1943, of the 1,200 daily papers, 500 weekly magazines, and more than 10,000 irregularly published newspapers that had existed in 1937, only 55 remained.[167]

The one-paper-per-prefecture rule was mutually beneficial for the state and the dominant national newspapers. By forcing the combination of competing papers in the prefectures, the state gained greater control over the dissemination of official information. At the same time, this policy reduced the number of competitors in the market, an action of considerable benefit to larger national daily papers such as the *Asahi*, the *Mainichi*, and the *Yomiuri*. In a relatively short period of time, then, the Japanese state, together with a group of influential daily newspapers having historically close ties to it, was able to affect a level of concentration in the Japanese newspaper industry that even the fierce competition of the 1920s had not been able to achieve. This level was incomparable to that of any other advanced industrialized country at the time; comparable levels would not be realized elsewhere until the 1960s.

The Newspaper Union also worked with the government to devise a system for licensing journalists. Once this system was put into place, reporters had to "clearly grasp the national spirit (*kokutai*) and be righteous and upright" and have at least a high school education and "sufficient knowledge and experience" to be eligible for a government license to practice journalism.[168] Fewer than eight thousand of the estimated fifteen thousand journalists who applied for government licenses to practice journalism were found to have sufficiently "grasped the national spirit." Those who were ineligible were left without jobs: without a license they could not participate in the press clubs, and without access to the clubs, they had no access to important war-related information.

Having reduced the number of competing papers and practicing journalists, the Newspaper Union began to work with the government to achieve their long-desired mutual objective of reducing the autonomy of the press clubs. This they carried out by introducing a number of important reforms, including reducing the number of clubs to one per government agency, establishing a standardized method for naming the clubs,[169] limiting the number of newspapers that could belong to a given club to ten nationwide, and limiting the number of journalists each eligible newspaper could dispatch to a club to no more than four (eight to the clubs in the Army and Navy ministries).[170]

One additional reform introduced by the Newspaper Union was the standardization of club regulations (*kurabu kiyaku*) and their forced adoption by the clubs. Prior to the introduction of this reform, each club had independently drawn up its own regulations, which varied considerably from club to club. The new regulations the clubs were forced to adopt stated that their main purpose was to "carry out the national mission (*kokkateki shimei*) of the press *in cooperation with the government.*"[171]

Having compelled the clubs to adopt the new regulations, the Newspaper Union assumed responsibility for imposing sanctions if a journalist violated them, removing that role from the clubs. Club journalists were to report to the union any violations of news story and photography agreements, and slander or libel of the club by a club member. In the event of a violation, club regulations provided for the imposition of the following sanctions: (1) warning, (2) suspension, (3) expulsion, or (4) cancellation from the reporters' list (the new registration list drawn up by the association).[172] As outlined in chapter 4, similar types of punishments (particularly 1–3) still exist today, though generally the club or the source (not the newspaper company) imposes sanctions.

In 1955 the postwar newspaper association—the Japan Newspaper Publishers and Editors Association (Nihon Shimbun Kyōkai)—noted in its ten-year history that, in spite of the reforms introduced by the wartime association in 1941, "the *kisha* clubs still had a distinctive influence. In addition to demanding the right for self-government and refusing to abide by company regulations, they had other undesirable tendencies, including acquiring news that the government had not officially released." To remedy these remaining problems, in December 1943 the Newspaper Association (the successor to the Newspaper Union) and the Cabinet Information Bureau joined together to introduce a number of additional reforms. The CIB established a room within the bureau where announcements from all of the government ministries and agencies were to be made. From that point on, none of the press clubs in any of the other ministries was recognized, even though they continued to exist in name. Second, the CIB announced that while regularly scheduled press conferences were held for the mutual convenience of government agencies and journalists, the government was not obliged to hold them, nor did journalists have a right to demand that they be held. Third, the Newspaper Association reiterated its stance that club newsgathering agreements were not valid unless they had been approved by the association.[173] Finally, the association took over the accounting and management aspects of the clubs.

By joining together, the Newspaper Association and the Japanese state introduced a series of reforms that limited the number of newspapers having access to official information, reduced the number of press clubs that these competitors could participate in, and restricted the number of journalists in the clubs. By severely limiting the clubs' independence of action, these reforms made the state's wartime propaganda efforts much easier. In 1955, the postwar Japan Newspaper Publishers and Editors Association noted only the positive aspects of these wartime reforms, arguing that they effectively rid the industry of the " 'corrupt journalists' (*akutoku kisha*) who had made inroads into government offices" and the "harmful intraclub agreements, which had become more powerful than orders from company headquarters."[174]

Prewar and wartime reforms had a significant impact on postwar journalism. A high level of industry concentration, management of the clubs by company headquarters, and government protection of the dominant media companies either resulted from or were reinforced by these reforms.[175] In addition, the large national dailies with ties to the state, including *Asahi*, *Mainichi*, and *Yomiuri*, increased their circulations as a result of the forced consolidation of their competitors in the prefectures. These three largest newspapers were also given new territory as the war progressed. According to Coughlin, "control of the Java press was assigned to *Asahi*, the Philippines to *Mainichi*, and Burma to *Yomiuri*."[176]

In introducing these reforms, the Newspaper Association helped the state establish an efficient system for the control of information and the dissemination of government propaganda.[177] This system, composed of three key players—the government, the Newspaper Association, and the press clubs—played an important role in providing the wartime Japanese public with a standardized, homogenized, and sanitized version of the news, leaving little room for the expression of alternative interpretations of the war. This coordinated system for the "manufacture of consent," to borrow a phrase from Chomsky, is responsible for the fact that when the Occupation officials first arrived in Japan after the end of the war, they discovered that, "for the most part, the people knew nothing of the steps which had led the nation into war, nothing of the causes of defeat, nothing of the atrocities committed by Japanese troops. Belief that Japan's defeat was due solely to the atomic bomb was widespread."[178]

Postwar Kisha *Club Renascence: The Argument for Institutional Continuity*

After Japan's defeat in 1945, the Occupation authorities quickly moved to abolish wartime press controls and remove all governmental barriers to the free flow of information in Japan. In a directive entitled "Disassociation of Press from Government," General MacArthur sought to abolish the 1909 press law, one of the key legal mechanisms used to control the press preceding and during the war. He also ordered an end to "government control of, or interest in, Japanese newspapers."[179] While the Supreme Commander of the Allied Powers (SCAP) also might have been interested in the exclusionary press clubs and the degree to which the government maintained control over them, the clubs were not mentioned in this directive and do not appear to have been among the early concerns of the General Headquarters (GHQ).

Perhaps this is understandable. The focus of the Occupation's early democratization efforts was on the formal, legal barriers to democracy. Thus, SCAP worked to guarantee that Japan had a free press by ridding the country of repressive legislation and formal censorship. However, they all but ignored informal mechanisms of informational control such as the exclusionary, cartelized practices of the press clubs and the considerable power that sources still maintained over them at the end of the war. Although the press clubs would eventually come to the attention of those in charge of democratizing the nation, SCAP forced no true reorganization of the club system. One result is their continued existence today, more than a century after their introduction. In form as well as function, the modern press clubs differ little from those first described by early press critics in 1911.

With the removal of wartime constraints by SCAP, most of the prewar press clubs were quickly reestablished. However, membership was limited to those companies that had belonged to the clubs before or during the war, and only one or two of the large number of newspapers founded immediately after the war were allowed to join them. This is one of the reasons for their failure. Writing in 1952, Coughlin noted, "In a fiercely competitive and rapidly expanding postwar news field, the tightly monopolistic control which a few newspapers held over the Reporters' Clubs gave them a decisive edge."[180]

Newly established papers could not succeed in a publishing world in which they had no direct access to the main resource from which their product was made—official government information. Even the nation's number two news agency, the Jiji Tsushin, was excluded from all but a few of the clubs. Although the war had ended, the government still maintained a considerable degree of control over club activities. While state control over them was not as great in the postwar period as it had been during wartime, it may have been greater than before the war. This was in part due to the severe shortages the nation was experiencing at this time, and to the state's ability to requisition goods for which journalists (and other citizens) had a need. Coughlin notes that "the government's hold on the Reporters' Clubs increased in direct ratio to the various shortages, as government ministries passed out rationed cigarettes, free train passes, tinned food, shoes, uniforms and so on to the club members."[181]

While the GHQ did not move to abolish the clubs, they eventually recognized early on the danger in allowing the government to remain in control of them, and the undemocratic nature of many club practices. In November 1945, in an attempt to reduce government control over the clubs, SCAP backed a group of club journalists who were attempting to gain access to the committee meetings of the House of Peers. (The press club attached to the Upper House had been given access to plenary sessions but not to committee meetings.) After the government refused to respond to their demands for access, SCAP forced the House of Peers to make the committee meetings accessible to the press, just as the Lower House already had.[182] However, this move allowed Diet access only to those journalists who first of all had access to the clubs.

Another area SCAP sought to influence involved the press club rules, including the clubs' ability to expel members who refused to follow them. In May 1946 the managing editor of the *Yomiuri-Hochi* and vice-president of the newspaper federation, Suzuki Tomin, and a journalist from the same paper took part in a food demonstration sponsored by the Communist party. These journalists pitched a tent outside the prime minister's official residence for three days in an effort to get the prime minister to increase the supply of food, but they gave up the demonstration once it became clear that SCAP would not support their efforts. Not long after this incident, club members in the prime minister's office club (the Kantei club) expelled the newspaper from the club, claiming that its journalists had "impair[ed] the honor and dignity of the club" by participating in the demonstration. The expulsion of the paper did not last long, however; as soon as SCAP officials learned about the incident they forced the club to reinstate the paper, claiming that the expulsion was "an undemocratic action." Major Imboden, the SCAP official responsible for reforming the Japanese press, criticized the club's action as follows:

> Any action by anybody, official or non-official, which denies access by any legitimate newspaper to governmental news sources cannot be reconciled with the democratic concept of a free press. It is a disappointment to the Press and Publications division that the Japanese press, which has a paramount interest in the establishment and maintenance of freedom of access to news, has failed to use its power to make impossible any such restriction of this freedom as apparently has been imposed on the *Yomiuri*. What is tolerated in regard to one newspaper may be inflicted later on any newspaper. It is hoped that the Japanese press will act immediately to correct this situation in order to make it unnecessary for *some other agency* to act in its behalf."[183]

Although the club complied with SCAP's demands by lifting its restrictions on the newspaper in question, it did not lift the ban on the two individual journalists. This move was supported by Major Imboden, who felt that the club "had a right to discipline its individual members as long as such action did not affect the operation of an entire newspaper."[184]

A number of incidents involving the press clubs over the next three years led Major Imboden to inform the newly formed Japan Newspaper Publishers and Editors Association in August 1949 that it either had to reform the press clubs or dissolve them altogether. Since the latter was unacceptable, the association implemented perfunctory reforms, eventually drafting a proposal outlining its official position on the press clubs. In an effort to appease SCAP, the association stated in this document that the clubs were organizations "for friendship and socializing," not for newsgathering. The policy statement also noted that the clubs should permit nonmembers to participate freely in joint press conferences and, in what was perhaps the biggest contrast with the wartime association's statement regarding press-state relations, that government bureaucrats had a duty (*gimu*) as public servants to report their activities to the public. The mission of the newspaper journalist was to communicate government activities to the public; government organizations should provide rooms and phones for the press, not as favors but as an *obligation* to the public.[185] After Major Imboden approved this draft proposal, it was passed by the association's standing committee[186] and disseminated to all club members and official organizations on October 18, 1949. Eventually, the new policy was adopted by the clubs and incorporated into each club's regulations.

Six years after making this initial policy statement on the function and role of the press clubs, the association conceded in its own summary of its first ten years that, "although the character of the clubs has changed, in reality the notion that the clubs are a place for the gathering of news remains."[187] In spite of this concession, for quite sometime the association stood firmly by its official statement that the clubs "did not have a newsgathering function," though fully aware that their primary purpose was as a mechanism for newsgathering by a select group of mainstream journalists. As noted in chapter 5, the 1949 statement was only the first of a series of periodic statements the association would issue to deny the newsgathering function of the press clubs. This denial was important: it helped give the national papers sufficient time to continue the incursion into the local areas and allowed them to deny that they were exclusionary cartels.

The association struggled for the next four decades over the issue of determining the precise function of the press clubs and their true relationship to the Japanese state. The initial policy statement would haunt it for many years and would be revised on numerous occasions. In its commentary on the degree of similarity between the wartime and postwar roles of the *kisha* clubs, the Japan Newspaper Publishers and Editors Association made the following evaluation:

During the long course of the war the press clubs in the government agencies had been nothing more than organizations for the transmission of official announcements to the journalists stationed in them. When it came to the publication of official news reports, the custom was to make agreements that restricted publication to a certain day and time, and free competition in newsgathering was practically nonexistent. That custom remains even in the postwar period: Press clubs have the tendency to be moved more by the wishes of the government agencies or by the ideas of the club members themselves than by the wishes of their companies. Club members make promises based on mutual agreements and have built walls so that those not included in the club are not able to carry out newsgathering in government agencies.[188]

Although this summary of the postwar press clubs was written in 1955, most of it describes the way they operate today, forty-five years later. Indeed, as we shall see in the chapters that follow, the hundred-year-old relationship between press and state that was institutionalized with the establishment of the press clubs has remained virtually unchanged.

The Importance of Path Dependency

When Japanese leaders of the late Tokugawa and early Meiji periods imported the Western institution of the press, they brought it into a political and social environment quite unlike the milieu in which it had evolved. Consequently, in spite of similarities in the formal structure of the medium as a commercial enterprise, the press that developed in Japan and the political and social purposes it served have frequently differed in important respects from the model it emulated. Perhaps this is unsurprising: research shows, after all, that instances of cross-cultural organizational borrowing frequently involve innovation.[189] "Underdeveloped countries are not," as Herbert Passin once noted, "*tabulae rasae* waiting virginally for Western ideas to be inscribed. Each has a long history, a set of predispositions which select out, under specific historical conditions, the particular Western influences to which they will respond."[190] In short, institutions anywhere develop along "path-dependent" trajectories.

What is noteworthy in the case of the development of the Japanese press, then, is not institutional differentiation per se, but rather the process through which variation occurred and the impact that the resultant institutional configurations had on political outcomes in prewar, wartime, and postwar Japan.[191] I have sought to explain here how a medium with a long and rich history in the West as a vehicle for political dissent and a major opponent of government policy became first a tool of a modernizing developmental state, then briefly the agent of a political movement, and finally a commercial enterprise adopting an "impartial and nonpartisan" editorial position in order to minimize its political role while maximizing its economic position. A second area of interest has been to try to understand the reasons behind the maintenance of this socially inefficient (in terms of its impact on the development of democracy and free speech in Japan) institutional form. In other words, given the undemocratic nature of many of the institutional arrangements that have developed for gathering and disseminating the news in Japan, how can we explain their preservation? As I have argued here, institutional stasis is largely a function of the close relationships that have developed between the Japanese press and the state and their mutual interdependencies. The impact of these relationships becomes more readily apparent in subsequent chapters detailing the ways in which the information market in Japan is cartelized. This cartelization is mutually beneficial both to the select group of media outlets that belong to Japan's news cartels and to the state. Naturally, both of these actors have a substantial stake in the maintenance of the status quo.

As in the American case, "news" in Japan gradually came to be "self-consciously regarded as a safe alternative to political debate and polemic."[192] In the United States, however, one could endorse "news" over "partisanship" because there were other institutions firmly in place for the expression of partisan viewpoints. In a nation such as Japan, devoid of democratic institutions and lacking a well-defined civil society, however, a "safe" press was not necessarily a better press.

Additionally, while the Western press had made a similar shift away from a partisan political press toward more information-oriented and commercial papers, the impetus behind this shift differs substantially from that in Japan. In the West, this transition had taken place as part of a process that involved the democratization of politics, not its devaluation. As Schudson notes in his work on the American press, in the United States the shift toward an information-based press had occurred as part of, and coterminous with, the "democratization of politics, the expansion of a market economy, and the growing authority of an entrepreneurial, urban middle class," or, in other words, the rise of a "democratic market society."[193]

In Japan, however, the masses are never brought into the political framework before the advent of newspaper commercialization, nor do we see the successful establishment of a legitimate arena for political discourse. In short, while market forces played an important role in the rise of the facts- and news-oriented commercial press described in this chapter, the reality of political democracy is less clear. Indeed, an important and ongoing element of the shift from a political to a commercial-information press in Japan was the state's attempt to hold in check the rise of civil society by formal (legal) and informal means. As Barshay has noted, after 250 years of seclusion and control during the Tokugawa period, civil society in Meiji and Taishō Japan was not easily distinguishable from the state. The state sought to "bind the 'public' to itself, along with the authority to define the identity and values of its subjects."[194] And the press was one of the mechanisms the state relied on to do this. Their success in this endeavor was already manifest by the 1930s, and by 1940 there was no going back. By that point, the Diet was no longer functioning as a representative assembly, the political parties had voluntarily disbanded, and the press was well on its way to serving as an important ideological weapon on the state's behalf.

In sum, to those who seek to understand why in the process of its introduction into Japan the news medium was flipped on its head, becoming not an adversarial champion of citizens' rights nor a bulwark against tyranny but rather the voice of a modernizing elite and the purveyor of government policy in a period of rapid change, I offer the words of Robert Putnam: "where you can get to depends on where you're coming from, and some destinations you simply cannot get to from here."[195]

Three

Japan's Information Cartels

PART I. COMPETITION AND THE CLOSED SHOP

> To the adage that if one wishes to enjoy either sau-
> sages or politics, one should not see how either is
> made, one can now add the news.
>   (*Aaron Wildavsky*)

> It was just these womblike conditions that gave
> rise to the notorious phenomenon called "pack
> journalism" (also known as "herd journalism"
> and "fuselage journalism"). A group of reporters
> were assigned to follow a single candidate for
> weeks or months at a time, like a pack of hounds
> sicked on a fox. Trapped on the same bus or
> plane, they ate, drank, gambled, and compared
> notes with the same bunch of colleagues week
> after week. Actually, this group was as hierarchical
> as a chess set. . . . But they all fed off the same
> pool report, the same daily handout, the same
> speech by the candidate; the whole pack was iso-
> lated in the same mobile village. After a while,
> they began to believe the same rumors, subscribe
> to the same theories, and write the same stories.
> Everybody denounces pack journalism, including
> the men who form the pack. Any self-respecting
> journalist would sooner endorse incest than come
> out in favor of pack journalism.
>   (*Timothy Crouse*, The Boys on the Bus)

HEGEL once argued that it was "senseless to talk of an absolute or objective reality without connecting with the procedures through which such
a reality could be established as real by us."[1] Given that modern media
organizations play a major role in constructing our daily reality, we should
strive to understand the procedures, rules, norms, and institutions that
guide the media as they perform this role.[2] Media scholars have deter-

mined that most of the news that gets reported by the American press emanates from official sources. In a study of the *New York Times* and the *Washington Post*, for example, Leon Sigal found that public officials were the sources of close to 80 percent of all news stories reported in these two papers.[3] In Japan the figure is even higher. Hara Toshio has suggested that as much as 90 percent of all news in Japan comes from official sources, a fact that takes on added significance given the distinctive structure of relations between news sources and journalists, a subject taken up in more detail in this and the following chapter.[4]

Because so much of our "reality-constructing" news comes from these sources, the patterned relations they have with journalists and news organizations, and the tacit and formalized rules governing their relations, have been a frequent subject of academic inquiry. Less studied, but nonetheless important, are the relationships among journalists from rival news organizations and those among the news organizations themselves. To comprehend how the media function in contemporary society, then, we must first understand the process through which sources and journalists balance such conflicting goals as access and autonomy, publicity and secrecy, protection of sources and readership trust. We must also consider the ways that rival journalists and news organizations cooperate to share and minimize the risks inherent in their profession, and examine the forms such accommodation and cooperation take. Finally, we need to consider how these practices may differ cross-nationally and analyze their impact on the political process.

Competition, Cooperation, and the "Information Marketplace"

The late Nobel laureate economist George Stigler defined competition as "a rivalry between individuals (or groups or nations) [that] arises whenever two or more parties strive for something that all cannot obtain." Suggesting that competition is "at least as old as man's history," Stigler points out that Darwin adopted the concept from Malthus and "applied it to species as economists had applied it to human behavior."[5] This broad concept has been used to explain many different kinds of relationships, whether economic, political or social.

When applied to the media, the concept of competition has become the cornerstone of the most frequently recurring media metaphor—that of a "marketplace of ideas." This metaphor envisions an open arena in which buyers and sellers of news and information bargain and compete. Even our normative image of journalism, which assumes both an intense rivalry among media outlets for information and audiences and adversarial relations between sources and reporters, is based on the market concept. With its assumption of unconstrained competition in informational transactions, the metaphor has also been used by free-speech advocates in the United States, setting boundaries within which debate about important free speech issues is carried out. Former U.S. Supreme Court Justice Oliver Wendell Holmes, sounding like a not-so-distant relative of Adam Smith, offered an eloquent summary of the idea when he opined that "the ultimate good desired is better reached by free trade in ideas—that the best test of truth is the power of the thought to get itself accepted in the competition of the market."[6]

On numerous occasions, the metaphor has been extended to debates involving government policies toward the media industry. Framing these discussions is the idea that media competition is important to the development of an informed citizenry, that "a vigorous and diverse marketplace of ideas . . . offer[s] numerous benefits to the social and political life of [a] nation."[7] Earlier generations used this notion as the basis for seeking to limit state interference in the free trade of ideas. As Curran points out, "traditionalist liberal thought argues that . . . only by anchoring the media to the free market is it possible to ensure the media's complete independence from government."[8]

More recently, the question has been how the state might act to correct market failures and reduce restrictions on informational exchange imposed by *private* interests—that is, by the media industry itself. The policy issue here has been whether and to what extent the state should intervene in order to foster or nurture the competition in ideas thought necessary to a democratic society. In the United States, the answer seems to be the same as it is with state involvement in the rest of the economy—namely, that it should be kept to a minimum. It is probably for this reason that chain ownership of broadcast stations and other potentially anticompetitive practices are not as vigorously pursued in government antitrust policy as they have been in the past, even as the process of concentration continues and a decreasing number of cities offer the public competing papers.[9]

The most noteworthy example of attempts by the U.S. government to protect idea diversity was the Fairness Doctrine. Seeking to provide the means for competing ideas to enter the marketplace, the doctrine required television stations to provide air time for the expression of alternative viewpoints. This doctrine was abolished, however, when the Federal Communication Commission decided a number of years ago that there had arisen a "genuinely competitive market that will guarantee diversity and autonomy in political information more effectively than government regulation ever could."[10] As one critic of state intervention put it, "doesn't every regulation converting the media into a 'neutral forum' lessen its capacity to act as a partisan gadfly, investigating and criticizing government in an aggressive way?"[11]

Many Western European governments, including those in Sweden, Norway, Italy, and France, apparently disagree with this argument, providing operational subsidies to newspapers in order to foster competition and diversity of ideas in the media marketplace.[12] Lent argues that in Sweden such subsidies have boosted the scrutinizing function of the press, stemmed concentration, and fostered the establishment of new newspapers—all while "complementing the market system." He explains Swedish subsidies this way: "The purpose of the Swedish system of subsidies is to encourage newspapers in the performance of their function to promote the formation of political opinion in the widest sense. The system reflects the idea that newspapers play (and should continue to do so) an important part in the democratic system and that this requires a multiplicity of newspapers."[13] Although competition would be meaningless without such diversity, it is unclear whether a state-subsidized media can remain truly impartial.

Despite the popularity and power of the marketplace metaphor as a Weberian ideal type, competition within the information market is rarely the "pure" competition of economic textbooks. The focus on competition represents an incomplete view of market systems, for markets, both informational and other, require rules to order and govern the relations between buyer and seller and among competing groups of buyers and sellers. Sometimes rules are mandated by government and are intended either to reduce excessive cooperation among competitors (as in the case of antitrust measures) or, conversely, to enhance competitiveness (as in the case of the operating subsidies referred to above). More often they take the form of tacit understandings among competitors that order behavior, reduce competitive excesses, and enhance cooperation. Rules thus change the nature of competition by providing the framework within which it takes place. They are so much an institutionalized part of marketplace behavior that they frequently go unnoticed.

In the media context, rules have an impact on information and idea diversity at at least two stages—information gathering (between journalists and sources) and information dissemination (within the media industry). Although both are important, the focus of this and the following chapter is on rules and procedures as they relate to information gathering.

In his path-breaking study of American media practices, Leon Sigal suggests that relationships between reporters and sources are based on a curious mix of motives, and that "overt competition coexists with tacit cooperation." Sigal points to the existence of certain rules "which seek to limit, but not do away with competition on most beats."[14] These rules, which at times include embargoes or agreements with sources not to disclose their identity, limit competition for news and may mean that information is framed in comparable, homogenous ways and reported simultaneously by a large number of news organizations. As a consequence, newspaper companies in the United States have tried to limit cooperation at the news-gathering level by establishing their own rules, such as those regulating the attribution of sources. In many cases, journalists must justify the non-attribution of a source both to editors and to readers.

The journalist-source relationship is not, however, the only media relationship based on mutual understanding and a delimited sense of rivalry. Competing journalists covering the same beat have also been known to cooperate under certain circumstances, exchanging information out of expediency by relying on such practices as pool reporting (one reporter or a group gather information that is then shared with the rest of the reporters) and "blacksheeting" (in precomputer days this entailed handing out carbon copies of one's dispatch to other reporters).[15] It was this kind of cooperative behavior among journalists covering U.S. presidential elections that led to the coining of the pejorative term "pack journalism." But such cooperation among American journalists is the exception and not the norm. Pool reporting, for example, is utilized only in the most extreme of situations, such as wartime, and is generally imposed on journalists by military or other sources, as it was during the Persian Gulf War. Furthermore, presidential elections happen only once every four years.[16]

Jeremy Tunstall's analysis of the British media also supports the cooperative characterization of journalists' relations with sources and with each other. In his study of political journalism in Britain, Tunstall suggests that information gathering entails an "active element—of personal interaction with news sources which involves notions of implicit *bargaining and of exchange.* . . . Firstly, in [the journalist's] role as newsgatherer in relation to news sources, there is an exchange of information for publicity; secondly, in relation to competitors working for other news organizations there is a colleague [*sic*], or helping, type of exchange of information for other information."[17] As detailed in chapter 6, British political reporting relies on a high level of cooperation: to gather information on Westminster, for example, one must belong to a proprietary newsgathering association known as the "lobby." Still, these characterizations of the American and British press appear incompatible with our normative image of journalism—that of an intense rivalry for information and audiences in an open market, of adversarial relations among journalists, sources, and competitors. With the establishment of rules, the nature of competition in the newsgathering process changes.[18] Adversarial relationships are mitigated by those of cooperation, exchange, and reciprocity. As a consequence, relations become more symbiotic than competitive.

One result of rule-based competition is that the information market-place becomes less an open arena where competing interests collide than a well-orchestrated auction in which information is a powerful and coveted commodity and the media act as "information brokers" between the state and society.[19] While the media have been "hired" by society, in their role as brokers they must develop close relationships with information holders (the state) and with other information brokers seeking the same informa-tion. How they develop and maintain these relationships without being co-opted by sources or compromising society's interests has been a long-standing dilemma for the media everywhere.

As the above discussion indicates, there are inherent problems with the marketplace metaphor, as cooperation and collective activities are as much a part of the information marketplace as competition. It also raises im-portant questions about the media's ability to carry out their watchdog function in a democracy and the viability of the watchdog image itself, which is predicated on the existence of free-wheeling competition and an open market, not the rule-based cooperation suggested here. While those who work in the information market—journalists—hold tenaciously to the belief that the media are both adversarial and competitive, the reality of rival buyers and sellers in the marketplace of ideas is, as we shall see, quite different.[20]

No one questions the necessity of rules for exchange. Without them, social chaos would ensue. The dilemma for the social scientist is to deter-mine where useful rules end and pernicious rules begin. What differenti-ates legitimate cooperative efforts aimed at preventing market chaos and those that create anticompetitive cartels? As the examples of the United States and Britain suggest, the institutional coordination of media activi-ties through the establishment of rules and procedures is a generic aspect of the newsgathering process in advanced democracies.

At the same time, for a number of reasons—historical, structural, and institutional—both the form that such rules have taken and the impli-cations they have for the state-media-society relationship differ across countries. What, if anything, for example, distinguishes the rules and procedures governing newsgathering in Japan from the kinds of coopera-tive-competitive media practices found elsewhere? And what are the impli-cations of these differences for the amount and type of news that gets reported? It is to these issues that we shall now turn.

The Postwar *Kisha* Clubs and Club-Based Journalism

In Japan (and to a lesser extent in Britain), the information-gathering process takes place within a "closed shop" made up of journalists having proprietary access to information and sources. Contact with official sources is limited to a select group of individuals or organizations that have established a clearly defined, if not codified, set of rules and practices. The perpetuation of the closed shop is guaranteed by the enforcement of sanctions or the threat of their enforcement. These define the basic features of what I term Japan's "information cartels."

The focal point for these interactions is the *kisha* club. Today's clubs are located in most major governmental, political, and business organizations. In Tokyo they can be found in every ministry, the headquarters of all of the major political parties, important economic organizations such as Keidanren, and other sports, entertainment, and consumer organizations. In the prefectures and larger cities, clubs are located in local parliaments, police headquarters, the courts, and chambers of commerce. They can also be found in research hospitals and major universities.[21]

Although some of Japan's larger corporations have meeting rooms (*ōen-shitsu*) that they call *kisha kurabu*, in general private companies do not have their own press clubs.[22] Exceptions include the clubs attached to Japan Railways (JR) and NTT, two companies that were privatized in the 1980s. "Semiprivate" organizations—private companies providing public services—such as the Japan Atomic Energy Headquarters and the Tokyo Electric Company—also have clubs attached to them. Likewise, NHK, a private nonprofit corporation established by the government in 1950, has its own press club and is unique among media organizations in this respect.[23]

The exact number of press clubs in Japan is not known. Kawai Ryōsuke, a media scholar, has suggested that there are as many as 1,000 clubs nationwide, while Japan Newspaper Publishers and Editors Association (NSK) documents generally use the considerably lower figure of 400.[24] The actual number probably falls somewhere in between. Nishiyama Takesuke, a former journalist and editor for Kyodo Tsushin, writes that in 1986 Kyodo dispatched journalists to 612 clubs throughout the country, 99 of which were in Tokyo.[25] A more recent article on the press clubs published by *Asahi shimbun* states that there are as many as 700 clubs throughout Japan and that *Asahi* journalists are dispatched to approximately 73 in Tokyo alone.[26]

Although one might expect the industry association in charge of the overall management of the clubs—the NSK—to keep a record of all the active clubs in the country, representatives of the association have repeatedly claimed that no such list exists. Consequently, the list of 121 Tokyo-based press clubs provided in table 1 had to be compiled by combining ten separate lists published in a variety of sources (including thirty-year-old NSK documents). While it is possible that a small number of the clubs on this list are no longer active, have merged with others, or have changed their names and have been unintentionally duplicated, the list still represents the most comprehensive registry of the Tokyo-based press clubs currently available.

As indicated in table 1, some ministries and organizations have more than one club. This phenomenon first began to appear during the early part of the Shōwa (1925–1989) era when disputes between large and small (national and local) papers and the wire services resulted in the division of clubs along functional lines.[27] This practice continued into the postwar period, and even today some ministries, such as the Ministry of Construction and the Ministry of Finance, have one club for industry and/or local newspapers and another comprised of mainstream print, broadcast, and wire companies. Still, the clubs comprising the national newspapers and their affiliated broadcast stations are treated preferentially by sources.[28]

In some instances the broadcast media, which did not gain access to the clubs until after the war, have formed their own clubs. The Ministry of Foreign Affairs, for example, for a long time had three clubs, one comprised of mainstream newspapers, wires, and NHK (the Kasumi Kurabu), one made up of commercial broadcast stations (the Minpō Hōsō Kisha Kurabu), and a third for foreigners. Similarly, the Ministry of Transportation, which has a number of clubs, has one specifically for commercial broadcast stations (the Unyushō Minkan Shimbun Kishakai) and another for industry newspapers (the Unyushō Senmon Shimbun Kishakai). In some cases, separate briefings and press conferences are held for each club in a given organization, though an explicit hierarchy exists, with the mainstream national and bloc papers having a preferential place.

In spite of the postwar efforts by the NSK to limit increases in the number of *kisha* clubs, several new clubs were established during the 1970s, including those in the Environmental Agency (itself established in 1971) and the Tsūsan Kishakai Shakaibu Bunshitsu, located in the Ministry of International Trade and Industry (MITI).[29] The newest club, the Renritsu Yotō (coalition government) club, housed in the party headquarters of the New Japan party (Shinseitō), was created after the LDP lost its majority in the Lower House in 1993 and a new coalition government came to power for the first time in almost four decades. Other relatively new clubs include seven that have been established throughout the postwar period exclusively for magazine journalists and photographers. Magazine journalists are excluded from participation in the regular clubs attached to most official organizations and consequently formed their own association in 1956 for the express purpose of lobbying for access to official sources.[30] A list of the clubs to which its members belongs is provided in table 2.

With the exception of a category of journalists known as *yūgun* or roving reporters, the *kisha* clubs serve as home base for the majority of Japanese journalists. Typically arriving at their respective clubs in early to mid-

TABLE 1
Major *Kisha* Clubs in Tokyo

Affiliation	*Club Name*
Political Organizations	
Diet	Kokkai kishaka
	Kokkai shashin kisha kurabu
House of Representatives	Shugiin kisha kurabu
House of Councilors	Sangiin kisha kurabu
Cabinet	Naikaku kishakai
Liberal Democratic Party	Jiyūminshutō kisha kurabu
Social Democratic Party of Japan	Shakaitō kisha kurabu
Clean Government Party	Kōmeitō kisha kurabu
Democratic Socialist Party	Minshatō kisha kurabu
Japan Communist Party	Kyōsantō kisha kurabu
Ruling Coalition (established in 1993)	Renritsu yotō kurabu
Ministries	
Agriculture, Forestry, and Fisheries	Nōrinshō nōsei kurabu
	Nōrin kishakai
	Shokuryō kishakai
	Rinsei kisha kurabu
	Suisanchō kisha kurabu
Construction	Kensetsu kurabu
	Kensestushō senmon shimbun kisha kurabu
Education	Monbushō kisha kurabu
	Monbu kishakai
	Nankyoku kishakai
Finance	Zaisei kenkyūkai
	Zaisei kurabu
Foreign Affairs	Kasumi kurabu
	Minpō hōsō kisha kurabu
	Gaijin kisha kurabu
Health and Welfare	Kōsei kishakai
	Kōsei hibiya kurabu
Home Affairs	Naisei kurabu
International Trade and Industry	Tsūsan kishakai
	Tsūsan kishakai shakaibu bunshitsu
	Tsūsanshō pen kurabu
	Tsūsanshō toranomon kurabu

TABLE 1 *(continued)*
Major *Kisha* Clubs in Tokyo

Affiliation	Club Name
International Trade and Industry *(continued)*	Tsūsanshō unemekai
	Chūshō kigyōchō pen kurabu
	Shigen kisha kurabu
Justice	Hōsō kisha kurabu
	Hōmushō kisha kurabu
Labor	Rōdōshō kisha kurabu
	Rōsei kisha kurabu
Posts and Telecommunications	Yūsei kisha kurabu
	Yūseishō terekomu kishakai
	Iikura kurabu
	Denpa kishakai
Transportation	Unyōshō kisha kurabu
	Nihon kōkūyū testudō kisha kurabu
	Nihon kōkūkyoku kurabu
	Kōtsū kishakai
	Unyōshō senmon shimbun kishakai
	Unyōshō minkan hōsō kisha kurabu
	Kōtsū seisaku kenkyūkai

Government Agencies and Other Organizations

Administrative Management Agency	Gyōseikanrichō kisha kurabu
Defense Agency	Bōei kishakai
	Bōeichō kisha kurabu
	Hinokichō kisha kurabu
Defense Facilities Administration Agency	Bōei shisetsu kishakai
Economic Planning Agency	Keizai kikakuchō kisha kurabu
	Keizai kenkyūkai
	Sangyō kishakai
Environment Agency	Kankyōchō kisha kurabu
	Kankyō mondai kenkyūkai
	Kankyōchō kankyō kishakai
	Kankyō hozen kenkyūkai
Hokkaido Development Agency	Kaihatsu kurabu
Imperial Household Agency	Kunai kishakai
Management and Coordination Agency	Sōmuchō kisha kurabu
	Somucho kankei kisha kurabu
Maritime Safety Agency	Kaijō hoanchō kisha kurabu
	Kaijō hoanchō muroto kisha kurabu

TABLE 1 *(continued)*
Major *Kisha* Clubs in Tokyo

Affiliation	*Club Name*
Meteorological Agency	Kishochō kisha kurabu
National Diet Library	Kokuritsu kokkai toshokan
National Land Agency	Kokudochō kisha kurabu
	Kokudochō senmonshi kisha kurabu
	Kokudo seisaku kenkyūkai
National Personnel Authority	Naisei kisha kurabu
National Tax Administration Agency	Kokuzeichō kisha kurabu
	Kokuzei kisha kurabu
Okinawa Development Agency	Sōrifu kisha kurabu Okinawa kaihatsu-chō tantō yokakai
	Okinawa sōgō jimukyoku kisha kurabu
Prime Minister's Office	Sōrifu kisha kurabu
Science and Technology Agency	Kagaku gijutsu kisha kurabu
	Kagaku kishakai

Courts and Police

Metropolitan Police Headquarters	Keishichō kisha kurabu
	Nanashakai
	Keishichō nyūsu kishakai
National Police Agency	Keisatsuchō kisha kurabu
Supreme Court	Saikō saibanshō kisha kurabu
	Saikōsai shihō kisha shitsu
Tokyo High Court	Shihō kisha kurabu
Tokyo District Court	Tokyo chiban kisha kurabu

Economic and Business Organizations

Bank of Japan	Kinyū kisha kurabu
The Federation of Economic Organizations (Keidanren)	Keizai dantai kishaka (enerugi/energy)
	Keizai dantai kishakai (jūkōgyō kenky-ūkai/heavy industries)
	Keizai dantai kishakai (kikai kurabu/machinery)
	Keizai dantai kishakai (zaikai-chūshōki-gyō/finance and small business)
Japan External Trade Organization	Bōeki kishakai
Japan Tobacco Industry	Nihon tabako kisha kurabu

TABLE 1 *(continued)*
Major *Kisha* Clubs in Tokyo

Affiliation	*Club Name*
JR Higashi Nihon kaisha	Tokiwa kurabu
	Tetsudō kishakai
NTT	Aoi kurabu
Tokyo Chamber of Commerce	Tōshō kurabu
Tokyo Stock Exchange	Kabuto kurabu
Commodity Exchange	Hinoki kurabu

Other Organizations

Agricultural Coop. Assoc. (Nōkyō)	Nōkyō kisha kurabu
Fire Defense Agency	Naisei kurabu
	Shakai kurabu
Haneda Airport	Tokyo kōkū kishakai
Japan Atomic Energy Headquarters	Genshiryoku kisha kurabu
Japan Central Horse Race Assoc.	Tokyo keiba kishakai
Japan Gymnastics Association	Taikyō kisha kurabu
Machinery Industry Promotion Assoc.	Kikai shinko kaikan kisha kurabu
Monopoly Corporation	Senbai kisha kurabu
Narita Airport	Narita kōkū kishakai
NHK	Rajio-terebi kishakai
	Tokyo hōsō kishakai
Science Council of Japan	Gakujutsu kishakai
Social Insurance Agency	Shakai hoken kenkyūkai
Tokyo Electric Company	Katei kishakai joninkai
Tokyo Metropolitan Government Office	Yuraku kurabu
	Kajibashi kurabu
Tokyo University	Tokyo daigaku kisha kurabu

Sources: Kawai Masayoshi, *Nyūsu hōdō shuzai no shikumi ga wakaru hon* (Tokyo: Asuka, 1992), 178; *Shimbun Kenkyū*, March 1966, 86–92; Inaba Sabuo and Arai Naohiro, eds., *Shimbungaku* (Tokyo: Nihon Hyoronsha, 1988), 96.; Kawai Ryosuke, *Yoron to masu komyunikēshiyon* (Tokyo: Bureen Shuppan, 1989), 142; Inaba Yutaka, *Kisha kurabu o kiru* (Tokyo: Nisshin Hodo Shuppanbu, 1978), 193–96; *Asahi Shimbun*, February 2, 1993; *Mainichi datebook*, 1994; Sendenkaigi, *Masukomi denwachō 1994-han* (Tokyo: Dendenkaigi, 1994), 275–76; Puresu nettowaaku 94, *Shimbun no ura mo omote mo wakaru hon* (Tokyo: Kanki Shuppan, 1994), 51; Asahi Shimbun, *Asahi Shimbun Weekly AERA*, October 1, 1991, 28.

TABLE 2
Magazine *Kisha* Clubs

Location	Club Name
National Diet (JMPA)	Kokkai zasshi kisha kurabu
Imperial Household Agency (JMPA)	Kunaichō zasshi kisha kurabu
International Airport (JMPA)	Kokusai kūkō zasshi kisha kurabu
JMPA (Sports)	Zasshi supōtsu kisha kurabu
JMPA (Arts)	Zasshi geino kisha kurabu
JMPA (Leisure)	Zasshi rejaa kisha kurabu
JMPA (Police)	Shoho-keisatsu zasshi kisha kurabu

Source: Nihon zasshi kishakai 25-nenshi, 1985.

Note: To be a member of these clubs a magazine must belong to the Japan Magazine Publishers Association (JMPA), which currently has seventy-nine member companies. These clubs differ from the newspaper clubs in that they are frequently headquartered in the JMPA offices. While individual newspaper *kisha* clubs draw up their own regulations, the JMPA has outlined a set of rules that apply to all of the clubs to which a magazine might belong.

morning, journalists begin their day by reviewing the morning editions of rival newspapers, checking for any missed information. This may be followed by attendance at a regularly scheduled news conference, a post conference *kondan* or informal briefing, a lecture (*rekuchaa*) on a related topic, or other activities having to do with the reporting of current events.

Journalists also leave the clubs to pursue stories and conduct interviews, but even these activities are frequently carried out in an institutionalized fashion, and often as a group. Younger journalists covering the major political parties or the police and prosecutors' offices, for example, often spend a considerable portion of their day conducting morning and nightly rounds known as *asamawari* and *yomawari* (also referred to as *youchi-asagake* or *satsumawari* in the case of the police). From early morning until quite late at night, groups of (often neophyte) journalists follow powerful individuals with whom they ultimately develop very close (and at times quite deferential) relationships.

Promising young political journalists, for example, are often assigned to cover LDP faction bosses. These journalists, known as "*ban* journalists" (*ban kisha*), frequently start their day by going straight to the politician's home, arriving at about 7:30 in the morning. Together with journalists from other news organizations, they greet the politician and then follow him or her around for most of the day, waiting for any tidbit of news that might be offered. In addition to gathering information, they often spend a good deal of time and effort developing friendly relations with the politician they cover. Indeed, as detailed later, the courting of sources by these journalists has been institutionalized to a remarkable degree, with emphasis placed on the development of long-term relations that may last well beyond the initial two- or three-year assignment. Though most *ban* journalists will eventually be invited into the politician's home, a journalist is said to have been successful when he or she has developed sufficiently close relations with a source to have been allowed to enter a room of the house other than the special waiting room provided for journalists.[31]

Certain types of club journalists spend a considerable portion of their day within the club as part of a group of journalists from their own company covering the same club (such as the club in the prime minister's official residence) or as part of a larger group of journalists from rival companies who are club members. By all accounts, the amount of time spent in the press club or at club- or source-sponsored functions has increased dramatically throughout the postwar period. Many journalists claim that they are now inundated with such large volumes of information from government and business sources that they rarely have time to check facts, not to mention searching out alternative viewpoints.[32] A survey published in the 1994 annual report of the NSK research institute and reproduced in figure 3 found that 41.6 percent of a total of 1,735 journalists interviewed agreed that they did not have sufficient time to carry out background analyses for their stories, while 76.9 percent said that they either agreed or somewhat agreed with this evaluation.[33]

In part, the fact that the journalists are inundated with such large volumes of information results from the concerted effort by the Japanese government to establish and strengthen public relations sections in important ministries and government agencies beginning in 1960, a year with considerable domestic turmoil over the renewal of the U.S.–Japan Security Treaty.[34] Nishiyama suggests that the PR system established by the police in 1964 has served as an important model for PR sections in key government agencies throughout Japan.[35] The creation and enhancement of these PR sections has been made possible by the Japanese Diet, which, since the early 1960s, has continually voted for budget increases for government PR activities. The volume of materials distributed to journalists in the clubs and the number of meetings and contacts they have with the PR rooms have increased significantly since the 1960s, making the press clubs an important and effective means for government management of the news.

Table 3 lists increases in the PR budget of the Prime Minister's Office from 1960 to 1972 and contrasts them with those of the Defense Agency during the same period. Although data for the intervening years is lacking, by 1985 the total PR budget for the Japanese government was twenty-four billion yen per year, placing it somewhere between the nation's eighth largest private advertiser—Nihon Denki—and its twelfth, Suntory.[36] While these funds were not earmarked specifically to cover expenses re-

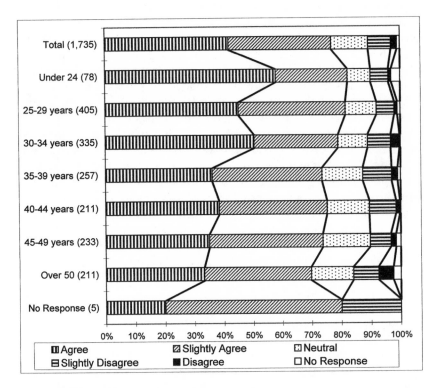

Figure 3. Survey of Journalists' Opinions on Newsgathering.
Number who responded that they did not have sufficient time to conduct
background research.
  Source: Nihon shimbun kyōkai kenkyūjō nenpo, vol. 12 (1994): 32.

lated to the management of journalists in the press clubs, at least a portion
of this budget was used to cover the cost of the permanent staff assigned
to the clubs and the staffing of the PR sections. These PR bureaus are
frequently located next door to the club room, and their staff develop close
working relationships with club journalists, particularly those assigned the
job of club supervisor (*kanji*).

Ministries may also use the clubs for their own PR purposes, especially
during the turf battles that erupt around budget time. Then, each ministry tries to get articles on its successful policies, future projects, and budget requirements published in the press in order to influence the Ministry
of Finance and gain bigger operating budgets for the following year.

The considerable financial resources of the government PR bureaus
make it it possible for state agencies to become quite adept in handling the
kisha clubs. Not only have government PR sections become sophisticated

TABLE 3
Comparing the Public Relations Budgets of
the Prime Minister's Office and the Defense
Agency (figures in million yen)

Year	Prime Minister's Office	Defense Agency
1959	100	n.a.
1960	179	n.a.
1961	308	n.a.
1962	430	n.a.
1963	500	n.a.
1964	580	130
1965	657	150
1966	740	193
1967	930	229
1968	1,220	244
1969	1,330	263
1970	1,610	285
1971	1,829	305
1972	2,021	317

Source: Kido Mataichi et al., eds., *Kōzō gendai
jaanarizumu II: shimbun* (Tokyo: Jiji Tsushinsha,
1973), 154.

writers of "news," their press releases often closely resemble both the style and format of Japanese newspaper articles. Occasionally they even include suggested headlines and subheadlines, leads and graphics.[37] One student of the Japanese press cites a "well-known chief cabinet secretary" who declared, "We are quite happy when club members spend their time sitting in the club. We give them all the information they need."[38]

In March 1971, as part of a strategy to gain greater control over the press, the MITI ministerial PR section (*daijin kanbō kōhōka*) published a set of detailed "guidelines" for handling journalists in the clubs. This forty-seven-page pamphlet entitled *A Notebook on Public Relations* (*Kōhō zakkichō*) included recommendations for managing the clubs, hints on how to guarantee that press releases would find their way to the front page, and ways to get rid of journalists conducting their nightly *yomawari* rounds. The *Notebook on Public Relations* is said to have been a secret best-seller in Kasumigaseki, the political center of the Japanese bureaucracy.[39]

The efforts to control the media through the utilization of the clubs are not limited to the large central bureaucracies. In the spring of 1991 the Saitama Prefectural Educational Division (*Saitama kyōikukyoku*) handed out a booklet to its 1,200 members entitled *How to Brief Journalists* (*Kisha happyō no hōhō*). This manual explained how to arrange press conferences with journalists and included points for drawing up press releases. One section, entitled "How to Respond to Interviews," is illustrative of the extent to which such organizations try to control the flow of information to the media, their attitudes toward journalists, and their support of the demand by club journalists for "fairness" in the divulgence of information that provides the basis for newsgathering in the club. The booklet tells members that "When journalists conduct newsgathering they are looking for a scoop. But if you divulge important information only to a certain journalist, this interferes with fair reporting. If an important item has been decided, promptly make arrangements with the club to make an announcement to all of the journalists. . . . If a journalist comes to interview you, always contact the PR supervisor and inform him or her of the contents of the interview."[40]

It has been argued that the homogeneity of Japan's newspapers and their tendency to provide excessively detailed accounts of a narrow range of issues while neglecting to provide explanations of the impact that government policies have on the public at large results from the heavy reliance by press club journalists on government press releases and their co-optation by government media handlers.[41] Both journalists and media scholars have criticized this practice, known cynically as "press release journalism" (*happyō hōdō*).

Tables 4 and 5 show the kinds and extent of public relations activities by the Ministry of Education and the Ministry of International Trade and Industry in 1984 and 1985, respectively. In 1984 the Ministry of Education sponsored an average of eighty-five PR activities (including conferences with ministers and vice-ministers, lectures, and press releases) a month, or close to three a day. The 1985 data for MITI reveal a similar pattern, and more recent data released in 1990 suggest that this has changed very little. The recent data also show the extent of the contacts between club members and their government sources, and the considerable volume of information conveyed to those having the privilege of belonging to the clubs.[42] From January to December 1990, for example, club journalists in the MITI club participated in 87 press conferences with the MITI minister and 69 with the vice-minister, attended 331 lectures and received 571 press releases. Having that information, however, is quite a different matter from acting on it, as we shall see shortly.

Journalists gain numerous benefits from participation in the clubs. As club members they have access to a large volume of information about government policies and activities. Additionally, they do not have to work hard to woo sources—as proximity to official sources is one of the benefits of membership, albeit a benefit shared by all members in common. One

TABLE 4
Public Relations Activities of the Ministry of Education

Year 1948	Minister's Conferences	Vice-Secretary's Conferences	Lectures	Press Releases	Total
January	16	2	22	52	92
February	11	0	21	84	116
March	10	1	9	84	104
April	8	1	13	67	89
May	8	1	12	60	81
June	9	0	14	50	73
July	9	0	16	81	106
August	6	1	13	49	69
September	7	1	19	37	64
October	9	0	17	52	78
November	9	0	6	51	66
December	11	1	24	49	85
Total	113	8	186	716	1023

Source: Kawai Ryosuke, *Yoron to masu komyunikēshiyon* (Tokyo: Buren Shuppan, 1987), 157. Original data collected by the ministry.

TABLE 5
Public Relations Activities of the Ministry of International Trade and Industry

Year 1985	Minister's Conferences	Vice-Secretary's Conferences	Lectures	Press Releases	Other
January	6	6	24	17	0
February	9	7	24	18	0
March	11	10	26	27	1
April	8	8	33	16	1
May	9	7	41	21	1
June	9	8	42	27	1
July	6	10	38	33	2
August	4	4	30	29	0
September	7	7	23	38	2
October	10	7	22	27	0
November	9	8	28	25	1
December	15	8	26	24	4
Total	103	90	354	302	13

Source: Kawai Ryosuke, *Yoron to masu komyunikēshiyon* (Tokyo: Buren Shuppan, 1987), 155. Original data collected by the ministry.

foreign correspondent in Japan suggests that "the club system circuits the journalistic process of cultivating reliable sources, in short, by providing them."[43]

Government ministries and agencies have also found it advantageous to have a large number of journalists from a variety of mainstream media outlets permanently stationed in their offices. As mentioned in the previous chapter, the Meiji state recognized the benefits to be had from providing early *kisha* clubs with a number of services, including desks, chairs, and other perquisites of the trade.[44] Today, as illustrated in figure 4, state and local governments, businesses, and other organizations still provide club members with a number of services (known as *bengi kyōyō*). These include the physical space for the club (the *kisha shitsu*), desks, tables, chairs, bookshelves, telephones, and payment for outside calls.[45] Frequently, television sets, subscriptions to popular magazines, and parking spaces or exemptions from parking restrictions are also provided. Free photocopies, fax machines, and copies of each of the papers' morning editions are other common items, as are mah-jongg, Shōgi, and Igo, popular games journalists rely on to wile away the time between scheduled events.[46]

In a survey conducted in 1993 by the labor union of the *Mainichi shimbun*, one of Japan's major national dailies, 60.8 percent of clubs surveyed stated that their government sources also provided and paid for a permanently staffed assistant (see figure 4). A breakdown of respondents reveals that all of the clubs located in the Diet and party headquarters have been provided with permanent staff. In addition, 89.4 percent of clubs in urban and rural prefectures (*todōfukenchō*), 87.5 percent of education-related clubs, 81 percent of the clubs in the metropolitan and local police headquarters, 75 percent of those located in general companies (*ippan kigyō*), and 68 percent of those in economic organizations also have been provided with a permanently staffed assistant. However, only 20 percent of sports and 29.8 percent of district police clubs had been provided with such staff. A minuscule 0.2% of journalists surveyed (one club) claimed that the source did not provide any services whatsoever.[47]

In terms of the fundamental requirement of journalism—that journalists maintain a suitable distance from their sources—it is somewhat astonishing to learn that 14.4 percent of respondents also said that sources had provided "free train passes for use on private railways and/or other entertainment passes." Some of the best gifts are provided not by government sources but by big business. During the gift-giving seasons of New Year and midsummer, the "big four" securities companies give journalists in the Kabuto club located in the Tokyo Stock Exchange gifts ranging from alcohol to coupons in order to show their gratitude. One journalist from the Kabuto club had this to say about relations in his club: "In the

Kabuto club we get a lot of product announcements and announcements about personnel changes. As far as the companies are concerned, we are their PR staff."[48] This is the case with many journalists from the economic bureaus of newspapers who are frequently invited to New Year and year-end parties by the companies, or go drinking with top executives. To foster close relations between the PR section and the club, club members are also often invited to parties when the head of a company PR section leaves and when a new head is appointed.

Automobile and airline companies are also well known for their generosity. Automobile companies, for example, take journalists on trips to new factories or make new product announcements about twice a month. These frequently require overnight stays in lush accommodations that are paid for by the industry. Other gifts (often redeemable coupons but sometimes fruit, soap, or other such items) may be sent directly to journalists' homes.[49] A separate, unpublished, informal survey compiled on February 2, 1992, by members of the labor union for the Kyodo wire service found that journalists in some of the local areas were given ski lift tickets, coupons for beer, neckties, and free passes for express trains. Local department stores also gave club members gift coupons, and at least one bank provided train passes that were valid in every prefecture.[50]

Most Japanese media outlets do not appear to have clear rules regulating the acceptance of gifts or meals at expensive restaurants, though the NSK has tried to set industrywide limits. In contrast, many American and European newspapers have strict rules against the acceptance of gifts from sources, however small. The *Washington Post*'s handbook for journalists, the *Deskbook on Style,* states that journalists are prohibited from accepting gifts from sources. A spokesperson for the newspaper indicated in a telephone interview that as a rule of thumb, journalists cannot accept gifts valued at more than twenty-five dollars. If a source sends a gift worth more than this, the gift is donated to charity and a note is sent to the source explaining why.[51] A representative of the *New York Times* also stated that while their journalists were not allowed to accept gifts, as a rule they could receive something valued at less than twenty dollars.[52]

While government sources in many industrialized democracies also provide journalists with basic services needed to carry out their jobs, the services provided in Japan are not only more extensive, they are provided only to a self-selected group of mainstream journalists. As is the case elsewhere, most of these services are paid for with public taxes. But a key difference in Japan is that only this select group has access to them—a fact that has become a rallying point for critics of the club system, including at least one very vocal citizens' group in Kyoto.

In 1991 Kyoto city residents filed a lawsuit against the prefectural government in which they challenged the use of public money to provide

Question: What kinds of services do sources provide for members of your club?
(More than one response allowed.)

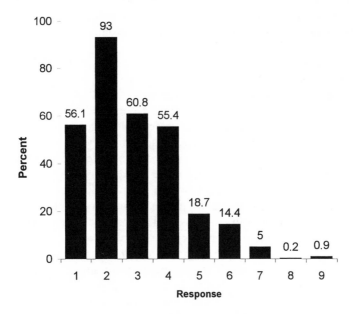

Responses: 1. Phone charges for outside calls
              2. Tables, chairs, and other furnishings
              3. Permanently stationed staff
              4. Parking spaces
              5. Stickers that allow journalists to park in restricted parking
                 spaces
              6. Free train passes for use on private railways and other
                 entertainment passes
              7. Other
              8. No services
              9. No response

Figure 4. Newsgathering Services Provided in *Kisha* Clubs.
Source: Honryū, August 26, 1993, 4–5.

special rooms to be used only by an exclusive group of private media companies. The suit claimed that, rather than serving as an information conduit, the press club attached to the Kyoto prefectural government "functioned to *deny* information about local administration to the public."[53] Although the local court ruled against the plaintiffs, declaring that "the provision of the *kisha* room does not contravene the law," in its decision the court stated that club rooms were provided as a public service and were to be used for the public good.[54] If this were truly an open market, public services paid for with public taxes would be available to all media outlets. But in Japan, one must be a "legitimate" news agency to gain access, and legitimacy is defined quite narrowly. As detailed in the next section, not only are the clubs inaccessible to the public, they are not even accessible to all of the public's proxies—particularly what are considered "illegitimate" media outlets, that is, those not belonging to the NSK.

One consequence of the "friendly" atmosphere cultivated in the clubs is the co-optation of journalists by sources. Club membership frequently results in a reduced sense of adversariness with sources and a high degree of cooperation with sources and with rival journalists. Though we suggest that this is a co-optative relationship, it is also a reciprocal, symbiotic one in which both sides gain significantly. Journalists establish close relationships with sources and get privileged information while sources get their imprimatur on the news. For journalists, membership also means that no one gets scooped, as all members receive virtually identical information in the clubs and frequently make agreements about how and when such information should be released.

There are a number of other ways in which clubs serve as the locus for the establishment and maintenance of close relationships between club reporters and their sources. Many clubs hold regular luncheons and parties, and club members get together for golf games or other social gatherings with sources that are paid for by the source. Figure 5 shows the results of a survey of the frequency of such gatherings and who pays for them. According to this survey, while 20 percent of club journalists responded that they rarely or never had such gatherings, another 20 percent responded that they had ten or more annually, or almost one social gathering a month. Clubs with more than ten social functions per year included 50 percent of those located in general companies, 36 percent of those in economic organizations, 33.3 percent of those in the metropolitan and local police offices, and 25.5 percent of those in the urban and rural prefectures. Among those clubs that responded that they rarely or never had such gatherings were those in the Diet and political parties (66.7 percent), judiciary clubs (50 percent), central government agencies (40 percent), special government agencies (36.4 percent), and education agencies (31.3 percent).[55]

When it comes to payment for such entertainment, about half of the clubs responded that the source paid or that they had an entertainment expense system (*kaihisei*) in which the individual companies paid. Some clubs responded that they refused to have such gatherings, while others replied that they would not participate in them if the source was paying. Sources paid for entertainment most often in the case of education-related clubs (73.3 percent versus 6.7 percent with an entertainment expense system), sports clubs (75 percent versus 25 percent), and the urban and rural prefectural clubs (42.2 percent as opposed to 28.9 percent). Those where the predominant form of payment was through an entertainment expense system included legal clubs (82.4 percent compared to 11.8 percent with the source paying), the Diet and political parties (66.7 percent as opposed to 0), the metropolitan and prefectural police (59.5 percent versus 21.4 percent), and the district police clubs (56.5 percent against 30.4 percent).[56]

The payment of meals and parties is not the only issue arising from these relationships. One journalist from the Kyodo wire service covering a local region told of a case in which, at the close of a party sponsored by the local chapter of the Liberal Democratic party, all of the journalists in the club were given packets, which he assumed contained press releases and other information about the party. Upon returning to his club, however, he discovered that in addition to public relations materials, the envelope also contained twenty thousand yen (approximately two hundred dollars at the time). The journalist promptly returned the money, although he said he was unsure what the other journalists had done.[57]

Other journalists, as well as former employees of the PR section attached to LDP headquarters, have corroborated such stories, telling of even larger sums of cash being paid to individual journalists, presumably for writing favorable stories.[58] As previously mentioned, there have also been a number of well-publicized scandals in which allegations were made that large corporations had paid journalists to write favorable stories. Most notable are a scandal involving payments a Hokkaido construction company allegedly made to executives in the regional *Hokkaido shimbun*, and the charge in the Itoman loans-for-favors scandal that the company had a "corroborator" inside the *Nikkei* who also was paid to write favorable articles about the company.[59] In all probability, however, if such a person existed (and that has never been proven), this person was not an acting press club member, but a more senior journalist in the company who was no longer participating in club activities.

Although these examples represent the exception and not the rule, and it can be assumed that most Japanese journalists would return cash and are not easily bribed, serious problems exist with a news system that emphasizes the creation of a "friendly" environment and "personal" relationships. One result is that the nature of acceptable, ethical practice is not always clear, to journalists and sources alike. In contrast to the situation confronting Japanese journalists, Joel Becchione, a spokesperson for the *New York Times*, said that journalists for his organization practice "situational ethics" based on company rules, but that in case there is any doubt, the *New York Times* provides its journalists with a "very liberal" expense account.[60]

The proprietary newsgathering practices made possible by the Japanese *kisha* club system have engendered caustic criticism from domestic pundits, media scholars, and foreign correspondents alike. Frequently, these critics have used the appellation "cartel" in describing the *kisha* clubs. One such critic is Amaya Naohiro, the well-known and highly regarded former MITI official, who had this comment about the Japanese press, the press club system, and cartels:

> It is my feeling that Japanese newspapers have an immense fondness for cartels. There can be no denying that the way subscription rates are set is clearly cartel-like. The *kisha* club system is also a kind of cartel. While I am not that familiar with the *kisha* club at the Fair Trade Commission, if the commission allows the club to limit the number of press-related enterprises and journalists that can enter and exit its own offices, then, in a real sense, the Fair Trade Commission is a partner to this crime."[61]

Note Amaya's pointed irony—that even the Japan Fair Trade Commission (JFTC), the agency delegated the job of vigilance against anticompetitive practices, has a *kisha* club housed in its headquarters.

Others argue that the existence of cartels in the Japanese news industry is by no means unique: the significance of cartels in Japan is widespread and pervasive across a range of industries. A recent work by Mark Tilton examines cartels in Japan's materials industries.[62] Other scholars have found cartels and cartel-like behavior in less traditional areas. Chalmers Johnson, for example, suggests that not only is the cartel "the characteristic institution of Japanese capitalism," it is a form of organization that pervades other noneconomic realms of Japanese society, resulting in the establishment of what he calls "cartels of the mind." Three of these are the closed nature of the university system, the legal system, and the system for gathering news.[63] Building on this thesis, Ivan Hall has recently published a powerful book in which he chronicles what he calls Japan's intellectual closed shop.[64]

Applying the concept of cartels to journalism in Japan opens up our analysis to a broader literary and conceptual apparatus. To understand the ways that Japan's *kisha* clubs work as information cartels, simultaneously controlling the content and flow of political and other news in Japan and limiting competition among rival news organizations belonging to the

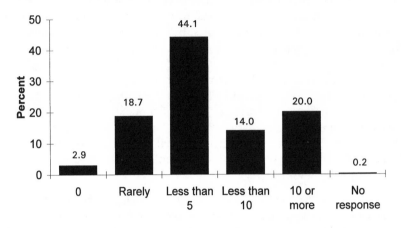

Question: How many times a year does your club have luncheons or parties, play golf, or have other social gatherings with sources?

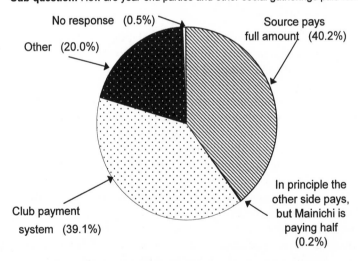

Sub-question: How are year-end parties and other social gatherings paid for?

Figure 5. Annual Number of Informal Gatherings with Sources.
Source: Honryū, August 26, 1993, 5.

clubs, I provide a conceptual framework based on three important aspects of cartels: an exclusive membership, rules governing marketplace activities, and the threat of sanctions against violators and the means to enforce them.[65] Each of these proves fundamental to understanding the press club and its impact on the flow of information in Japan. The first of these—limitations on membership—is discussed in the next section. The remaining two elements—rules and sanctions—will be discussed in the next chapter.

Closing the Shop: *Kisha* Clubs as Information Cartels

Although discussions of Japanese press clubs frequently touch on their exclusive, "clubby" nature, no consistent or cohesive theory of information cartels or of the cartelization of knowledge has been developed. In what sense can the word "cartel," a term normally employed by economists to describe socially inefficient (and in many countries illegal) business practices, be applied to an analysis of the news? And with what theoretical or explanatory value?

Webster's dictionary gives a number of different definitions for "cartel," of which the fourth is of most direct relevance here: "A voluntary often international combination of independent private enterprises supplying like commodities or services *that agree to limit their competitive activities* (as by allocating customers or markets, regulating quantity or quality of output, pooling returns or profits, fixing prices or terms of sale, exchanging techniques, trademarks or patents or by other methods of controlling production, price or distribution)."[66] A similar definition is provided by the *New Palgrave's Dictionary of Economics*: "Cartels may involve price fixing, output controls, bid-rigging, allocation of customers, allocation of sales by product or territory, *establishment of trade practices*, common sales agencies or combinations of these."[67]

What these definitions suggest is that cartels involve a wide range of mechanisms for organizing and controlling the activities of competitive enterprises. Most industrial organization economists focus on the formal analysis of industry-level controls on prices and/or output quantities—controls that are seen as ultimately increasing the prices consumers pay for goods or services, and thereby reducing social welfare. But cartels among competitive enterprises can also have other effects, among these the establishment of trade practices that effectively standardize products and limit consumer choice. It is this aspect of cartels—particularly the effects of their closed shop nature—that is of interest here.

A sign posted outside the door of most *kisha* clubs reads "Off Limits to Nonmembers" (*kankeisha igai wa nyūshitsu o kinjimasu*) and underscores the reality of the information-gathering process in Japan—namely, that it takes place within a "closed shop" made up of journalists having proprietary access to information and sources.

Limiting membership has always been an important feature of cartels because, as *New Palgrave's* notes, "as the numbers in a cartel grow, the gain from violating it generally increases faster than the loss from such punishment when detected."[68] The Japanese information cartel also has considerable impetus to limit membership, as an increase in numbers would require letting in news agencies and individuals whose understanding of the nature of the journalist-source relationship may be different from that of existing members. Were these journalists permitted to join, existing members might be less able to develop the kind of intimacy with sources that enables them to feel that they can speak freely "off the record." It would also become increasingly difficult to maintain some of the tacit rules of reporting that currently operate among journalists and between journalists and their sources, particularly the somewhat distinctive rules regulating source attribution. In addition, there are numerous other benefits to be had from a limited membership. As a foreign correspondent working for AP once noted, "by obtaining an exclusive proximity to sources it becomes easier for club members to digest press releases, to attend impromptu briefings and to develop close ties with newsmakers. These are all major advantages over those excluded."[69]

It is not surprising, then, that changes in membership criteria have been implemented infrequently since the broadcast media were permitted to join the clubs in the immediate postwar period. Although a significant modification of membership rules was made in the summer of 1993 when the NSK recommended that foreign journalists be given access, this ruling has had little impact on the day-to-day reality of those Japanese journalists hitherto excluded. With the exception of a few foreign journalists working for business news services such as Bloomberg, the ruling has not greatly affected the way that foreign correspondents gather news and write their stories.[70] Other than the seven magazine clubs listed earlier (which restrict membership to companies belonging to their industry association, the Japan Magazine Publishers Association, or JMPA, in much the same way as the NSK limits membership), access to Japan's *kisha* clubs has been limited to those journalists whose companies are members of the NSK.[71]

At the same time, although membership in a *kisha* club requires prior membership in this association, this is only a necessary, and not a sufficient, condition. Generally, in the case of the major clubs located in Tokyo, access to information is limited to an even smaller and more exclusive group of news organizations holding a virtual monopoly over sources through their tight control over the day-to-day management of the clubs. In other words, not only have foreign correspondents and Japanese journalists working for weekly and news magazines, industry newspapers, party organs, or as freelancers been excluded from the clubs by fiat, in practice only the major fifteen to twenty mainstream Japanese news organizations participate as regular club members in many of the clubs in Tokyo. Consequently, actual membership is much less diverse than one might expect given a multimedia industry association that in 1996 had 164 members—112 newspaper companies, 47 broadcast companies, and 5 news agencies.

Membership is also considerably less varied than the survey results provided in figure 6 indicate. Although 50.7 percent of respondents in this survey said that their clubs allowed members of the NSK, NHK, and local newspaper and broadcast companies to participate, the data are based on a nationwide survey that included many clubs in local areas that naturally would have a fairly substantial number of local media outlets on their membership lists.[72] Had the survey been limited to the key clubs in Tokyo, particularly those attached to central government ministries and agencies, the percentages would have been substantially lower, as a large number of Tokyo-based clubs restrict membership to members of the NSK and NHK. On closer inspection, only 4.3 percent of respondents said that their club had no limitations on membership, while 34.5 percent said that the club limited membership to those companies that either had belonged to a club from its inception, were members of the NSK, or were members of the NHK. All clubs, moreover, still exclude freelancers, journalists from news and other magazines, and those representing political or religious organs.

Most clubs have anywhere from 15 to 150 individual members, almost all of whom work for companies belonging to the NSK. There are exceptions, of course. The largest club in Tokyo, the Diet club, is said to have 5,000 individual members, but most of these are also NSK members. The Kantei or prime minister's club is in second place, having 467 members in 1985.[73] Even in these clubs, the establishment of rules and enforcement of sanctions are the responsibility of a much smaller group of companies—those having voting rights in the club general committee (*sōkai*). Club supervisors (positions that rotate every two to three months) are chosen from among the *sōkai* membership. Club supervisors are responsible for handling any problems arising within the club and calling emergency meetings of regular members whenever a major rule violation has occurred. This kind of meeting was convened in the case outlined in the preface, in which the *Asahi* attributed the derogatory comment about South Korea to then secretary general of the LDP, Ozawa Ichiro. As a consequence of these arrangements, control over the management and makeup of the clubs lies with a limited number of mainstream media outlets regardless of whom they let in. One author even goes so far as to suggest that the "big five"—*Asahi, Yomiuri, Mainichi*, Kyodo, and NHK—are "fighting it out for hegemony."[74]

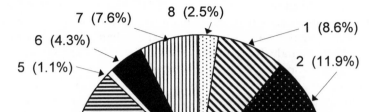

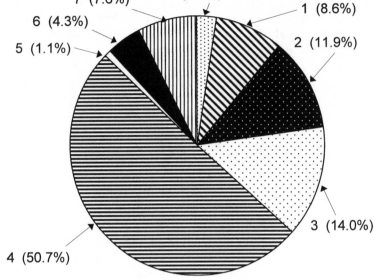

Responses: 1. Membership is limited to companies that have
                  belonged to the club since its inception.
              2. Membership is restricted to members of the Japan
              Newspaper Publishers and Editors Association (NSK).
              3. Membership is restricted to members of the NSK and
              NHK.
              4. Membership is restricted to NSK members, NHK, and
              local newspaper and broadcast companies.
              5. Club allows local minikomi (mini-community) papers to
              participate.
              6. There are no requirements.
              7. Other
              8. No response

Figure 6. *Kisha* Club Membership Eligibility Requirements.
Source: Honryū, August 26, 1993, 2.

Usually, approximately seventeen companies participate as regular members in a given club. These include the five national papers (*Asahi, Yomiuri, Mainichi, Sankei,* and *Nikkei*), the four bloc papers (*Hokkaido, Chunichi, Nishi nihon,* and *Tokyo*), two news agencies (Jiji and Kyodo), and six broadcast companies (NHK, TBS, Nihon Terebi, Terebi Asahi, Fuji Terebi, and Terebi Tokyo). However, the number of club members and their composition vary somewhat from club to club. As indicated in figure 7, there are two fewer regular members in the Imperial Household club, and two fewer in the club located in the Supreme Court.[75] The composition of clubs in the local areas also differs from that of clubs in the capital. While clubs outside Tokyo invariably include a large number of local newspaper and broadcast companies, generally the three major national papers and NHK are also members of these clubs, as illustrated by the justice club in Kitami (a small town in Hokkaido) in figure 7.

The fact that membership is limited to a score of mainstream news organizations does not mean that only fifteen to twenty journalists are dispatched to a given club at any one time. A media organization may send from one to ten of its journalists to a *kisha* club. Tables 6 and 7 show the distribution of journalists dispatched from NHK and *Asahi* to major clubs in Tokyo. In 1990 both companies sent a large number of journalists to clubs in several key organizations, including political parties, the police, and government offices. Both companies also sent six to eight journalists to cover the Liberal Democratic party and five to seven reporters to cover the opposition parties. They also sent nine to ten journalists to the prime minister's official residence, ten to sixteen to the police department, and four to the Tokyo metropolitan government.

Membership in one club does not guarantee access to any of the others. Journalists are usually assigned to a single club and cover only the issues arising from and related to the ministry or organization to which that club is attached. In most cases, they are refused access to press releases or news conferences sponsored by other clubs, even though other journalists from their company are members. A journalist generally remains in his or her assigned club for two or three years before being assigned to a new club in a different organization. One consequence is the considerable degree of sectionalism and territoriality that goes on between members of various clubs. Often a journalist will feel closer to a competitor in his or her own club than to another journalist from the same company. This is particularly the case when the other journalist comes from another bureau. The political and social affairs bureaus, for example, are known to have an intense rivalry, in part because of the different types of tasks assigned to them.

Sources are also aware of this intracompany sectionalism and use it to their advantage. As a rule, politicians and bureaucrats refuse to see social affairs journalists, while sources in the metropolitan police headquarters

FIGURE 7

Regular Members of Various *Kisha* Clubs.

Newspapers (7)	TV Stations (6)	News Agencies (2)
Yomiuri ←→	Nihon Terebi	Kyodo
Asahi ←→	Terebi Asahi	Jiji
Mainichi ←→	TBS	
Sankei ←→	Fuji Terebi	
Nikkei ←→	Terebi Tokyo	
Tokyo (Chunichi)	NHK	
Hokkaido		

Figure 7a. Regular Members of the Imperial Household Press Club.
Arrows indicate ties between television stations and national papers.
Source: Maruyama Noboru, *Hōdō kyōtei — nihon masukomi no kamman na jishi* (Tokyo: Daisan shokan, 1992), 10.

Newspapers (7)	TV and Radio Stations (7)	News Agencies (2)
Yomiuri ←→	Nihon Terebi	Kyodo
Asahi ←→	Terebi Asahi	Jiji
Mainichi ←→	TBS	
Sankei ←→	Fuji Terebi	
Nikkei ←→	Terebi Tokyo	
Tokyo (Chunichi)	NHK	
Hokkaido	Bunka Hoso	

Figure 7b. Regular Members of the Supreme Court Press Club.
Arrows indicate ties between television stations and national papers.
Source: Nishiyama Takesuke, *Za riiku: shimbun hōdō no ura-omote* (Tokyo: Kodansha, 1992), 170.

Newspapers (5)	TV Stations (5)	News Agencies
Yomiuri	NHK	None
Asahi	Hokkaido Hoso	
Mainichi	Sapporo Terebi Hoso	
Hokkai Taimuzu	Hokkaido Bunka Hoso	
Hokkaido shimbun	Hokkaido Terebi Hoso	

Figure 7c. Regular Members of the Kitami Judicial Club.
Source: Regulations for Kitami Judicial Club, September, 1987.

(which has historically been the territory of social affairs journalists) will not talk with political journalists or journalists from other clubs. This practice also explains why social affairs, rather than political, journalists generally write about scandals involving politicians. The social affairs journalists are not encumbered by the ties to sources and the rules, that a political journalist would be, though this also means that it is much more difficult for them to get information—even information that their "colleagues" in the political bureau may well have, but for obvious reasons can't write about.

Some clubs have provisions in their club regulations (*kurabu kiyaku*) for additional types of membership, and may allow participation by non-regular members and "observers." With the exception of foreign correspondents, who have been handled as a special category, historically even non-regular members and observers must belong to the NSK, or at the very least be endorsed or sponsored by a member company, although this is gradually beginning to change. Club regulations for the Prime Minister's club (the *kantei* club), for example, expressly exclude "journalists from news magazines, weekly magazines, government, political party and labor organs as well as industry papers."[76]

Figure 8 provides the results of a survey of press clubs conducted by the *Mainichi shimbun* labor union in 1993. According to these results, only 7 percent of the clubs surveyed allowed nonmember individuals to be present during press conferences and participate in the same way that regular members did, while 26.4 percent did not allow nonmember individuals and 34 percent did not allow nonmember companies to participate in such conferences. A fairly large number of the clubs that allowed attendance by nonmember journalists during press conferences placed conditions on that attendance, with 7.9 percent stipulating that outsiders were not allowed to say anything or ask questions. A small percentage of the clubs surveyed (1.1 percent) even went so far as to require that nonmember journalists get approval in advance for any statement they wished to make during a press conference.

Although some efforts have been made to reduce these restrictions on attendance, and there have been calls to reform the *kisha* club system, the organization responsible for implementing reforms—the NSK—has viewed the *kisha* club "problem" (*kisha kurabu mondai*) mainly in terms of how to give access to foreign journalists while continuing to exclude those Japanese journalists who have always been prohibited.

One high-ranking member of the reform committee, referring to these Japanese journalists as the "semiyellow journalists of Japan," said that the "problem" as the committee saw it was to figure out how they might develop criteria that would give access to the "foreign 'bona fide' press, but exclude the local indigenous press." In other words, the committee

TABLE 6
NHK's Dispatch of Reporters to Major *Kisha* Clubs (1985)

Kisha Club	*Political Reporters*	*Social Affairs*
Parliament	2	
Liberal Democratic Party	6	
Opposition Parties	5	
Supreme Court		5
Prime Minister's Residence	9	
Ministry of Justice	1	
Ministry of Foreign Affairs	3	
Ministry of Finance	1	
Ministry of Education	1	2
Ministry of Health and Welfare	1	2
Ministry of Construction		1
MITI / Ministry of Agriculture and Forestry		1
Ministry of Transportation		1
Ministry of Posts and Telecommunications	1	1
Ministry of Labor	1	3
Ministry of Home Affairs	1	
Defense Agency	2	1
Environmental Agency		1
Science and Technology Agency		1
Imperial Household Agency		1
National Railway		1
Subtotal	34	21
Metropolitan Police Board		16
Police Department		2
Metropolitan Government		4
Haneda Airport		1
Total	34	44

Source: Kawai Ryosuke, *Yoron to masu komyunikēshiyon* (Tokyo: Buren Shuppan, 1987), 133.

felt compelled to include "legitimate" foreign newspapers and such magazines as *Time* and *Newsweek* but wanted to continue to exclude Japanese newspapers that were not NSK members as well as Japanese magazines.[77] Yet Japanese weekly magazines—including *Bungei shūnju*—are precisely the ones that carry out investigative journalism and are responsible for breaking many corruption and other scandals involving politicians and bureaucrats. With the notable exception of the Recruit stock-for-favors scandal, which, in spite of its political nature was uncovered by a group of

TABLE 7
Asahi's Dispatch of Reporters to Major *Kisha* Clubs (1990)

Kisha Club	Political Reporters	Economic Reporters	Social Affairs
Parliament	3		2
Liberal Democratic Party	8		
Opposition Parties	7		
Courts			6
Prime Minister's Residence	10		
Ministry of Justice	1		
Ministry of Foreign Affairs	5	2	
Ministry of Finance	1	4	
Ministry of Education	1		1
Ministry of Health and Welfare	1		1
Ministry of Agriculture/Fisheries	1	2	1
Ministry of International Trade and Industry	1	3	1
Ministry of Transportation		1	1
Ministry of Posts and Telecommunications	1	1	1
Ministry of Labor—Labor Unions	1		1
Internal Affairs*	3	1	2
Defense Agency	1		1
Environmental Agency	1		1
Economic Planning Agency		1	
Imperial Household Agency			3
National Tax Board			1
Subtotal	28	15	15
Metropolitan Police Board			10
Police Department			7
Metropolitan Government			4
Finance		6	
Securities		4	
Industries/Business Groups		12	
Other locations/Tokyo branch offices		12	25
Unattached roving journalists (*Yugun kisha*)			25
Total	46	49	94

Source: Leviathan 7 (Fall 1990): 44.

Note: Reporters may be counted in more than one section/category. Managers and editors are excluded.

* Includes Ministry of Home Affairs, Ministry of Construction, and the National Land Agency.

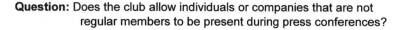

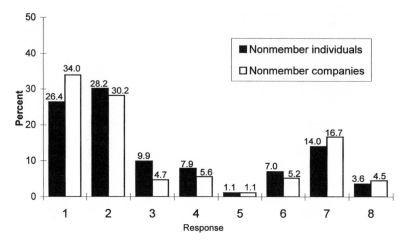

Responses: 1. It is not allowed.
                   2. Depending on the subject of the press conference.
                   3. Depending on the company.
                   4. They can come as observers but are not allowed
                       to say anything or ask questions.
                   5. They can come as observers but they must get
                       prior permission for any statement they would like
                       to make.
                   6. They can participate in the same way that regular
                       members do.
                   7. Other
                   8. No response

Figure 8. Presence of Nonmembers at Press Conferences.
  Source: Honryū, August 26, 1993, 3.

mainly social affairs journalists from *Asahi* working in a local office in
Kawasaki city, such magazines have broken a large number of political and
other scandals, including the Lockheed scandal involving former prime
minister Tanaka Kakuei, and the more recent exposé that resulted in the
ouster of former prime minister Hosokawa. That these scandals were written by journalists and media organizations excluded from the *kisha* club
is not, as we shall see, merely coincidental.

Table 8 shows which clubs allowed access by foreign correspondents
as of October 1991, and whether or not this access was conditional. As
mentioned earlier, as a result of the policy recommendation issued by the
NSK in June 1993, a number of these clubs now have provisions for mem-

bership by the foreign press, but it is assumed that foreign correspondents will not have the time to take on the duties of regular members and will therefore as a matter of course be nonvoting members of the clubs.[78] Although foreign journalists in any country have less access to important sources than the indigenous press, the extent to which the foreign press has been excluded in Japan is remarkable. More important, not only do many of the clubs that now allow foreign access do so conditionally, most of these clubs (and many others) still refuse access to the "semiyellow" Japanese journalists who are not NSK members. Moreover, because the clubs still do not allow participation by domestic or foreign religious and state organs, media outlets such as the *Christian Science Monitor*, the *Seikyō shimbun* (the organ of the Sōka Gakkai, a Buddhist sect), the BBC, and the *People's Daily*, among others, are still excluded.

Now that foreigners have been granted a degree of access to important clubs, the information cartel appears to have little incentive to open up the clubs any further. Having passed this face-saving measure allowing access by the foreign press, representatives from the NSK say that the organization is not currently pursuing the possibility of giving access to those Japanese journalists who continue to be denied entry. The NSK's Subcommittee on the *Kisha* Club Problem (Kisha Kurabu Mondai Shōiinkai) does not meet on a regular basis.[79] This is not surprising. As Jong Bock Lee phrased it some years ago, "The NSK itself does not want to destroy the system of the press clubs because of the privileges these groups receive from the news sources."[80]

Conspiring against the Public

The issue of source-journalist trust is a key reason given for maintaining the existing size of the information cartel. Outsiders, particularly foreigners who presumably come from a different "journalistic culture" (i.e., they have different rules and institutions governing behavior with sources), are not trusted. Considerable caution is taken on those occasions that they are allowed into briefings, and they are given access to background or other briefings of a more sensitive nature only on a limited basis. The member of the NSK subcommittee cited above had this to say about why the NSK was hesitant in allowing "outsiders" (both Japanese and foreign) into the clubs: "If, for example, we were to invite *Akahata* (the organ for the Communist party) to join, they would ask questions and say bad things. That would change the whole thing."[81]

A final point needs to be made about the relationship between Japanese journalists or organizations that are excluded from the clubs and those that belong. One might expect a degree of animosity between the NSK

TABLE 8

Kisha Club Membership by the Foreign Press (October 1991)

Foreign Press Allowed as Members[a]	Membership Never Requested	Membership Not Recognized
Nagata Club (Cabinet *Kisha* Club)	House of Councillors *Kisha* Club	Economic Research Group[b]
Cabinet, Prime Ministers Office, Management and Coordination Agency	Hokkaido Development Agency Club	Economic Planning Agency
Science *Kisha* Club	Yusei *Kisha* Club	Science and Technology *Kisha* Club[b]
Science and Technology Agency	Ministry of Post and Telecommunications	Science and Technology Agency
Justice *Kisha* Club	Nanasha Club	Kasumi Club[c]
Ministry of Justice	Metropolitan Police Board	Ministry of Foreign Affairs
Natural Resource *Kisha* Club	Machine Industry *Kisha* Club	Finance Research Group[b]
Energy Resource Agency	Machinery Industry	Ministry of Finance
Iikura Club	Trade *Kisha* Club	Finance Club
Ministry of Post and Telecommunications	Narita International Airport *Kisha* Club	Ministry of Finance
Internal Affairs *Kisha* Club	Science Council *Kisha* Club	Education *Kisha* Club[c]
Ministry of Home Affairs	Travel *Kisha* Club	Ministry of Education
		MITI *Kisha* Club[c]
		MITI

Source: Asahi Shimbun Weekly AERA, October 1, 1991, 28.

Note: In July 1993 the NSK revised its policy on *kisha* club membership by the foreign press and recommended that all clubs should in principle give the foreign press access. As a result, some clubs now allow foreign journalists limited access. Club selections are given below club names.

[a] Includes clubs that place conditions on membership.

[b] Nonmembers may attend press conferences.

[c] Nonmembers may attend press conferences, but restrictions apply.

TABLE 8 (*continued*)
Kisha Club Membership by the Foreign Press (October 1991)

Foreign Press Allowed as Members[a]	*Membership Never Requested*	*Membership Not Recognized*
Hibiya Club	Tokyo Sports *Kisha* Club	Construction *Kisha* Club[c]
Ministry of Health and Welfare	Sports Association Subcommittee Japan Sports Federation	Ministry of Construction
		Ministry of Justice *Kisha* Club[c]
	National Land Agency Specialty Newspaper *Kisha* Club	Supreme Court, Tokyo Supreme Court, Regional Court, Summary Court, Family Court, Prosecutor's Office, Ministry of Justice
	Ministry of Transportation Specialty Newspaper *Kisha* Club	Metropolitan Police Headquarters[b] *Kisha* Club
	Labor Administration *Kisha* Club	Economic Federation *Kisha* Club[b]
	Ministry of Labor	Keidanren
	Yuraku Club	Kabuto Club[c]
	Tokyo Metropolitan Government	Tokyo Stock Exchange
		Aoi Club[c]
		NTT, etc.

Source: Asahi Shimbun Weekly AERA, October 1, 1991, 28.
Note: In July 1993 the NSK revised its policy on *kisha* club membership by the foreign press and recommended that all clubs should in principle give the foreign press access. As a result, some clubs now allow foreign journalists limited access. Club locations are given below club names.
[a] Includes clubs that place conditions on membership.
[b] Nonmembers may attend press conferences.
[c] Nonmembers may attend press conferences, but restrictions apply.

(the newspaper association) and the JMPA (the magazine association), given that the latter was established expressly because the NSK had excluded magazine journalists from key clubs. However, when the NSK was deliberating over the issue of giving access to foreigners, it contacted the JMPA to learn whether or not it would register a complaint if foreigners—including foreign magazines such as *Time*—were given access to clubs that JMPA members themselves did not have access to. Contrary to expectations (but understandable given the business linkages between major newspapers and magazines in Japan discussed in chapter 5), the JMPA replied that it would not oppose this decision.[82] Though the response might seem counterintuitive, as a result of the informal arrangements magazine companies and reporters have with individual newspaper and broadcast journalists in the clubs, the magazines have not felt a great need to demand access. They obtain information and stories another way: by paying journalists in the clubs to leak information, or, more commonly, by having club journalists write stories for the magazine anonymously or under a pseudonym.

Although newspaper companies frown upon such practices, the fact that many club journalists moonlight in this way is widely recognized. The arrangement is mutually beneficial for the press club journalists and the magazines. Journalists gain an extra source of income and an outlet for some of the information they have obtained but cannot write about due to club embargoes and other tacit agreements with members of the club and sources. The magazines, which have smaller budgets and fewer reporters, find that developing close relations with newspaper journalists with access to important sources in the clubs and hiring them to write such stories makes bottom-line sense: it is more convenient and cheaper than sending some of their own rather limited staff, who would have great difficulty obtaining information anyway. In a sense, though not a direct party to the information cartel, those excluded have their own reasons for doing relatively little to see that it is dismantled.

But there is a price for having information filtered in this way—a price paid by the public. Under this arrangement, because the magazine has obtained such information second or third hand, either the story is written as rumor or, because it is written anonymously and/or does not include an attribution of sources (a practice followed by club members and nonmembers alike), its news value and believability are seriously diminished.

In sum, closing the shop not only means placing limitations on the metaphorical marketplace for ideas, it has also resulted in some unusual press practices in Japan. Obviously, there has been limited internal pressure for change, as the relationship is a cozy one for members and sources alike. But neither has there been substantial pressure from the outside, except for the pressure applied by foreign journalists. Those excluded from the clubs have not behaved as one might expect, in part because gaining membership would require them to follow the club "rules" outlined in the following chapter and would also make them subject to the sanctions imposed for breaking such rules. This lack of enthusiasm to change the closed nature of the newsgathering system, not only by club members but also by those who have been denied access, explains in large part the maintenance of these arrangements throughout the postwar period.

The lack of external challenge to the system does not mean that it is without harm or that it should not be changed. A newsgathering system that deliberately limits either the number or makeup of those having access to official information is in many ways no better than a system of official censorship, a point forcefully argued by Hedrick Smith. When asked about censorship in the Soviet Union during his tenure as a Moscow correspondent for the *New York Times* in the 1970s, Smith responded that, while there had been no official censorship, "the most effective censorship of all is not the deleting of words, sentences and paragraphs but *the denial of access*—stopping information at the source before I could learn it."[83]

Four

Japan's Information Cartels

PART II. STRUCTURING RELATIONS THROUGH
RULES AND SANCTIONS

> Rare indeed is the capitalist nation that has print
> and broadcast media that carry such uniform
> news as Japan. If you were to hide the masthead,
> it would be virtually impossible to tell from the
> contents which newspaper you were reading.
>   (*Yamamoto Taketoshi*)

THE JOINING together of a loose group of competitors is a necessary but incomplete step in the creation of the information cartel. The formation of a group with similar interests and goals leads to two other requirements: the establishment of rules to standardize and regulate behavior among group members, and the provision of effective sanctions to be enforced in the event a member breaks these rules. Rules, formal and informal, serve to set the framework within which information is gathered, interpreted, and disseminated. While they differ from legal controls and government-imposed censorship, they can have similar effects and may be equally binding. Thus, the lack of overt press controls in a country, though important, does not guarantee an unrestrained press. Self-imposed and tacit rules can also pose a threat to the preservation of press freedom in a democracy by placing limitations on the watchdog, agenda-setting, and investigative roles of the media, and by serving as barriers to a truly open information marketplace. In short, rules can, and often do, serve as an alternative form of censorship.

I. Formulating Rules of Interaction

The rules established by the Japanese information cartel generally involve membership criteria, acceptable behavior, and sanctions. Although the media industry has also been known to regulate pricing and distribution, the key element regulated here is the production of news. Most rules, therefore, entail agreements between sources and journalists or among rival journalists within the clubs. They can regulate the newsgathering activities of the entire industry, or they may only regulate the behavior of journalists within a single club. Two distinct categories of rules are considered here: (1) those that are formal and codified—including membership rules, "blackboard agreements," and "press agreements"—and (2) other, mostly informal and tacit rules. Both types of rules set the parameters for acceptable behavior for club members and sources, fostering a newsgathering environment that is more symbiotic, reciprocal, and cooperative than adversarial or competitive.

Formal Rules

CLUB REGULATIONS

All clubs have a written list of regulations (*kurabu kiyaku*) such as those provided in appendices A and B, outlining the basic guidelines for the operation and management of the club. These documents usually include the name and location of the club, its purpose, membership criteria (e.g., that members must belong to the NSK), and managerial procedures. Although newsgathering rules are rarely specified, the sanctions for breaking them frequently are. Most *kisha* club regulations include a section on sanctions describing what may happen to members who "harm the honor of the club," a euphemism for breaking written and unwritten club rules. As detailed later, sanctions can range anywhere from a verbal warning to expulsion from the club. Generally, however, when journalists or sources mention "club rules" or "the rules," they are not referring to these regulations but to the written and tacit rules governing newsgathering behavior described below.

BLACKBOARD AGREEMENTS

A second category of formal rules, and the most common type of written rule, is known as the blackboard agreement (*kokuban kyōtei*).[1] These agreements generally involve the members of a single club, though they also can be binding on the entire news industry. Kawai describes blackboard agreements as follows: "The term 'blackboard agreement' refers to the practice of listing the schedule of upcoming press conferences and briefings on blackboards provided in the *kisha* clubs. Once these schedules have been posted on the blackboard, and as long as no objections are raised, journalists are no longer permitted to conduct independent newsgathering or reporting that might allow them to obtain a scoop on the posted item."[2] In most cases the blackboard listing will include a precise date and time for the release of information, broken down by news medium.[3] Nishiyama explains the rationale for concluding such agreements: "Given that in a single day a club will have three or four press briefings and lectures on various topics, it is understandable that the government side will want to have these printed in an effective manner. The *kisha* club, the recipient of these announcements, also hopes to have a smooth flow of articles and wants to be sure that they don't become inundated with information."[4]

Without the "adjustment function" (*chōsei kinō*) of blackboard and other agreements, the role played by the *kisha* clubs would be severely limited.[5] Ministerial press sections utilize these agreements to coordinate the release of information at the best possible moment and to make sure that it is presented in the best possible light. Often during the interim between the release of an item and its embargo date, the ministry or government agency will hold a series of lectures or form research or study groups (*kenkyūkai* or *benkyōkai*) to ensure that journalists understand the issues as the ministry would like to have them understood. Adjustment and coordination are also important for competitors in the club, though for different reasons. Journalists from rival organizations in the club want to be sure that they don't get scooped (what is known as *nukegake*), and the easiest way to guarantee this is by making written or tacit agreements with competitors in the club to make sure that every party in the cartel gets identical information, that no one tries to obtain additional independent information, and that all members release the information they have at the same time.

One of the important functions of blackboard agreements, then, is to restrict the flow of information coming from official sources and to reduce competition among rivals for information on certain topics. Frequently, a group of rival reporters in a club will decide (often through a representative or during a general meeting of regular members) in consultation with the source precisely when a story will break. These practices give new meaning to the word "news": it is not really new; it is quite planned. Blackboard agreements are also important for the chilling effect they have on independent newsgathering and investigative reporting, and for the role they play in coordinating the dissemination and slant of news. The practice also fosters a newsgathering environment based on a high degree of cooperation between ostensible competitors and sources, an environment that often works to limit, rather than increase, the flow of information to the public.

Although blackboard agreements are made between the members of a single club and their sources, all journalists within a given news organization are expected to abide by them, even if they do not know about them. Consider, for example, a case in which a member of the club in the public prosecutor's office was expelled after his newspaper published a report claiming that the former president of the Heiwa Sogo Bank was about to be implicated in a scandal.[6] The members of the club had made an agreement with sources in the prosecutor's office not to write the details of this case. When club members discovered the article in this journalist's newspaper, they promptly expelled him. But the journalist in question had actually abided by the agreement: the article had been written by a roving reporter (*yūgun*) from his own paper who had not known about the embargo. This kind of incident used to happen with considerable frequency in the early postwar period and eventually led to a NSK ruling that individual club members could not make agreements among themselves or with sources without getting the prior approval of their managing editors. But in actual practice this ruling has had a limited impact on the newsgathering routines of many clubs, where blackboard and other agreements to embargo information are made on a daily basis, often without the knowledge of managing editors.

Figure 9 lists the average number of blackboard agreements made by various clubs per month as reported by a nationwide survey conducted in 1993 by the labor union of *Mainichi shimbun*. At first glance, the numbers would seem to suggest that such agreements are fairly infrequent—with 42.6 percent of clubs overall responding that they do not have them, and 38.8 percent claiming that they have them only once or twice a month. But when the responses are broken down by type of club, they reveal a different picture. Certain types of clubs, including those in central government agencies and prefectural government offices, have an exceptionally large number of blackboard agreements. Of the clubs located in the central government ministries and agencies, for example, 53.3 percent said that they had more than six agreements a month, while 13.3 percent said they had three to five agreements per month. Additionally, 34 percent of the prefectural government clubs said that they had from three to five agreements per month, 31.9 percent said that they had one or two such agreements, and 8.5 percent said that they had more than six cases a month. Other organizations with a large number of blackboard agreements include legal clubs (33.4 percent have three to six or more agreements a month), clubs in special government agencies (27.3 percent), educational clubs (25 percent) and economic clubs (24 percent).[7]

The original study does not offer any explanation for the large number of blackboard agreements in these clubs. However, the reason may lie in differences in the types of news stories coming out of a particular organization. Press clubs in the national and local police headquarters, for example, have reported the fewest number of blackboard agreements. This might be explained, in part, by the fact that news reports coming from such clubs are generally straight reports of crimes (such as the fact that

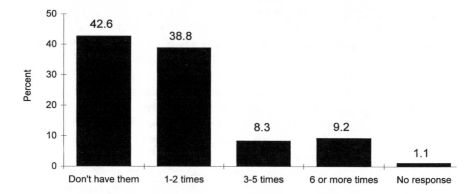

Question: Does your club ever make "blackboard agreements" or agreements with sources to set in advance the date and time a particular item can be reported? If you have such agreements, how many times a month are they made?

Figure 9. Number of Blackboard Agreements per Month.
Source: Honryū, August 26, 1993, 2.

someone has been murdered or a suspect caught), and not the more politically sensitive stories covered by journalists in clubs located in central and local government organizations, where news management is seen as a fundamental requirement. Additionally, as detailed below, the police have other rules that may make the establishment of blackboard agreements unnecessary.

While many blackboard agreements resemble the agreements between journalists and sources in other countries to embargo a particular item, there are important differences. To begin with, they differ in terms of the active role played by journalists in deciding to embargo an item, in the setting of very specific embargo times for different types of competing media, and in their frequency. Second, they differ in terms of what happens when a media outlet ignores the embargo (an issue discussed in more detail in the following section). In Japan, breaking an embargo can result in expulsion from the club—not by the source, but by rivals who have been scooped as a result of the violation. In contrast, a group of competing news organizations in the United States would be hard pressed to prevent a rival from having access to a news source, even if that rival had disregarded an embargo. Sanctions, such as they are, would be imposed by the source, not rival journalists. Finally, they differ in terms of their ultimate purpose. Although the aim of many embargoes—in Japan and elsewhere— is to give journalists enough time to review lengthy documents such as government White Papers or to protect innocent victims, in Japan they are also frequently used as a means to reduce "excessive" competition and to create a level playing field among cartel members. For sources, they have the additional function of reducing the possibility that journalists will carry out investigative reports involving certain government agencies or their policies.

It is in sources' manipulation of the clubs' willingness to agree to such embargoes that the distinction between overt press control and self-censorship begins to blur. In some instances, as soon as a source discovers that a journalist is investigating a certain topic, they request that an embargo be placed on the story. Fearful of being scooped, club members find it in their best interest to agree to the embargo, and in some cases they have even been known to request an embargo themselves precisely for this reason. Eventually, the source provides details of the story to all the journalists in the club, albeit only those details that the source is willing to have released to the public. In one case, a journalist had obtained information about a plan to form a team to work on the establishment of a new medical school in the Defense Agency. While hardly a scoop, when the journalist asked a source in the Defense Agency about this rumor, he was told to wait before pursuing the story further. A short while later, the source gave a lecture to the entire club about the plan and the journalist lost his "scoop."[8]

The practice of stopping investigations or queries early on means that the journalist carrying out an independent investigation will be unable to write what he or she has already learned and discourages investigative reporting altogether. It also gives sources time to come up with ways of presenting information in the most favorable light. Why do club members agree to the placement of an item on the blackboard, particularly in cases where it is clearly being used as a means to control them? Club members abide by, or even seek to establish, such agreements because they recognize them as a convenient means to reduce the possibility of getting scooped. In other words, it is the fear of being scooped by a competitor that compels media companies and journalists to enter into collusive agreements with sources and with each other. As a result, blackboard agreements have become one of the classic ways officials and media companies in Japan collude in order to manage the news.[9]

PRESS AGREEMENTS

The most formalized way that competition in the information market is regulated and the content and flow of information controlled is through "press agreements" (*hōdō kyōtei*). These agreements limit newsgathering activities for a specified period of time, are generally formulated under unusual circumstances, and represent an extreme form of binding group self-control. Unlike blackboard agreements, which are usually drawn up by members of a single press club, press agreements frequently (though not always) require the intermediation of Japanese media industry associations, such as the Japan Magazine Publishers Association (JMPA) and the NSK. These agreements are also generally binding at the industrywide level and involve negotiations between the newspaper, broadcast, and/or magazine associations and one of several powerful sources, including the Ministry of Foreign Affairs, the Imperial Household Agency, and the police. The latter two institutions have perhaps the most draconian control over the Japanese media and, not coincidentally, are the locations of two of Japan's oldest press clubs.[10] Although the NSK (or the JMPA in the case of magazines) frequently serves as the major media representative in negotiations with sources over the formulation of these agreements, they also have a considerable impact on journalists in the press clubs who must use them as guidelines in their newsgathering and reporting.

One of the earliest and best-known postwar press agreements was that between the NSK and the Imperial Household Agency in 1956 to limit reporting on then Prince Akihito's search for a bride. As detailed in chapter 5, a generation later, in 1992, newspapers, magazines, and broadcast stations made similar agreements, abiding by an Imperial Household Agency request to refrain from reporting the details of Prince Hironomiya's search for a wife. Originally intended to last three months, these agreements were extended on two separate occasions and ultimately remained in effect for almost a year. In the end, it was T. R. Reid, an American journalist from the *Washington Post* not party to the cartel agreement, who wrote the story that led to its collapse. Underscoring the degree of formality involved in such agreements, even after the news of the prince's engagement was already out, members of the Editorial Affairs Committee of the NSK had to convene an emergency meeting just to declare the agreement officially null and void.

Press agreements and other somewhat less formal written agreements are a common feature of the media–Imperial Household Agency relationship. Appendix C provides a chronological list of some of the agreements made between magazines belonging to the JMPA and the Imperial Household Agency from 1960 to 1983. The list serves as a fascinating illustration of the extent to which information from a single source is both cartelized and controlled in Japan. Though no similar list is available for agreements between the IHA and the newspaper and broadcast media, in return for access, these media also make numerous agreements with the IHA over how and when to release information on the imperial family.[11] Among the agreements detailed are those regulating the use of photographs of the royal family on magazine covers (including the sanctions to be imposed in the event that such rules are not observed), prohibition of news coverage of the Numazu and Karuizawa residences of the imperial family, coverage of Prince Hironomiya at school, and use of the imperial family symbol. There was even an agreement prohibiting the publication of directions to, and the location of, Prince Hironomiya's residence while he was studying in England. While the agreements on this list apply mainly to magazine journalists, some of them are also binding on the newspaper and foreign media as well.

It is not surprising that the IHA would seek to control the flow of information in the most efficient way available to it. By making agreements that bind the entire news industry, it is able to have the maximum degree of control over the publication of information on the royal family. No doubt the British royal family wishes it could impose a similar system of control on its own press. Because stories about the imperial family are a major revenue source for newspapers, and especially many Japanese magazines (particularly women's magazines), having access to the imperial family through membership in the IHA *kisha* club, however limited, is considered better than no access at all. But one consequence of the almost complete reliance on the IHA for information about, and photographs of, the imperial family is that press agreements are numerous, while violations are relatively rare. The contrast between the way the Japanese media handle incidents involving Japanese royalty and the British tabloid press's treatment of the British royal family could not be more striking. In the former case, the press shows undue deference to the wishes of the royal family in the name of "protecting privacy," while the British tabloid press seems to have taken notions of free speech and the public's right to know to their utmost limits. Obviously, neither is ideal.

The police are another media source that is a frequent party to press agreements. Agreements with the police often involve high-profile kidnap cases or other cases where police officials feel that the divulgence of information may harm their investigation, or result in the injury of a victim. In 1984, after the president of the Glico Corporation, one of Japan's largest candy manufacturers, was kidnapped, the press acquiesced to police requests for restraint. In this case, the press wound up signing two consecutive agreements not to make public the details of the case, the first of which lasted eight months.

In another less well-publicized but more common case, the press agreed to police demands to withhold information on the abduction and murder of a young girl, even after her body had been found. One eager journalist from the *Chunichi shimbun* found himself in a bind, having relayed the story about the discovery of the body to newspaper headquarters hours before the club and local police reached an agreement to withhold publication.[12] Although the article was already in press, the *Chunichi* editorial affairs board agreed to halt publication in spite of the considerable expense to the company. Publishing the story would have meant breaking the press agreement and may have resulted in the expulsion of the journalist and the newspaper from the club.

Often what happens when the press makes an agreement with the police to withhold information or refrain from pursuing a story, and clearly what was happening in the cases above, is that they are provided with the most up-to-date information on the police investigation and police activities related to the case. But the quid pro quo is that they cannot publish this information. While club journalists have become part of an elite group having proprietary access to events and information, one of the responsibilities as members of that group is to ensure that certain categories of information do not flow downward to the public.

Agreements with the police are not limited to these kinds of situations. In many cases, the reason for concluding an agreement to withhold information from the public is less obvious to outsiders. Frequently, for example, the police will ask the club to withhold information about suspects. In Japan, the press is not permitted to interview those arrested or under suspicion of having committed a crime. Although police officials say that the reporting of certain types of information related to a crime may harm their investigation, the withholding of information can also be viewed as an infringement on the rights of suspects, who are often treated by both the police and the news media as guilty until proven innocent. Criminal suspects in Japan have little opportunity to voice their views once arrested, and since journalists are prohibited from interviewing them (and are expelled from the club if they do), news stories are frequently based almost entirely on information handed to them by police officials in the relevant press club.

It is important to recognize, that while it may have legitimate uses, the practice of making agreements with sources and relying almost solely on them for information has become so routinized that it is frequently relied upon in situations where the need to protect sources—especially government bureaucrats and politicians—is less clear. While it is not difficult to imagine situations in which the media, recognizing the power they have to influence the public and events, might choose for very legitimate reasons not to exercise that power (for example, in the event of a kidnapping or hostage taking), in other cases, the press extends the legitimate use of such "self"-restraint to situations where there seems to be little reason for having done so. It is not just that journalists make agreements with sources to withhold information; they also implicitly agree not to seek additional information. A particularly egregious example of the misuse of this practice and the excessive reliance on the police for information is cited by Helen Hardacre in an article published in 1995. Professor Hardacre's study of the religious sect Aum Shinrikyō, responsible for the sarin attacks on Tokyo subways in March 1995 and earlier attacks in Matsumoto City, includes a telling example of press overreliance on the information, viewpoints, and biases of the Japanese police. In this case, the press repeatedly wrote damning and supposedly factual reports about Kono Yoshiyuki, a suspect in the gas attack in Matsumoto City on June 27, 1994. According to Hardacre, "The media passively accepted the police's lame suspicions about Kono and did nothing to press for an investigation of Aum at that time." Although this man's wife was in a coma as a result of the gas attack and there was no evidence linking him to it, the press continued to write about Mr. Kono as though he was guilty. More than a year later, Hardacre notes, "Every major newspaper and the regional papers published apologies to Kono for their role in his continuing ordeal."[13]

Journalists in other liberal democracies have also been known to practice self-restraint in the event that a victim of a kidnapping or hijacking might be harmed by the publication of certain kinds of information, but this has nothing to do with conspiring to suppress or not seek the truth, and everything to do with the desire to protect human lives. Critics of police-press and other press-source relationships in Japan (Asano Kenichi, for example) have argued that the Japanese press has shown itself much too willing to make open-ended agreements with sources, that their willing compliance has made the press liable to manipulation and co-optation by those sources (as the Aum example shows), and that their close, institutionalized relations with sources have impeded their ability to protect the public's right to know.[14] One particularly vociferous critic of these agreements, Hara Toshio, making a slight play on the Japanese word for "press agreements" (*hōdō kyōtei*), refers to them as "illegal agreements" (*fuhō kyōtei*). Another critic calls them "agreements to prohibit reporting" (*hōdō kinshi kyōtei*).[15] In spite of these criticisms, press agreements are an important and institutionalized part of the newsgathering process in Japan, and agreements with such organizations as the IHA and the police appear to be on the rise. In recent years such agreements have regulated news reports involving the death of emperor Hirohito, the marriage of the current emperor's second son, and the search for a bride and marriage of Crown Prince Hironomiya.[16]

Informal and Other Rules

So far we have examined written agreements between sources and journalists in the clubs. Many other agreements and practices, frequently referred to as "rules," are unwritten and less conspicuous. These rules affect and reflect the understanding that journalists have of their jobs and are an important aspect of the professionalization of journalism in Japan. While rules reduce the risks inherent in the profession, they also come at a hefty price: the manufacture of a standardized, inferior product.

ESTABLISHING INFORMATION EQUALITY AND A LEVEL PLAYING FIELD

One important rule regulating press-source relationships is the emphasis placed on "equality" in the provision of information. That is, all club members expect to be given exactly the same information, and they expect that the source will not favor one journalist over another by preferentially releasing information that has not been provided to everyone else.[17] One result of this practice is that exclusive interviews are relatively rare in Japan. Indeed, in the past club members have been expelled by their rivals in the club for having obtained one-on-one interviews with sources without receiving prior permission from the club to do so. Even in cases where sources have given "exclusive" interviews to foreign correspondents or nonclub Japanese journalists, the informal understanding is that the source is obligated immediately to relay the contents of the interview to journalists in the relevant club. The Tokyo correspondent for the *Economist* underscored the impact of these practices when he described in 1991 what happened in one case when foreign correspondents had been given access to the prime minister: "A handful of foreign correspondents in Tokyo (this one included) recently saw their own words being relayed by a Japanese wire service minutes after interviewing the prime minister, Toshiki Kaifu. Rival foreign newspapers were doubtless delighted."[18] One official from the LDP press section complained in an interview that club members in the Hirakawa club (the club covering the LDP) frequently put pressure on him not to release information to nonclub members, including editors and writers of the party's own organ. Although the official expressed his disapproval, he also recognized that the arrangement was based on reciprocity: journalists agreed to withhold information from the public and to not attribute sources only if the sources agreed not to give the same (or other) information to outsiders. It also reveals the degree to which the information cartel is sanctioned and supported by sources (or the state). In short, the rule that the source must provide information to all club members in an equitable manner and that they must give club members any information also given to nonclub members (such as foreign correspondents) is a key element of the cartelized news system.

THE "PREVAILING MOOD" AND A CONGENIAL NEWS REPORTING MILIEU

This brings us to an important point involving the nature of the environment within which relationships are formed and rules made, and the ways

in which professional roles and journalistic norms become institutionalized in Japan. I refer to the effort made by club members and sources to
create a "friendly" atmosphere and establish cordial relations among club
members and with sources, the resultant deferential attitude club journalists often have toward official sources, and the cooperative relationships
they have with each other.

The emphasis on the establishment and maintenance of a congenial
newsgathering environment and on relation-building can be found in internal company guidelines for newsgathering produced by various newspaper companies. It is also nurtured early on by the system of training
neophyte journalists in Japan: young recruits are dispatched to local areas
for several years, during which they become members of *kisha* clubs
attached to local government offices and police organizations. It is here
that journalists first learn of the importance of forming close relations
with sources and with competitors, and that sources often wield considerable power over clubs comprised of mostly neophyte reporters. Although
journalists everywhere try to cultivate relationships with important
sources, as we shall see, in Japan the practice differs in terms of the extent
to which journalists are willing to ingratiate themselves in order to develop that "special" relationship.

In a sense, the development and maintenance of a friendly atmosphere
is the defining rule of the *kisha* club. Yayama Taro, a veteran political
journalist, supports this assertion in an article originally published in *Chūō
kōron* in which he suggests that there is a "prevailing mood" in the clubs
that is "somehow shared by all club members." Yayama claims that "this
mood dictates, as it were, which issues and what kind of slant given in
reporting these issues the members think will most appeal to the readers of
their newspapers." He concludes that "the worst problem of the reporters'
clubs is not [their] exclusivity, but the fact that they are controlled by the
'atmosphere.' "[19] Although the creation of this kind of "atmosphere" or
"mood" is not a rule in the strict sense, it is important in that it regulates
behavior much as rules do.[20] Indeed, it regulates the establishment of
rules—what they are and what purposes they serve.

Though this is a difficult assertion to prove, documents from two different newspaper companies would seem to support the contention that priority is placed first and foremost on establishing intimate relationships
with sources and rivals, irrespective of the social costs or the price paid by
the public. Asano Kenichi, the well-known Kyodo social affairs journalist
and author of numerous books on criminal reporting in Japan, describes
an in-house booklet published in 1986 by *Yomiuri shimbun* entitled *A
Handbook for Police Reporting* (*Satsumawari nyūmon*). In this booklet,
the newspaper company likens the police to the *danka*—wealthy families
that provide financial support to temples—suggesting that the police are

similarly important as major supporters of newspaper companies—not as direct financial supporters, but as the suppliers of information. The booklet points out that the establishment of friendly relations with official sources is of such import that police club journalists should take along a bottle of whiskey when they make their nightly rounds to police officers' homes (a procedure known as *yomawari-asagake*) in order to develop such relations.[21]

Asano also provides excerpts from a second book published in April 1988 by another media company, the *Mainichi shimbun*. This book also argues that journalists should try to establish close relations with police officials. One rather lengthy section suggests that one way for journalists to develop an intimate relationship with a police official is by getting close to his family members:

> The most important thing you should do is to make sure that the police officers' families—their wives and daughters—do not dislike you. You must maintain friendly relations with the family. There are many ways to do this. While some journalists offer their services as home tutors, what will make family members really happy is a present that comes from the heart. During such occasions as wedding anniversaries, the wife's birthday, the daughter's celebration for entering a good school, a necktie, scarf or fountain pen make nice, thoughtful gifts. It is best to leave these presents while the police officer is away at the office, as they will be more naturally received this way. . . . You should try to be the kind of journalist the family will come to think of not as a "journalist who makes visits in terms of his own interests and benefits" but rather, as a "journalist who comes visiting as an intimate friend." Human relations formed in this way become the journalist's own personal asset. . . . If your opposite number likes alcohol, take along some whiskey or other alcoholic beverage; if they don't drink, take candy or fruit."[22]

Though these examples refer to relations between police club journalists and their sources, they are representative of the kinds of relationships that journalists are encouraged to establish with sources in other clubs as well. One author has described similar behavior among journalists in the prosecutor's office club who try to develop close relations with the prosecutor, usually as a group: "If the prosecutor is known as someone who likes to climb mountains, suddenly all of the journalists become alpinists. If he likes bowling, a bowling game is held with all the journalists from all the companies."[23]

But the example that best illustrates the extent to which relation-building has become an institutionalized part of the newsgathering process in Japan is that of the group of political reporters known as *ban* journalists. These reporters have historically covered influential members of the ruling Liberal Democratic party, such as the secretary general, faction leaders (these journalists are known as the *habatsu kisha*, or faction reporters), and the heads of such important committees as the Policy Affairs Research Council (PARC) and the Party Executive Council. They also cover other key political elites, including the chief and deputy-chief cabinet secretaries and the prime minister. Generally, an individual *ban* journalist (often a neophyte political reporter) is assigned to cover a single prominent official. As described in chapter 3, this reporter is expected to follow that individual around throughout the day, showing up at his house in the early morning and once again late at night. But the *ban* journalist is rarely alone: he or she can usually count on the company of other *ban* from rival firms assigned to cover the same important figure. These journalists form a tight-knit group with a distinctive set of rules and routines regulating the gathering of information about the individual with whom they are in daily contact. Feldman has gone so far as to suggest that the group of *ban* journalists is actually "a press club within a press club."[24]

The close relations political journalists have with their sources make it very difficult for them to write unfavorable pieces about them.[25] In fact, political journalists in Japan have been known to feel quite protective of the political "bosses" they cover. As Mori Kyozo pointed out after magazine journalists broke the scandal involving former prime minister Tanaka Kakuei, "some reporters exclusively covering the Liberal Democratic Party often become more LDP oriented than LDP members. The same applies to the reporters who have been assigned to LDP factions."[26]

Political reporters in Japan, particularly the faction and *ban* journalists described above, have been known to brag that they have much closer relations with important political sources than do their counterparts in the United States. How many American political reporters can say, for example, that they have been in the president's bedroom, or that they have followed him around all day long, greeting him when he awakes and chatting with him before he goes to bed at night? In contrast, entering the prime minister's living and sleeping quarters is not such an uncommon occurrence among "trusted" political journalists in Japan. While some Japanese political journalists have suggested that this is evidence that they get much closer to their sources than do American political reporters, proximity comes at a high price—the ability to write what one knows.[27] Perhaps the most famous example of this involved the relationship between Tanaka Kakuei and the journalists who covered him. After a non–club member magazine wrote an exposé that led to his downfall, a number of political journalists confessed that they had known about his transgressions but had chosen not to write about them for fear of falling in disfavor.

It is clear from these examples that newspaper companies, and consequently club journalists, place a high priority on the development of long-term and stable relationships with sources. This emphasis fosters close relations not only with sources, but also with rivals in the club seeking similar types of information from a similar (and limited) supply of official sources. An important distinction exists, however, between this kind of group-based cultivation of sources and that carried out by individual journalists in other countries. Unlike the cultivation of sources by individual, independent journalists, the group-based and rule-bound efforts of journalists in the *kisha* clubs make it easier for sources to manipulate a much larger number of journalists than they could otherwise. An important consequence of this practice, then, is the high level of homogeneity of news accounts in the Japanese press.

While the practice has obvious advantages for both parties, sources have been particularly adept at using the emphasis journalists place on maintaining close relations with them to persuade club members to keep certain kinds of information out of print. One example of a case where the source asked the press to refrain from reporting an incident involved the *kisha* club in the Tokyo metropolitan government offices during the reign of Tokyo's socialist Governor Minobe in the 1960s and 1970s. On one occasion when Minobe was speaking to a group of youths in Tokyo, he was heckled so badly when he criticized the LDP that he was unable to complete his speech. Although the media were present at this debacle, not a single newspaper, television or radio station reported the incident. Why? The metropolitan vice-governor and the chief of general affairs had gone to the club afterward and requested that the journalists not write about the incident. The claque of journalists in this club complied. Later, the incident was raised by an LDP politician during a session of the metropolitan assembly, but this also was not reported.[28] Often, however, it is unnecessary for the source to make the kind of request documented here to withhold a story. Club members and sources alike understand that critical comments will go unreported. This is precisely what is meant by the establishment of a friendly environment.

Japanese defenders of the press club system like to argue that although journalists get close to sources, they rarely wind up in the proverbial vest pocket. In the sense that journalists are professionals with high moral and ethical standards, this may be true; they are rarely "bought" outright by their sources (though occasionally such allegations have been made). At the same time, there can be no denying that the close proximity to sources provided by club membership entails a greater obligation on the part of journalists to protect them. The closer one gets, the harder it becomes to write what one knows. Moreover, given that proximity is frequently achieved through membership in an exclusive group, the impact of such relations increases exponentially. There is no need for sources to "buy" Japanese journalists in order to get them to cooperate. Cooperation with sources and competitors is a fundamental aspect of club membership.

While the access-autonomy dilemma detailed here is confronted by journalists everywhere, as we have seen in the case of Japan, journalists are encouraged from the beginning of their careers as part of their early training to form close relations with rivals and sources, often without giving due consideration to the costs that cultivating such relationships might entail. As a result, there is a greater willingness among them to withhold information from the public or not attribute the source of a story than one might expect to find elsewhere.

Returning to the example of journalists in police-related clubs, Asano Kenichi, a veteran crime reporter, argues that while some journalists and police officials claim that their relationships are not overly close, he believes that "Japan's newspaper reporters have become public relations organs of the police authorities. As long as journalists are absorbed in a competition to deduce the identities of individuals the police are arresting, the essential task of journalism—namely that as the watchdog of the powerful—will continue to be impaired."[29] Similar comments have been made about the newsgathering practices of political and economic journalists and the relationships they have with their sources.

The emphasis on maintaining close relationships with sources and withholding information from the public that might reveal a less-than-favorable image of the source also explains why, on numerous occasions—even when politicians have made absurd comments *on the record*—journalists have not reported them. Asano tells of a case where a journalist was scolded by both the source and club members for having reported comments made on record. In May 1987, the Kyoto prefectural governor made a disparaging comment about the people of Okinawa in an on-record press conference. Apparently, a fierce typhoon had destroyed many of the sugar cane fields in Okinawa, and the governor suggested that it would now be easier to protect the country against radicals—implying that Japanese radicals hide in the sugar cane fields of Okinawa. Although a dozen or so journalists were present when the governor made this comment, only one, a young social affairs reporter from the Kyodo news service, wrote about it.

Even though the wire service journalist had chosen to leave the pack and write the story, none of Kyodo's subscribers in the Kansai region (the region surrounding Kyoto) nor the national mainstream papers or their affiliated broadcast stations published the account. The only papers that picked up the story were the *Hokkaido shimbun* in northern Japan, which wrote about it on its social affairs page, and the local papers in Okinawa, the *Ryukyu shinpō* and the *Okinawa taimuzu*. Although the rest of Japan had not yet heard of the incident, it became a significant enough political issue in Okinawa that the Kyoto governor had to fly to Naha (the capital of Okinawa) to apologize. It was not until after he made this trip that the mainstream national and local newspaper companies began to report the event.

But the story does not end there. The day after the Kyodo journalist wrote and filed his report, the chief of the press section of the Kyoto prefectural government asked the journalist to join him at a coffee shop to talk about his story. During that meeting, the section chief told the journalist that while the governor's remark had been on the record, it was only part of a larger conversation and "did not represent the governor's true feelings." Moreover, he pointed out, all of the other journalists in the club had taken this into account and had not filed the story. In summarizing the conversation between the journalist and the government official, Asano claims that during the course of the hour-long conversation "the official said something that epitomizes the relationship between the modern mass media and the authorities." According to Asano, in explaining why the journalist should have refrained from writing the story, the official made the following comment: "The Kyoto prefectural *kisha* club is a 'friendly club' (*nakayoshi kurabu*) and maintains friendly relations with the government. Because it is a friendly club, it is not that club members cannot write stories about things that might be disadvantageous to the Kyoto governor or the Kyoto government, but that the club somehow manages to gloss over these. Even things that might make the farmers in Okinawa angry are hushed up."[30]

Informal Rules and Pack Journalism

FUNCTIONAL SPECIALIZATION: "HARD" AND "SOFT" NEWS

For over a hundred years, Japanese journalists have been divided into two broad categories: those covering "hard news" (*kōha*)—journalists from the political and economic bureaus—and those covering "soft news" (*nampa*)—the social affairs (*shakaibu*) journalists. The distinction between these two categories of news is not always clear to the outsider. Political or economic journalists, for example, frequently cover a relatively narrow range of topics. In the past, as a result of the practice of assigning political journalists to cover individual faction leaders, much of the political news covered by political journalists focused on the inner workings of the LDP or inter- and intrafactional disputes of the ruling party.[31] While political journalists (particularly *ban* journalists) have covered politicians quite closely, they have not generally been responsible for covering (or uncovering) the political scandals in which these politicians have frequently been involved. This role has been taken on by the social affairs journalists, who ironically do not have access to the politicians involved in the scandals they report. Likewise, economic journalists have generally focused their attention on a fairly narrow range of topics, providing detailed analyses of personnel shifts in major corporations, or announcements of new products and corporate business strategies. Critics have often accused them of being mere extensions of the PR bureaus in major corporations—the major sources of many of their stories.

In contrast, journalists in the social affairs bureau, the largest bureau in a newspaper, cover a much broader range of topics, many of which touch on issues related to both politics and economics.[32] While social affairs journalists cover such issues as environmental pollution, urban crises, and natural disasters (earthquakes and typhoons)—in other words, the kinds of topics that might come to mind when we hear the term "social" affairs—they also cover the Imperial Household Agency, the police, the public prosecutor's office, and important ministries such as the Ministry of International Trade and Industry, the Ministry of Education, and the Ministry of Post and Telecommunications. *Shakaibu* journalists are almost always the first newspaper journalists to investigate or write about a political or economic scandal, even though in many cases it is non–*kisha* club journalists—particularly the magazine press—who are responsible for breaking these scandals in the first place.[33]

This explains why political scandals, when they break at all, are frequently found on the social affairs page of a newspaper rather than the political or front page, at least in their early stages. This "division of labor" also explains why social affairs journalists are not well liked by businessmen, politicians, bureaucrats, and journalists from the other two bureaus. Japanese politicians frequently refuse to talk with journalists from the social affairs desk, in part because, in contrast to the *ban* journalists described earlier, these journalists are thought to be "untrustworthy." One media critic and former political journalist, Honzawa Jiro, cites a politician's secretary as saying that "even a phone call from a social affairs journalist can send shivers down our spines."[34] Another reason why politicians do not talk to social affairs journalists has to do with a tacit understanding they have with political journalists that they will not divulge information to journalists in the social affairs or other bureaus.[35] In this way, politicians and bureaucrats use the existing rivalries between political and social affairs journalists—rivalries intensified by the press club system—to their benefit.

One consequence of the arrangements described here is that none of the major political scandals in the last decade have been uncovered by political journalists; several of them were not even uncovered by the newspaper press. The the only true example of investigative reporting by the newspaper press in Japan in the postwar period, the uncovering of the stock-for-favors scandal involving the Recruit company, was by local social affairs journalists in Kawasaki city, far from the main centers of power in Tokyo. The scandal involving former prime minister Tanaka Kakuei mentioned above was uncovered by a monthly magazine, *Bungei shunjū*, and was not even picked up by Japanese newspapers until it had been covered by the American press.[36] Even then, the Japanese papers initially cited the English-language press and not the original (magazine and non-club member) source. What is interesting about this scandal is that many political journalists later conceded that they had known about the information contained in the *Bungei shunjū* piece. Finally, more recent revelations about former prime minister Hosokawa's relations with the Sagawa Corporation that brought down his administration in 1993 were also initially reported by *Bungei shunjū*, not by the mainstream press.

The fact that social affairs journalists are the first newspaper journalists to write about scandals might lead one to conclude that they have fewer constraints or are subject to fewer rules than, say, journalists from the political or economic bureaus. But this is not necessarily the case. With the exception of the special category of roving reporters, both "hard" (political and economic) and "soft" (social affairs) journalists are first and foremost *kisha* club members. As such, they are subject to the newsgathering rules and other constraints imposed on them by club membership. The stories they write, and the way they write them, are controlled to an exceptional degree by their membership in the club. While it is true that the *shakaibu* journalists are free of some of the specific constraints imposed on journalists in some of the political clubs, they have other, equally binding rules and conventions that they must follow. These journalists are also accused of getting too close to sources, and of withholding information from the public.

THE MINISTRY OF EDUCATION CLUB: A CASE STUDY

An incident in 1982 involving the Ministry of Education (MOE) club serves as a revealing case study of what can happen when rule-based journalism is the norm and club journalists follow the pack rather than their instincts. Each year the Ministry of Education authorizes forty or fifty textbooks for use the following year in classrooms nationwide, and each year the authorization process has pitted the leftist Japan Teachers Association against the conservative LDP and the MOE bureaucracy. The issue is not a new one, but 1982 marked the first time media reports of the domestic dispute over textbook content served as a catalyst for an international incident.

In this case, a problem arose over putative changes that the Textbook Authorization Committee had made in a passage involving the war with China. Members of the MOE *kisha* club had uniformly reported that the committee had replaced the word "invasion" with "advance," rewriting history in such a way as to suggest that Japan had advanced into North China rather than invading it. Naturally, the Chinese were angered when they learned of the alleged change. But it was not until after they had successfully extracted a promise from the Japanese government to rewrite the offending portion of the textbook that it was discovered that the initial reports had been in error. That year, the textbooks had not been altered in the manner reported by the MOE club (although they had in other years). Given a limited time frame and the fact that the ministry provided the club with only one copy of each textbook to be reviewed, the sixteen members had made an agreement to share the burden of reviewing some forty-odd textbooks. It was this sharing of the workload that had led to the unanimous error.

In an article on the textbook controversy originally published in *Chūō kōron* and later translated in the *Journal of Japanese Studies*, Yayama Tarō, a veteran political journalist, explained the arrangement as follows: "With only a single copy, and working under a very tight time pressure—[journalists] are given the books only a few days before the material is made public—review and analysis presents a major problem for the members. . . . Currently, each reporter is responsible for an assigned part of the texts. Given the situation the ministry gives them to work with, it seems a reasonable, perhaps inevitable, approach to the problem at hand." Still, it is hard to imagine a group of competing journalists in the United States agreeing to get together to share a similar workload.

Not only had the journalists in the MOE club agreed to share the task of analyzing the texts, they had also implicitly agreed to accept the conclusions of any given member of the group, and to make those conclusions their own. Once one of the club members claimed to have found a major revision in a textbook, following club rules, he presented his "scoop" to all members. As Yayama points out, "since all the findings of all the facts found by a member are common property of all the members, this fact was immediately used by all." Not one journalist in the club bothered to verify the claim. Instead, they all quickly wrote the story and sent it to their respective head offices.

The tale does not end here. By sharing the task of reading and analyzing the textbooks, and accepting the results at face value, members of the club also shared in the responsibility for having written an inaccurate story. No one knows for sure when the club realized that the story was inaccurate, but for almost two months a kind of pack mentality held sway in the club. As Yayama points out, "as club members, no one dared say that reporter colleagues from other papers had made such a monumental mistake." Eventually, information on the MOE club's activities made its way to the nonmainstream press—those not party to the cartel—and they had a field day. On September 8, 1982, almost two and a half months after the original story had broken and only after several weekly and monthly publications, including *Shūkan bunshū* and *Shokun*, had exposed the club's error, *Sankei* (a national newspaper and club member) broke ranks and published an article in which it apologized for the mistake, noting that the original report had been inaccurate and informing its readers that the error had resulted from the agreement by rivals in the club to share the task of reviewing the textbooks.

In letting its readers know what had gone on inside the club, *Sankei* broke an unwritten rule that member organizations are not to refer to club practices or compromise the integrity of participating news organizations. As a consequence, the day after *Sankei* issued its correction and apology, the club called a general meeting, or *sōkai*, in order to impose sanctions on *Sankei*. After nearly three days of deliberations, the *sōkai* finally voted on whether or not to expel *Sankei* from the club. Ultimately, no sanctions were imposed in this case.[37] However, the journalist from Nihon Terebi responsible for spreading the original story in the club is said to have been transferred to the sports bureau (*undōbu*), in what represented a serious demotion. The reporting error may have permanently damaged this journalist's career.[38]

In sum, this incident reveals that club rules are many and varied. Some are explicit, such as the agreement by the MOE club to divide the workload, while others are merely implicit, such as the rule that when an error has been made (as it was in this case), all members are bound by this rule to act in the interest of the club as a whole, even if that means withholding vital information (the truth) from the public. As a member of the cartel, one's primary obligation is to protect the group; serving the interests of the public is secondary.

INFORMAL RULES GOVERNING POLITICAL *KISHA* CLUBS

Let us now turn to some of the informal rules regulating the reporting of political or "hard" news. While there are many types of rules regulating political news reporting, here we will consider only two: rules regulating press conferences with the prime minister, and rules regulating informal (though systematized) briefings, known as *kondan*.

Press Conferences with the Prime Minister

One of the rules of the club located in the Prime Minister's Office (the Kantei club) is that all meetings with the prime minister are joint conferences (as opposed to exclusive interviews) and may be attended only by *kisha* club members.[39] In principle, press conferences with the prime minister are supposed to resemble the open free-for-all that takes place during White House press briefings; but the reality is quite different. Frequently, a select group of journalists in the club (directed by the club supervisor) comes up with questions in advance in consultation with the Prime Minister's Office. These questions are then given to the prime minister several hours before the scheduled press conference in order to allow him time to "prepare meaningful answers."[40] Once the conference begins, the club supervisor, as the representative of all members of the club, asks the questions.

Commenting on Japanese-style press conferences involving the prime minister and other important officials, a former political bureau chief made the following observation:

> There is no room for a "happening" to occur. It is a complete farce. There are many instances where official press conferences involving political journalists and the prime minister, bureaucrats, and party officials are based on mutual agreement. The *kisha* clubs are the root cause of this. . . . As a result of the *nemawashi* [literally, root binding, but in a sense, advance agreement] that is carried out between the official holding the press conference and the club supervisor representing the mass media, the substance of the conference is diluted all the more.[41]

On May 10, 1990, I had the opportunity to observe a press conference held by then prime minister Kaifu Toshiki that is supportive of this general characterization of press conferences in Japan. This press conference was distinctive in several respects. First, only six of the sixteen members of the Kantei or Prime Minister's Office club (NHK, *Asahi, Mainichi, Yomiuri,* Kyodo, and a regional newspaper, *Nishi Nippon*) were allowed to ask questions, with each media company permitted to ask only one question apiece. These questions were then compiled into a single list that was provided to the Prime Minister's Office ahead of time in order to give him time to prepare his answers. In the end, the prime minister gave his "impromptu" and candid responses to the six questions, all of which were asked by a single representative of the club. That evening, the press conference was broadcast by all the major network television stations. The Japanese public never knew that they were watching a staged event. In short, press conferences in Japan, particularly those involving the prime minister, are notoriously not spontaneous affairs, and the rule-based practices outlined here go far in explaining why.

Rules Governing Postconference Kondan Briefings

The most distinctive in comparative terms of the various institutions guiding reporting in Japan's *kisha* clubs, particularly those attached to important ministries, government agencies, and political parties, are the rules regulating the attribution of comments made during what are known as *kondan* (literally, "chats"), the structured background briefings commonly held by ministers, deputy ministers, and key party officials in their offices immediately after regularly scheduled press conferences.[42]

There are two types of *kondan*—on record and off record. Even in the case of the former, the speaker is not on record, only the information he or she has provided. In other words, in the case of "on record" informal briefings, journalists can report the contents of the meeting but may not attribute them. In the case of "off record" *kondan*, none of the information garnered can be reported. In most *kondan*, tape recorders and note-taking are not permitted. As a result, when the *kondan* is over, the group of rival journalists frequently gathers together to reconstruct what was said and to coordinate their summaries of the meeting. This practice is known as *memo-awase* or "the coordinating of notes" (memos) and is another reason why news reports in Japan are remarkably similar. On occasion, particularly at the close of background briefings held in the various ministries, the source may allow journalists to take notes—a practice known as *memokon*. As Suzuki points out, however, "although the *memokon* are extremely convenient for the news gatherers, journalists become satisfied just by having been allowed to take notes. As a result, they neglect to carry out direct newsgathering and interviews. There is a good chance that these journalists are liable to manipulation as a result. The benefits for the information provider are also clear—they can be assured that information will not be scattered in all directions and that the news is released in a uniform manner."[43]

Though many journalists contend that the purpose of these briefings is to enable them to obtain deep background information, they also serve as a very effective means for sources to manipulate the news. Given that most of the mainstream news and broadcast organizations in Japan are generally represented at the *kondan*, the source can be assured that any story resulting from information supplied during them will be distributed throughout the country in a uniform manner. The source can also be assured that he or she will not be held responsible should there be an unfavorable public reaction to what has been reported.

The practice of holding *kondan* immediately after regularly scheduled news conferences also has serious implications for the way news is gathered and reported in Japan. As indicated in table 9, in some clubs, such as the MITI club, *kondan* have become an important and institutionalized (as opposed to ad hoc) part of the newsgathering process. In the process of becoming a regular part of the newsgathering process, however, the *kondan* have reduced both the impact and the importance of official press conferences in Japan. Press conferences are frequently staged events, while *kondan* have become an important means for officials to manipulate the news behind the scenes, co-opting journalists along the way.

TABLE 9
Press Conferences and Informal Briefings at the Ministry of International Trade and Industry

	Press Conferences				Informal Briefings (Kondan)			
	Time	Location	Duration	Media Members Present	Time	Place	Duration	Media Members Present
Minister	Tues., Fri., after cabinet meetings	Conference room	10 min.	20–25	Mon., Thurs. evenings 4:30 p.m.	Minister's room	30 min.	30
Deputy minister	Mon., Thurs., after dep.min. meetings after 2p.m.	Conference room	20–30 min.	20–25	Tuesday 5:00 p.m.	Deputy minister's room	40 min.	30
Chief secretary	—	—	—	—	Friday 3:00 p.m.	Chief secretary's room	30–40 min.	30

Source: Kawai Ryosuke, *Yoron to masu komyunikeshiyon* (Tokyo: Buren Shuppan, 1987), 154.

How do regular press conferences and *kondan* briefings differ? In an incident I witnessed in May 1990, Ozawa Ichiro (then secretary general of the LDP) came to the regularly scheduled news briefing, sat down, and, stating that he had no comment to make that day, asked reporters if they had anything they wanted to talk about. When no one raised a question, Ozawa rose and said, "Well, I guess there's nothing for us to talk about today." As he began to walk out of the room, approximately fifteen journalists ran after him, and an unofficial, "off record" *kondan* was held immediately thereafter in the room next door. In fact, they had all had questions—they just were not questions that could be asked in the more formal setting (and in front of television cameras) where Mr. Ozawa's comments would be on record.

As this example reveals, there is a clear distinction in the minds of both the source and journalists about what issues and topics can be discussed in official briefings and what must wait for the unofficial briefing held immediately afterward. This distinction follows very closely the distinctions Japanese often make between *tatemae* (official viewpoints) and *honne* (one's real intentions). Still, while some journalists contend that the *kondan* are important because they give them the opportunity to learn what politicians and bureaucrats are thinking but unwilling to say on record (that is, the *honne*), others have claimed that journalists never learn the truth in these meetings, and that the main purpose of *kondan* is to co-opt journalists, letting them think that they are part of an inner circle of elites so that they will agree to act as protectors of that group and refrain from writing what they know. These critics suggest that journalists are given little information of substance in the *kondan* briefings, and that even when they are given important information, tacit rules of behavior make it impossible for them to include it in their stories. In short, if a journalist feels that the public somehow has a right to know about an important issue discussed during the *kondan*, the only options are to leak it to outsiders, particularly journalists from the magazine press who are not party to or constrained by the cartel arrangements (a practice that occurs fairly frequently), or to write about the incident pseudonymously for the non-newspaper-affiliated magazine press.[44]

As a participant observer of the *kisha* club in the Prime Minister's Office in 1990, I was given the opportunity on one occasion to observe a *kondan* held by Ozawa Ichiro and to get a firsthand look at one of these informal "chats." During this *kondan*, the group of journalists sitting around the table with Mr. Ozawa (his *ban* journalists, or journalists assigned to cover important political figures) treated him with extreme deference during the entire twenty-minute meeting. They spoke about his summer vacation and commented about his wife. But the questions, responses, and overall tenor of the meeting were all quite formal, more akin to relationships between bosses and their clients (*oyabun-kobun*) than relations of equal parties, or of adversaries. Clearly, this was a lopsided, asymmetric relationship in which the source (Ozawa) was in the position of power. I observed much more *tatemae* than *honne* during this *kondan*, and there was no question as to who was in control of the situation. Ozawa's comment to me, one of two foreigners observing in the corner, was also quite telling. The secretary general turned to me and asked whether or not the scholarship I was receiving provided me with enough money to live on. I have always wondered what might have happened had I told Mr. Ozawa that I did not have enough money.

INSULATING SOURCES FROM PUBLIC SCRUTINY

One of the most important aspects of the *kondan* are the tacit rules regulating how information obtained during them can be reported. These rules have a considerable impact on the way that political issues and public policy are reported in Japan and frequently serve to insulate political and bureaucratic elites from outside scrutiny. As a result, political information is often reported in a vague and unsubstantiated way. In Japan, a country where journalists have traditionally had bylines only when they go abroad and become foreign correspondents, not only does the public not know who has written a story, they often do not know where the story or the ideas and quotes contained within it come from. The practice of not attributing sources has been institutionalized to such a high degree that journalists often wind up protecting sources even when something has been said on record. It has also resulted in the use of extremely vague expressions in news articles, particularly those about political events.

A leaked copy of notes written up by one media company after some of these *kondan* reveals that often one of the first things decided during a *kondan* is how the meeting is to be reported, for example, whether it is completely off record, or whether journalists can cite the information using several common phrases such as *seifu suji* (government sources) or *seifu kōkan suji* (a high-ranking government source). Those in the know (generally, politicians, bureaucrats, and journalists) can often decipher articles containing these phrases and know precisely who has made a statement. But the public-at-large has little idea who is being referred to when, for example, an article attributes a statement to "one of the heads of the LDP." Consider, for example, the following phrases commonly found in Japanese newspapers and to whom they actually refer:[45]

> The term "government heads" (*seifu shunō*) usually refers to the chief cabinet secretary (*kanbō chōkan*) or the prime minister. If the source is one rank below the chief cabinet secretary, the vice–cabinet secretary (*kanbō fukuchōkan*), for example, the journalist will use the phrase "government sources" (*seifu suji*).

If an article mentions the "head of the xx ministry" (*xx-shō shunō*), it is referring to one of two individuals—either the xx minister (*xx-daijin*) or xx ministry vice-minister (*xx-shō jimujikan*). If, for example, a story mentions a "MFA head" (Gaimushō *shunō*), it is referring either to the minister (*daijin*) or the vice-minister (*jimujikan*) of that ministry.

The phrase "LDP heads" (Jimintō *shunō*) generally is used to refer to one of three individuals also known as the "three key officials of the party" (*tōsanyaku*). These are the LDP party chief secretary (*kanjichō*), the head of the Policy Research Committee (Seichō Kaichō) or PARC, and the chairman of the Party Executive Council (Sōkaichō). If the source is someone other than a politician holding a ministerial position, the journalist will use the phrase "party executives" (*tōkanbu*). When the source is the head of PARC, journalists will sometimes refer to him as "an LDP head in charge of policy" (*seisaku tantō shunō*).

"Sources close to the prime minister" (*shunō sokkin*) refers to the prime minister's personal secretary. Sometimes journalists will also use the phrase "those near the prime minister" (*shunō shūhen*) to refer to the prime minister's personal secretary.

"Xx ministry officials" (*xx-shō kanbu*) usually refers to the director or chief of a bureau (*kyokuchō*) or someone of higher rank. Sometimes this is used to refer to the press secretary (*hōdōkan*). "Xx-ministry circles" (*xx-shō suji*) refers to individuals who are section heads (*bu-kacho*) in the ministry.

"Xx ministry is" (*xx-shō wa*) or the phrase "the LDP government is" (*seifu wa/ seifu jimintō wa*) is a broad phrase that can include bureaucrats from the related ministry or the chief cabinet secretary (*kanbu chōkan*).

"Informed circles" (*shōsoku suji*) refers to embassy personnel, while "sources in the prime minister's office" (*kantei suji*) refers to the cabinet vice-secretary (*kanbō fukuchōkan*).

"Xx faction heads" (*xx-ha shunō*) usually means the top two members of the faction.

As these examples reveal, the rules governing the *kondan* (particularly rules regulating the attribution of sources) can have a considerable impact on how news articles are written in Japan. Rather than trying to force sources to go on record, efforts are made in the other direction—to protect sources—even when such action is unwarranted or unnecessary. This means that businessmen, politicians, and important government officials are frequently not held accountable for what they say. Although journalists in other countries use similar types of phrases as a means of protecting sources when the release of the source's name might prove harmful, in general they must be able to justify this to their editors and readers. Nonattribution is supposed to be the exception, not the norm.

Recent evidence suggests, however, that the practice of nonattribution is much more indiscriminately used and widespread in Japan than it is elsewhere. There have been numerous instances, for example, where comments introduced in the newspaper as having been made by "a head of the LDP" were from speeches made on the record and broadcast on television the same morning. Those who had watched the television program knew precisely who had made the statement, while those who had only read the newspaper did not.[46] Tase has suggested that not only are these phrases used in protecting the identity of sources and insulating them from public scrutiny, but journalists have also been known to misuse them in other ways—using nonattribution when they do not actually have a source, for example, or when they have heard something but have not had the time to check its veracity or accuracy. He also suggests that they have been known to use this convention when they are merely expressing their own viewpoints and opinions about an issue.[47]

In an article in *Shimbun kenkyū*, the trade journal published by the NSK, Suzuki Kenji, a member of the editorial affairs board of the *Mainichi shimbun*, reports the results of an analysis he made of articles appearing on the front page of the *Mainichi shimbun* for the month of December 1989 with regard to their use of the kinds of phrases listed above (that is, phrases that do not reveal the actual source). Suzuki concludes that such terms as "heads of the party" (*tōshunō*), "government sources" (*seifu suji*), and "those affiliated with the *zaikai*" (*zaikai kankeisha*) were used excessively in articles about domestic politics.[48] Moreover, not only were such phrases used when the writer had a legitimate need to conceal the identity of the information provider, in many instances the practice of not attributing sources was unnecessarily abused, particularly in articles about politics.

Informal briefings and the informal mechanisms of protecting those making statements during them are an integral part of the newsgathering routine of many press clubs and have a tremendous impact on the way political stories are written in Japan. Although the *kondan* are a convenient means for journalists to gather information, Suzuki concludes that they "can be an extremely dangerous trap. . . . Official news conferences become nothing but mere skeletons and the legitimate newsgathering activities of the press become distorted. . . . Unlike the pointed follow up of foreign press conferences, official press conferences in Japan are closed and lack impact." He is also critical of Japanese journalists' misuse of vague phraseology in their effort to conceal the identity of those making comments during *kondan*, and he suggests that the practice "makes newsgathering too easy and results in the relaxation of the necessary tension between interviewee and interviewer." The mass media, concludes Suzuki, "should strive to bring out the true intentions (*honne*) of the subjects of their interviews. To practice sophistry through the use of these phrases is merely currying favors with sources."[49] Although many of the comments made during the *kondan* are of little consequence and their attribution would not harm the source in any way, that smaller subset of press club journalists who have exclusive access to politicians and officials through their participation in *kondan* tend to rely on nonattribution at all costs.

The Function of Rules: A Brief Summary

The rules established by the information cartel govern not only the behavior of the competitors in the press clubs, but also the relationships cartel members have with news sources. Rules make it possible for members to cooperate with each other and with sources, to develop informal, long-term relationships, minimize risks, and reduce competitive "excesses." The advantage of rules for both sides is obvious: they make each of their jobs easier by limiting unexpected events and outside competition. But the newsgathering and reporting rules outlined here have negative aspects as well, not the least of which is the price paid by the public. The numerous levels and networks of ties between the media and their elite sources and one another, as well as deeply ingrained practices for gathering the news (both of which are influenced by rules), frequently serve to reduce the adversarial potential and the other normative functions of the press. It is not that conflict does not occur, but, as Richard Samuels has suggested, it becomes routinized—ordered by the rules of interaction that exist within ongoing relationships among stable elites.[50] With the routinization of conflict, however, the tension between information gatherer and information provider diminishes. Sources can more easily manipulate the news, while journalists lose their ability to act as government watchdogs and are more likely to support the status quo than to challenge it in any significant way.

The Key Role Played by Sanctions

While the establishment of rules is an important part of the cartelization process, rules are meaningless without the means of enforcing them. Once rules have been instituted, consideration has to be given to a third requirement in the creation of an effective information cartel, namely, rule enforcement. As *New Palgrave* notes, "Enforcement is a crucial aspect of cartels. This requires (a) detection of violations and (b) sanctions on violators. . . . Once a violator is 'found out,' he can be deprived of the gain from collusion and, perhaps, access to the objects being bid for."[51] In this section, I discuss two distinct types of sanctions—club-imposed and source-imposed—and suggest ways in which they reinforce the cartel arrangements outlined earlier, ensuring conformity among group members and minimizing defection.

Club-Imposed Sanctions

Although sanctions are frequently included in the regulations that the members of each club draw up, nowhere do these regulations state that they are to be imposed when a member has broken club rules. Club regulations merely claim that sanctions will be enforced when a member of the club has done something to damage the club's reputation. Regulations for the Kantei club in the Prime Minister's Office, for example, provide for the imposition of four different sanctions when club members or participating companies "harm the honor of the club."[52] These include apology, warning, temporary expulsion, and removal from the club.[53] Other clubs also impose similar sanctions when a member has broken club rules.

In the case involving Secretary General Ozawa's "prostration comment" (*dogeza hatsugen*) described in the preface, in which one of the club members defected by attributing the statement to Ozawa Ichiro, the group of competitors in the Hirakawa club (attached to Liberal Democratic party headquarters) held a general meeting (*sōkai*) attended by representatives from all of the companies in the club in order to decide what sort of sanctions to impose against *Asahi*. After the conclusion of this meeting, the representatives handed the journalists from *Asahi* the following list of demands:

1. They stated that they would take a "wait and see" attitude with respect to punishing *Asahi* by prohibiting access to the Diet (a punishment known as *tōin teishi*), or taking other (unspecified) measures.

2. They threatened that if similar problems arose in the future they would implement such sanctions.

3. They demanded that an "appropriate" representative from the political desk at *Asahi* write an apology to the club.

4. They asked *Asahi* to send an "appropriate" person to apologize to Secretary General Ozawa in person.

5. Finally, *Asahi* was told that its affiliated publications (which are supposed to have independent editorial rights) were not to refer to "Secretary General Ozawa's 'prostration statement.' "[54]

Both *Asahi* and its affiliates abided by these demands. Several weeks after this incident, the journalist who had been responsible for covering Mr. Ozawa and attending his briefings (his *ban* journalist) was transferred to a club in the Labor Ministry. Officials at *Asahi*, however, maintained that the transfer had been planned prior to this incident.

While descriptions of cases where club members have sanctioned a competitor are sometimes leaked to nonmember magazine journalists, who relish the opportunity to attack the mainstream press by revealing some of the more dubious press club practices, it is next to impossible to obtain empirical data on the frequency with which a particular sanction is imposed. A survey conducted by the labor union of the *Mainichi shimbun*, however, provides a fairly good idea of the types of sanctions that are most likely to be imposed when journalists break one type of club rule—the blackboard agreements described earlier.[55]

As part of a study to ascertain conditions in the *kisha* clubs and draw up a proposal to reform the club system, members of the *Mainichi* labor union asked journalists in clubs all over the country to respond to a series of questions about newsgathering practices in their respective clubs. These responses were later compiled and published in the labor union's organ, *Honryū*. One of the questions included in the survey asked club journalists, "What measures are taken when a blackboard agreement is broken?" The responses to this question are detailed in figure 10, below. According to the survey results, the most common type of sanction imposed by the club when a journalist has violated a blackboard agreement is expulsion or suspension. This sanction was noted by 36 percent of the respondents, followed by 14.6 percent who listed a verbal warning from the club supervisor and 13.2 percent who answered that journalists would be given a strict written warning by the club supervisor.

In terms of which clubs were more likely to impose the kinds of sanctions listed in the figure, 60 percent of clubs in the central government agencies, 50 percent in educational clubs, and 56 percent in economic-related clubs responded that they would impose such sanctions. Clubs where the sanctions imposed were relatively lenient or infrequently enforced included those in city halls, special government agencies, and law-related clubs. Of the 216 city hall clubs, however, only 18 said that they had no sanctions whatsoever, and 30 said that at a minimum, a verbal warning would be given.[56]

What is striking about these responses is that sanctions are most often imposed by competitors in the club, not by sources, underscoring the important role played by the cartel. These results are also in stark contrast to the noncartelized news-source relations found elsewhere, where one would expect the source, not competitors, to refuse access to a journalist who has broken an embargo or an agreement that certain statements were to remain off record. This alternative sanction (though more common in other advanced industrial democracies)—refusal *by the source* to continue to provide information—was selected only 2.5 percent of the time by the

Question: What measures are taken in the event that a blackboard agreement is broken? (May answer more than once.)

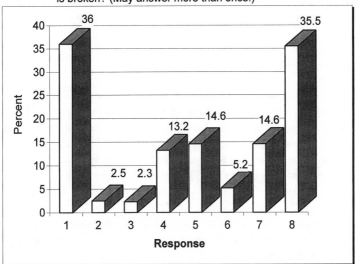

Responses: 1. Internal punishment by the club such as expulsion for a set amount of time.
2. Attendance prohibited by the source.
3. Refusal by the source to provide information.
4. A strict written warning by the club supervisor.
5. A verbal warning by the club supervisor.
6. There are no sanctions.
7. Other
8. No response

Figure 10. Measures Taken When Blackboard Agreements Are Broken.
Source: Honryū, August 26, 1993, 2.

clubs surveyed here. Likewise, expulsion by the source was selected only 2.3 percent of the time.[57]

One of the reasons that it is the cartel rather than the source that imposes penalties when such agreements are broken has to do with the fact that it is members of the club (and not sources) that suffer most from these kinds of violations. Because blackboard agreements frequently involve agreements about when a certain official announcement will be published, those who violate the agreement by publishing that information early do not generally harm the source, which has given the club the information to publish anyway. But they do harm their competitors by "scooping" them. This is not to suggest that sources do not sanction violators of club rules; as shown below, in certain clubs they do. They just don't sanction violators of blackboard agreements very often. It may be significant, too, that the clubs having the smallest number of blackboard agreements overall, namely, the police-related clubs, are also those where it is more common for the source (rather than the club) to impose a sanction.

Source-Imposed Sanctions

In sharp contrast to the situation described above, where club members punish those who violate blackboard agreements, in certain clubs, including those in the public prosecutor's office, the metropolitan police headquarters, and sometimes the Ministry of Foreign Affairs, powerful sources often play an important role as sanctioners. Using the existing cartel arrangements and journalists' dependency on them for gathering information, these sources use sanctions as means to control the flow, content, and slant of information. Not coincidentally, many of the rules for which these powerful sources enforce sanctions have been imposed by the source in exchange for access, underscoring the considerable power many sources have over club members.

What kinds of sanctions do sources generally rely upon? The most common sanctioning mechanism used by sources is known literally as "entry and exit prohibited" (*deiri kinshi*) or, more accurately, access denied.[58] One veteran journalist from the club in the prosecutor's office describes how this sanction affected his club: "In a word, *deiri kinshi* is a pronouncement from the top that limits and prohibits newsgathering within the Tokyo District Public Prosecutor's Office. This includes a prohibition on interviewing sources, gathering information, and participating in press conferences."[59] The source best known for imposing sanctions on club members is the special investigations unit (*tokusabu*) in the Tokyo prosecutor's office, Japan's powerful investigative organ.[60] Journalists in this club, the Shihō club, or judicial club, are frequently sanctioned for having obtained a scoop or for breaking one of the following club rules:[61]

> **1.** Members of the club are prohibited from talking with anyone other than the director or assistant director (*buchō* or *fuku-buchō*) of the special investigations unit.[62]
> **2.** Members of the club are prohibited from conducting interviews with suspects, or interviews that "interfere with an investigation."
> **3.** Members of the club are prohibited from conducting interviews that might "*destroy the relationship of trust* with the special investigations unit."[63]

If a journalist breaks one of these rules and speaks with the public prosecutor or deputy prosecutor (or even one of the secretaries in the public prosecutor's office), interviews a suspect, or conducts other interviews that the prosecutors find offensive, he or she is likely to be expelled from the club or given a strict reprimand. Once a reporter has been prohibited from entering the club, none of the journalists from that media organization are permitted to carry out newsgathering activities, participate in regular press briefings, or attend the informal *kondan,* for the duration of the penalty. During high-profile investigations, the prosecutors office imposes these sanctions frequently and indiscriminantly, making it difficult for journalists to know precisely what are acceptable newsgathering practices. Nishiyama points out, moreover, that "in some cases journalists are expelled from the club fairly frequently merely for having written articles that the authorities have not liked." Naturally, in most of these cases, the articles that resulted in a journalist's expulsion were scoops.[64]

An interesting case where the prosecutor's office imposed this sanction frequently and repeatedly is described by a former Shihō club journalist who was present when six of the sixteen members of the club were expelled over a period of about two weeks. Not surprisingly, the author of this detailed account wrote it under a pseudonym, lest he be expelled from the club (or worse) for having divulged club "secrets."[65] This incident took place in 1987 when the special investigations unit of the Tokyo public prosecutor's office was pursuing an important bribery scandal involving a politician from the Democratic Socialist party, Okute Fumio, who was suspected of having taken bribes from the Association of Labor Unions for the Japan Twine Industry (Nihon Yoriito Kōgyō Kumiai Rengōkai). Because this was the first time in more than a decade (since the Lockheed bribery scandal) that a politician in office had been investigated for taking a bribe, the prosecutor's office was quite sensitive about how the press might report the developing scandal. As a result, they exerted considerable control over the release of information related to the investigation.

It is somewhat understandable why the public prosecutors would want to limit the flow of information about their investigation, particularly given the history of relations between the prosecutor's office and the justice minister (a political appointee) in Japan. It seems that Japan's public prosecutors have had rather bitter experiences when it comes to arresting politicians, particularly from the LDP. In the Zōsen scandal of 1954, for example, after the prosecutor's office had made out a warrant for the arrest of then LDP secretary general Sato Eisaku, the justice minister exercised his "right of judicial authority" (*shikiken*) and effectively crushed the investigation into the scandal. Apparently, he had learned of the prosecutors' plans to issue the warrant from the press. As a result, journalists in the prosecutor's office club were forced to agree not to report the details of ongoing investigations until they are given the go-ahead by the prosecutor's office. This agreement (rule) is still in effect today and has made it possible for the prosecutor's office to use the media as leverage vis-à-vis the justice minister and the Justice Ministry in an effort to ensure that undue pressure is not placed on them while they conduct important investigations of prominent politicians, bureaucrats, or business people. At the same time, in agreeing to side with the prosecutor's office in its power struggle with the justice minister, the media have become active participants in efforts to keep information from the public.

In the case described above involving the politician from the Democratic Socialist party, eventually six media organizations were expelled from the club for having violated various club-source agreements. The first two media companies that the prosecutor's office expelled from the Shihō club—Company A and Company B—were expelled for a week for having incorrectly reported the imminent arrest of the politician. Given their past experiences, the prosecutor's office had decided to act cautiously in this case, ordering only that the politician in question remain under house arrest. They were not about to arrest him as the news accounts had stated.

Because the Diet was still in session at that time, they could not have legally arrested him anyway, a fact that these journalists evidently forgot. The deputy public prosecutor who expelled these two companies from the club explained that they were being punished because they had filed mistaken reports claiming that the politician in question would be arrested shortly, and had consequently "misinformed the public." While their stories were indeed inaccurate, a more practical response might have been for the prosecutor's office to request that the newspapers revise or correct their stories, or for the newspapers to have done so independently once they realized their error.

The day after this infraction, two other companies—companies C and D—were expelled from the club for having written that the prosecutors had conducted a simultaneous search of Mr. Okute's office and that of the politician occupying the office next door, a Mr. Inemura. Claiming that this was not true, the prosecutor's office ousted the journalists from both of these newspapers. That same day, Company E was also expelled from the club when prosecutors learned that a journalist from this company had interviewed the politician in question. His crime? He had violated the second rule above, namely, that club journalists are forbidden to interview suspects.

Only two days after the first two companies were expelled, Company F became the sixth company expelled from the club. This time, the prosecutor's office claimed that an article describing the events that had transpired when the politician had allegedly accepted the bribe was *too detailed*. The only way the journalist could possibly have obtained such a detailed account, they claimed, was to have interviewed one of the rank-and-file prosecutors investigating the case, a violation of the first rule outlined above.

Several days later, another journalist was expelled from the club for having written a story in which he repeated the suggestion that the second politician, whose name he included in the story, was also being investigated for bribery in the same case. This time, the prosecutors claimed that the publication of the other suspect's name might result in the destruction of evidence. But the author of this account points out that "there had been evidence all along that both politicians were involved in the bribery." Moreover, the politician concerned knew by this time that he was being investigated, and had he wanted to destroy evidence he would have done so long before his name made the papers.

Following this incident, companies H and A, which had just been allowed to reenter the club, filed similar reports based on Company F's story and found themselves expelled from the club a second time. According to the author of this account, who was present when these incidents occurred, the process of violation, expulsion, reviolation, and renewed expulsion was repeated numerous times during the several-week period before the two members of parliament were finally arrested and prosecuted.[66]

The case described above is only one of many in which the source is able to effectively muzzle the press by imposing sanctions. Another well-known example occurred during the investigation of the Recruit scandal. Here, the prosecutor's office frequently imposed sanctions on members of the club, eventually kicking out more than half of the fifteen companies in the club for things they had written about that investigation.[67] But what is perhaps the most infamous case of a source sanctioning club members occurred in the prime minister's Office club just before former Prime Minister Sato Eisaku was to make an official televised announcement of his resignation as prime minister on June 17, 1972. In this case, Prime Minister Sato, angry with the press for doggedly pursuing him over rumors that he was preparing to resign, refused to let journalists have access to his final press conference. In a dramatic incident televised live, political journalists from the newspaper press were forced to exit the conference hall, leaving Sato to deliver his resignation in front of the few remaining television technicians.[68] The following day, all of the major newspaper companies published the resignation speech in its entirety, having watched it on television themselves.[69]

Understanding Sanctions

What the situations described in the preceding passages suggest is the existence of two different types of relational priorities in Japan's *kisha* clubs.[70] In the first type, relations *among club members* are the primary concern, and it is the club that imposes sanctions against errant members. The key issue in the violation of a blackboard agreement, for example, is one of equality and standardization among cartel members. One of the implicit assumptions behind the kinds of arrangements outlined here is that members have agreed to have a standard product. As a result, everyone is expected to report a given story at the same time, and relations have been structured in such a way that it is next to impossible to get (or at least to publish) information that competitors do not also have. By not adhering to an agreement, a violator scoops the other members of the cartel. While sources are not disinterested in such violations (they are sometimes harmed by early publication), they have given the information to the cartel to be published anyway, and they expect the club to keep its own house in order, imposing sanctions for this kind of infraction on its own.

In the second instance, however, the primary relationship is the *source-club relation*. Here, powerful sources impose certain rules on newsgathering and reporting in the club, rules the club tacitly agrees to in exchange for access. These rules are designed to protect the source's interests and help it control both the flow of information and the way that certain types of stories are written. While the cartel is also hurt when a member violates these rules (they get scooped and/or the source gets angry and refuses to talk to any of them), it is generally a source-imposed rule that has been broken, and consequently it is the source that imposes the sanction.

What is interesting about this latter category of relations is that the club does not usually rally behind a sanctioned member. Indeed, it implicitly supports the sanction imposed by the source. Why? In most cases, by breaking one of these rules, not only has the violator scooped the other cartel members, frequently they have published a "real" scoop, not the kind of scoop that occurs when one has published a bit of shared information a day early, as in the case of a violation of a blackboard agreement.[71] There is no incentive, then, for club members to come to the aid of a source-sanctioned member by challenging the source's imposition of the sanction.[72] Quite the contrary, the newspaper desks (*desukku*) of the other member companies have probably demanded that their journalists in the club explain why they missed out on the story, and club members may pressure the source to take some sort of retaliatory measure as a result. Consider what happened in the following case cited in the *Economist* in 1991: "In April, 1991 TBS, the largest commercial broadcasting station, disregarded a Foreign Ministry edict against traveling to the Soviet-held islands north of Hokkaido that are claimed by Japan. TBS's punishment was to be banned from the ministry's briefings during Mr. Gorbachev's visit that month—but none of the *kisha*-club members at the Foreign Ministry muttered a word of protest."[73] But why should they? The competitors had missed out on a scoop.

Even when competitors in the club decide to impose sanctions against one of their members, they generally impose them not on the individual journalist responsible for an infraction, but on all of the representatives from a given media outlet that participate in that club. In other words, if the *Yomiuri*, for example, has eight reporters assigned to the Prime Minister's Office club, all eight would be suspended. This reflects in part the nature of group-based reporting in Japan, where articles are frequently written by the group of reporters, not by a single individual. One favorable aspect of this system—in terms of the individual journalists concerned—is that responsibility for a story is dispersed. But one of the downsides to the club system is that when it comes to sanctioning, more often than not the entire group is punished. Group sanctions are a much more powerful and effective means of control, whether put in place by the club or by the source. This practice may also result from the "fairness" norm discussed earlier. Without this rule, the larger and wealthier national papers would be able to take more risks than the smaller-staffed ones and would be less vulnerable in the event that an infraction were made.

In arguing that sanctions can be imposed in two different ways, we suggest that the power of the *kisha* club vis-á-vis state organs is clearly variable. At the same time, the evidence shows that while officials in certain state organs have overwhelming power over the club, rarely do the clubs gain a position of superiority in relations with sources. As mentioned earlier, this has been the case historically as well: the club-source relationship has always been one of either the club's cooperation with or subordination to its sources.

Finally, while sources can and do have legitimate reasons for imposing sanctions on journalists, many source-imposed sanctions step beyond the bounds of justifiably punishing an offending journalist for breaking an embargo or promise of anonymity, and into the realm of out-and-out censorship and control. Source-imposed sanctions in Japan fall under an altogether different category—one of explicit control by a powerful actor. Here, too, there is an implicit understanding that if the club does not keep its own house in order, the source may do so itself. The most important distinction between this kind of sanction and that imposed by the club is that it is carried out by an actor that, while not officially party to the cartel, has played an important role as rule maker and key supporter of the cartel arrangements. Sources are never passive bystanders to the information cartel; they play an active role at many levels, from rule making to rule enforcing. The degree to which they participate, however, varies. Some sources rarely impose sanctions on club members; others, including those described earlier, are powerful sanctioners.

Detecting Violators

Palgrave's notes that the detection of violators is key to the functioning of a cartel. In line with our emphasis on the establishment of trade practices by the information cartel, sanctions and their enforcement are key. However, unlike violators of other types of cartels (who violate by offering lower prices), in the case of the information cartel, violation entails writing or printing information that members (or members and sources) have agreed is subject to control. Detection is not very difficult: a violator of the trade practices established by an information cartel will have violated by publishing certain information that has been subject to group (or source) regulation. Detection merely requires reading rivals' morning editions (or, in the case of the source, reading the major dailies). More extraordinary—at least to a Western observer accustomed to the notion of open competition among an open press—are cases where rivals themselves have agreements to exchange advance copies of the first edition so that daily comparisons can be made, infractions can be caught, and one's own paper updated with any missed information. This actually happens: Japan's major dailies have agreed to share with one another their first editions. Because each paper has as many as ten different editions *each day*, it is easy to include in the next edition information left out in the final, Tokyo, edition. Of course, if any of the companies party to the exchange agreement feels that they have a scoop, they generally refrain from taking part in the exchange that day. This practice results in a considerable uniformity in reporting as individual papers "adjust" their stories in later editions to include information that had been previously left out.

The Negative Impact of Rules

The rules established by the information cartel are important for a number of reasons. To begin with, they foster an alternative and powerful form of censorship: group self-censorship. Second, they lead to the creation of a congenial newsgathering milieu in which journalists exchange autonomy for access, lending themselves to the ready manipulation and co-optation by sources, and to their active collaboration with the state in the management of information. Third, rules play an important role in restricting the flow of information to the public, severely limiting the extent of investigative and critical reporting among the Japanese press. Finally, although rules minimize risks, they often do so at a price, to both journalists and their readers.

Japan's information cartels—and the rules made by them—are interesting for reasons that go beyond what most industrial organization economists study: the effects of such collusive practices on "social welfare" or the public good, as defined by higher prices paid by consumers. There is an interest here as well in social welfare, but the primary welfare loss is associated with access to a limited range of information—that is, newspaper collusion results in the standardization of an informationally inferior product. The loss in social welfare comes less from higher prices than from the ineffectiveness of the fourth estate function played by the press. Consumers have less access to the information that would help them to become informed observers of the political process.

While the media everywhere formulate rules—both tacit and formal—to structure relations among themselves and with key sources, the rules established by Japan's information cartels represent institutional arrangements that have moved beyond simple convenience or efficiency for journalists and news organizations to a system in which information of relevance to the public is effectively restricted.

Five

Expanding the Web: The Role of *Kyōkai* and *Keiretsu*

> People of the same trade seldom meet together,
> even for merriment and diversion, but the conver-
> sation ends in a conspiracy against the public, or
> in some contrivance to raise prices.
>   (*Adam Smith,* The Wealth of Nations)

As ECONOMISTS and business historians have long noted, cartels can be unstable arrangements. Insiders may renege on their agreements, effectively introducing competition into the mix. Or producers that are outside the cartel, and therefore not bound by the cartel's rules and restrictions, may offer alternatives that also break down the cartel's barriers. Despite these hazards, Japan's *kisha* clubs have remained a remarkably durable and powerful force in the Japanese political process. To understand just how, this chapter focuses on two media institutions that have reinforced and extended the clubs' role: the newspaper industry association (*kyōkai*) and media *keiretsu*.

As with other trade associations in Japan, the Japan Newspaper Publishers and Editors Association (NSK) plays a central role in cartelizing its industry.[1] It coordinates media political interests, collects sensitive sector-level information, and provides an informal backdrop within which competing firms adjust prices, layouts, and other operational components of the newspaper product. Most importantly, it controls access of news organizations to political and other news sources by regulating entry and exit to the clubs themselves and has been the chief source of resistance in efforts to reform the club system by opening them to outside media (including the foreign press). As indicated in the case study of the news embargo imposed during the Crown Prince's marriage search in 1992–93, the NSK, like the *kisha* clubs, interacts with critical news sources to manage the news reporting process in Japan.

Media *keiretsu* are important for the way they extend the reach of Japan's national newspapers to the remainder of the media industry. These newspapers are the strategic center of a complex network of relations that includes television broadcasting, radio stations, and weekly newsmagazines. Their control over television is especially important, given the major role this medium plays in most democracies. Virtually the entirety of the commercial television broadcasting industry in Japan is under the control of one of the five national newspapers, which send executives to help with their management and own a substantial share of their equity capital. The early entrance into this new medium by the newspaper press was supported by state policies that encouraged the organizing of television stations under a vertical control structure, with the major newspapers at the top. The mutual interests of the state and the newspaper industry intersected: by linking the new broadcast media to a *keiretsu* led by club member newspapers, they could severely limit their ability to report news independently of their parent organizations and prevent the rise of an alternative mainstream media in Japan.

The Nihon Shimbun Kyōkai

Immediately after the end of the war, the major Japanese media gathered in Tokyo to discuss how they might transform themselves in a manner acceptable to Occupation authorities.[2] As a result of this meeting, they established the Japan Press Federation (Nippon Shimbun Renmei), choosing as their head then president of *Mainichi shimbun* Shingoro Takaishi. Occupation authorities soon realized that the new federation was unacceptable, in part because it was headed by one of the fifty-plus newspaper elites later purged for their wartime roles. As a thinly veiled re-creation of the wartime association discussed in chapter 2, it was clear that the federation would make a poor choice for carrying out SCAP directives to end censorship, introduce free speech, and disassociate the press from government. Consequently, in July 1946 SCAP "sponsored" its transformation into the NSK, as well as the adoption by the association of a code of ethics—the Japanese "Canons of Journalism." As Coughlin noted in 1952, however, both the NSK and its code of ethics were "about as Japanese as a Hershey bar."[3]

Despite its less than auspicious origins, the NSK gradually began to make some positive contributions to the democratizing role of the press in Japan: educating journalists about their obligations and responsibilities to society; publishing documents and holding seminars about free speech; and acting as the main representative of the Japanese press in its relationship with SCAP. More ominously, however, it also began to take on a number of other functions that gave it considerable power over the re-emerging industry. One of these was the role it played in developing rules for the distribution of scarce newsprint, which inadvertently gave it the power to limit entry into the market by newly established (and reestablished) newspapers. Even more important is the role it has played since its inception as the definer, legitimator, adjudicator, and maintainer of the press club system, and therefore of Japan's information cartels.

This latter role had a long-term impact. By deciding early on to allow the club system to remain virtually intact, the NSK—ignoring suggestions from SCAP that the clubs be abolished—provided the more powerful members of the industry with an effective means for limiting access to sources by rival companies. By restricting who could tap the "raw materials" (i.e., news sources themselves) needed by new and reestablished newspapers to compete effectively, they were able to maintain the high degree of industry concentration and perpetuate the close press-source relations that had been put in place during the wartime period. This decision also gave NSK members a powerful mechanism for keeping down the costs and risks associated with the gathering of information by giving club members exclusive use of public resources *at taxpayer expense*. But the decision to maintain the club system was one the association would repeatedly have to reevaluate and defend. Indeed, what the association began to refer to euphemistically as "the *kisha* club problem" has remained a constant thorn in its side throughout the postwar era.

The NSK's goal of promoting its own members' interests is clear. So too is the wide-ranging character of these interests. As the NSK explains on its own web page: "It often becomes necessary for newspaper companies to protect their common interests vis-à-vis *other media, society, or the government*. As a common-interest organization of newspaper companies, NSK, representing member press organizations, conducts activities to advance the interests of the entire newspaper industry in every field from editorial to business and technical aspects. NSK also mediates among newspaper companies when their interests conflict."[4]

In the half-century since its establishment, the NSK has grown to embrace a wide range of Japanese media organizations, including broadcast companies and news agencies. As of 1997 the association had 164 members, of which 112 were newspapers, 47 were broadcast companies (29 television stations and 18 stations in radio or radio-TV combination), and 5 were news agencies.[5] Dues are determined according to the type of media: for newspapers, whose dues cover more than 90 percent of the total budget, these are based on circulation numbers; in the case of broadcast companies, they are calculated by antenna output; and for news agencies, they are determined by the volume of news distributed.[6] Most of the association's expenses are covered by these dues, though a small proportion of expenses are paid with income earned through sales of the NSK's own publications.

Membership in the NSK is determined by a Board of Directors (thirty-five to forty-five individuals selected biennially) who base their decisions on a number of formal criteria, including that the organization agree to abide by the NSK's own Canons of Journalism and that it be of a minimum size (for newspapers, circulation in excess of ten thousand). In addition, there are several prerequisites to membership not formally listed, including that the organization not be affiliated with any political party or religious group. The most problematic unwritten rule, however, is the requirement that a member be a Japanese company: in 1952 the Board of Directors refused membership to a Japanese newspaper that was owned by a Chinese national, stipulating that no foreign-owned newspaper would be granted membership. As the foreign media have learned, this unwritten restriction, which stood for well over four decades, has been fundamental: if an organization cannot gain access to the industry association, it is next to impossible for it to gain access to the all-important *kisha* clubs on an equal footing with Japanese newspapers, and consequently to important news in Japan.

The NSK and the Kisha *Club Problem*

Although it was established in 1946, the Nihon Shimbun Kyōkai was not forced to confront the press club issue head-on until 1949. In the fall of that year, responding to an ultimatum it had received from SCAP to either democratize the clubs or abolish them altogether, the association's Editorial Affairs Committee met to discuss the problem, publishing its first "Guideline on the *Kisha* Clubs" a month later.[7] This nonbinding policy statement, the first of a series of statements the NSK would make in the ensuing half-century to clarify the roles, functions, and rules of the press clubs, covered four areas: (1) press conferences, (2) the press room, (3) press clubs themselves, and (4) grievance procedures.[8] This guideline set the framework within which all subsequent debates about the club system have taken place and is worth evaluating in more detail.

The first section of the 1949 guideline sought to clarify who should have access to official press conferences in Japan. While press conferences held in government ministries and agencies in most advanced industrial democracies are sponsored by the source (for example, the White House sponsors and arranges the press conferences held there), Japan stands as an anomaly in that, ostensibly at least, press conferences are sponsored by the relevant press club itself.

This has resulted in a remarkable "catch-22" for nonmembers. When nonclub journalists have made requests to sources for access, these sources have responded that they are not responsible for arranging briefings and therefore are unable to give nonmembers permission to attend. Instead, these officials tell would-be press conference participants to make their requests for access directly to the club. Once a request is made to the club, however, club members also turn them down by saying that they cannot allow nonmembers into the club (and therefore the press conferences) because club membership rules stipulate that members have to belong to the NSK.[9] In the event that the nonmembers go the extra step and request membership in the NSK (as Bloomberg did in 1992), they have been turned down by the association, which cites its own membership rules.[10] In this way, government sources, the *kisha* clubs, and the NSK have joined together in classic cartel fashion for half a century to restrict participation in official press conferences to a small group of elite news organizations.

Without commenting directly on the issue of whether or not the clubs should be allowed to continue to control access to and "sponsor" such briefings, the NSK noted in its defining 1949 policy statement that "press clubs and news companies should not impose restrictions on reporters or editors in their reporting of the press conferences and proceedings of public institutions." Reading this statement, one might assume that the association expected and desired the conferences to be free and open to all. Surely, that is how SCAP—which had argued that the clubs either be divested of their exclusionary practices or be abolished—must have understood the statement. But in practice, no substantive changes in the norm of excluding nonmembers from briefings resulted from the issuance of this or any succeeding guideline on the clubs in the intervening decades. In fact, although foreign journalists finally managed more than four decades later (in 1993) to gain access to a limited number of clubs and official press conferences (often only as "nonregular" members with limited rights), many Japanese journalists are routinely excluded by fiat. What's more, the clubs are still the official sponsors of press conferences in Japan, and NSK membership remains a primary requirement for access.

The second section of the 1949 policy guideline concerned the "press rooms," or the physical space occupied by press club members. This section reads as follows: "Public institutions deemed newsworthy by the press should provide press rooms that are equipped with the facilities required by journalists for writing and dispatching news reports, such as telephones, desks, and chairs. These facilities should be made readily available and without charge for use by *all* news companies" (emphasis added). Yet while this recommendation is clear about the need for open access, it also had little impact on actual practice. Government institutions in Japan even today continue to provide rooms and various accoutrements and staff exclusively to club members, at taxpayer expense—a practice that has resulted in a number of class-action suits brought against the government by individuals charging misuse of public funds.[11]

The third section of the 1949 guideline—that pertaining to the press clubs themselves—has given the association the most trouble in the ensuing decades. The goal here was to provide a definitive account of the function and character of the press clubs. This was done to allay SCAP's concerns about their undemocratic nature, especially their exclusivity and their tendency to sanction recalcitrant members by denying them access to sources. The key issue here concerned the definition of the clubs—that is, were they "newsgathering organizations" or merely "social organizations"? This was and remains a crucial distinction. If the association were to claim that the clubs were newsgathering organizations—the function the clubs have actually had since their creation in the Meiji period—they could not easily continue to justify or maintain their exclusivity, most assuredly not to SCAP, and would be forced to open them up to all interested journalists. If, on the other hand, they determined that they were merely social organizations, like any other "voluntary" organization, the clubs could continue to define their memberships as they pleased, excluding those whom they felt did not have the requisite qualifications to join their club.

Having managed during the prewar and wartime eras to reduce the number of competitors in the information marketplace, Japan's largest and most powerful newspapers—not incidentally also the most powerful members of the NSK—were in no mood to reopen the field to "excessive competition" (a common euphemism in Japan for open markets). The solution, as the association saw it, was to claim that the clubs were nothing but social organizations that had nothing to do with newsgathering.[12] Thus, section 3 states that "Press clubs have been established for the purpose of mutual enlightenment and friendship among reporters covering public institutions, and as such should not be involved in newsgathering." In making this statement, the association was able to guarantee the maintenance of the club system even under SCAP scrutiny and perpetuate the exclusive relationships of the information cartel indefinitely. The argument that the *kisha* clubs are voluntary, autonomous organizations whose membership decisions and activities are beyond outside control is one sources have also used in explaining why they cannot force the clubs to allow nonmembers to attend their press conferences and other briefings.[13]

In the fourth and final section of the 1949 policy statement, the NSK clarified procedures for resolving disputes within the clubs, reserving for itself the role as ultimate arbiter in cases where the clubs could not resolve disagreements on their own. Ironically, at the same time that it was claiming that the clubs were social organizations that had nothing to do with newsgathering, the association was also delegating to itself the role of handling disputes arising from the club system—disputes that mostly concerned violations of newsgathering norms and the appropriateness of the various sanctions applied. Additionally, while on the one hand touting the clubs' "voluntary" nature, the association was also trying to establish increasing power over them in order to guarantee that they did not become truly autonomous organizations outside of its control. This effort is evident in a number of subsequent NSK policy statements issued in the ensuing several decades, which sought to give the association greater control over the clubs by taking over their rule-making function, setting uniform rules in the clubs nationwide, and codifying relationships between sources and journalists and among journalists in the clubs.

The NSK's initial policy guideline on the press clubs was disseminated to all press clubs throughout the country as well as to government agencies in October 1949. Each club subsequently amended its regulations in line with the NSK recommendation, a process that would be repeated in the decades that followed as the NSK made successive attempts to revise and/or rephrase this critical defining document.[14] In 1957, for example, fearful that sources were gaining an upper hand in their relationships with club journalists, the NSK sought to limit the kinds of "benefits" journalists could receive from them. Similarly, a 1962 guideline tried to limit the clubs' ability to formulate independent agreements with sources to restrict the reporting of news and mandated that newspaper management be informed of such agreements in advance. Later policies tried to abolish "accompanied reporting" (*doko shuzai*), the practice whereby journalists who follow prominent politicians or officials on domestic and foreign trips were often either bought off with gifts or sequestered in such a way that they were unable to gather independent information. But as journalist Leslie Helm noted in a piece written for the *Los Angeles Times* in 1993, this practice—including the gift-giving component—is still a prominent feature of political news reporting in Japan today.[15]

Almost thirty years after it issued its first policy statement, the NSK appeared finally to have recognized the inherent newsgathering function of the clubs in a policy guideline written in 1978 in which it stated that "the purpose of the press clubs is to foster mutual enlightenment and friendship of reporters *through their daily newsgathering activities*" (emphasis added). In its appended notes, however, the NSK was less clear, claiming that while "the new guideline states that 'press clubs are permitted to carry out a small amount of regulation in order to promote smooth reporting activities. . . . This does not mean that press clubs are newsgathering organizations; they are organizations for socializing."

In 1985, after considerable pressure from the foreign media, the NSK issued a guideline recommending that the clubs allow greater access to the foreign press. In this document, the NSK states that "press clubs should do their best to cooperate with qualified foreign correspondents in newsgathering activities and allow them to participate in the formal press conferences held under the auspices of the clubs." While this may sound as though the NSK was moving toward a reconciliation on this issue, William Horsley, then chairman of the Foreign Press in Japan (FPIJ), noted at the time that the notes appended to the guideline "read like a re-run of the old 1978 Guideline which has been the subject of all our heartaches and efforts for the past 7 years. On the face of it we have been duped. We have been made to look like the dumb Yankee tourist lured into playing a card-game with the hawker outside a London tube station."[16] As evidence that the policy was not really intended to change anything, Hall notes that none of the clubs had provided access to the foreign (much less the Japanese) press by the end of that year.[17]

There was renewed hope that the association was finally moving forward on this issue in 1993 when it issued a similar guideline recommending that foreign correspondents be given access to Japan's press clubs. However, while some foreign media companies subsequently managed to obtain limited access to a number of clubs as nonregular members, this access was not extended to non-NSK-member Japanese newspaper companies. Ultimately this guideline, as those before it, did not effect a true alteration or reorganization of the club system itself, nor did it substantially change the role of the clubs in the cartelization of information or loosen the restrictions they place on the public's right to know. Perhaps this is not surprising: as the association representing the interests of Japan's mainstream newspaper media, it would have been incongruent for the NSK to have opened up the media marketplace to additional competitors, especially those trained in a very different milieu—one based on notions of open competition for information and ideas.

A Case Study: Managing the News in the Crown Prince's Marriage Search

The case of the request by the Imperial Household Agency in 1991–92 that the Japanese media refrain from reporting the crown prince's search for a bride illustrates graphically the role the NSK and its various subcommittees can play as part of a larger system of press coordination and control that includes the *kisha* clubs, sources, and the media conglomerates discussed later. When IHA bureaucrats wanted to place a complete nationwide ban on press reporting of the crown prince's search for a suitable marriage partner, they went directly to the peak media association and the group within that association that they knew would have the power to put such an embargo in place—the Editorial Affairs Committee (EAC) of the NSK. The EAC, which is dominated by the largest and most important media companies in Japan, is the specific body within the NSK most involved in regulating relations with news sources.[18] It was here that the IHA sought and successfully obtained an agreement by the mainstream mass media to censor their reporting on this important event. The details of the process by which NSK members drew up this "self"-censorship agreement in coordination with the IHA are worth reviewing as they demonstrate the ways in which news is cooperatively managed by media and official sources in Japan.

Negotiations between the major mass media represented by the NSK and the Imperial Household Agency began in the summer of 1991 when the director of the Imperial Household Agency, Shoichi Fujimori, went to each of the media companies in Tokyo to talk with their top management about establishing a "peaceful environment" for the crown prince to carry out his courting.[19] A short time later, Mr. Fujimori and his vice-director were invited to attend the 465th meeting of the EAC, where they made a similar appeal to assembled editors. Framing their plea as a criticism of the reporting by television entertainment shows and the magazine press, they asked that the newspaper media take the lead by showing prudence and exercising special care in reporting activities related to the crown prince's search. After deliberating, the EAC decided to form an ad hoc subcommittee to review the issue and come up with a "sensible" (ryōshiki) response.

The Subcommittee on Reporting the Crown Princess consisted of seventeen individuals: fourteen representatives of the national newspapers, wires, and broadcast companies, and three members of the Social Affairs Desk Editors Association (Shakai Buchōkai), the desk responsible for covering the IHA.[20] According to an NSK summary of the group's first meeting, some of those present felt that an agreement was not necessary since "members of NSK had hardly reported on the search for a bride in the first place." Others pointed out that the Japanese media would be looked on negatively by the foreign press (as they later were) if they concluded such an agreement. Although the NSK report describes the atmosphere of this meeting as "overwhelmingly negative," it also notes that the members decided that they had a duty to cooperate with the IHA in order to help a crown prince who by that time was beginning to move beyond the "marriageable age." In deciding to limit the reporting of news related to this event, they left the formulation of specific rules to the Social Affairs Desk Editors Association. In the end, the subcommittee drafted a document formulating a detailed set of procedures for managing reporting on this issue, which was then sent to the overall EAC for approval.

Shortly thereafter, the EAC held a meeting with the fifteen regular members of the club responsible for covering the IHA—the kunai kisha-kai—to explain the gist of an agreement whose main purpose was to limit this "voluntary" association's coverage of the crown prince.[21] Later, representatives of the EAC met with IHA representatives to explain the final details of the agreement and confirm the IHA's willingness to provide ongoing information to the NSK about the progress of the crown prince's search. The agreement and related details were confirmed one week later during the 501st meeting of the EAC and put into effect that day. A translation of the three major points in the agreement follows:

1. For a set period of time, news reports related to the prospective crown princess will be withheld. The time frame for this agreement shall be three months from the day the agreement is reached. News reports related to the prospective crown princess are defined as "reports that indicate the background details of either the prospective crown princess or individuals under consideration as prospective crown princess."

2. Details of the procedures for canceling this agreement will be decided separately.[22]

3. Careful consideration will be made to respect the human rights and privacy of the prospective crown princess, and news coverage will be carried out in moderation.

Indicative of the strength of the *keiretsu* ties described later in this chapter, soon after the NSK sent copies of the agreement to the Japan Broadcast Federation—whose membership largely overlaps with that of the NSK—it concluded a similar agreement to censor its reporting on this issue. Approximately one month later, the Japan Magazine Publishers Association, which also has many members who have close *keiretsu* ties to the newspaper press, did the same. Just as the IHA had anticipated, once they had obtained the agreement of the mainstream newspapers, broadcast stations, and news agencies belonging to the NSK to censor their coverage, the rest of the Japanese media quickly followed suit.

The agreement to limit coverage of the crown prince's search for a prospective wife was extended on three occasions (May 8, August 5, and November 12, 1992), remaining in effect for almost an entire year.[23] In early December 1992, however, rumors began to surface that a "candidate" had been chosen. On January 6, 1993, the trickle became a flood as word leaked that Owada Masako, a career employee of the MFA, had agreed to marry the crown prince. Soon a large group of reporters and camera operators gathered in front of her home, and while the Japanese press was as yet mum, the foreign press (the *Washington Post* in particular) and wires began to report the rumor. When word reached the Japanese press that CNN—available in Japan by satellite—was going to broadcast an announcement that evening, they were alarmed, particularly given that their own embargo was still in effect.

To be scooped on an important domestic story like this by the foreign press was truly embarrassing, especially for those media organizations that must have had prior knowledge of the crown prince's decision but were still bound by the agreement. Given the critical nature of the situation, but also exemplary of the group's willingness to abide by the managed-news-reporting features of the agreement, the head of the EAC convened an emergency meeting of the subcommittee responsible at 8:00 that evening officially to end the agreement, choosing the two Japanese news agencies, Kyodo and Jiji Tsushin, to report the news to the entire Japanese media at precisely 8:45.

And so one of the most restrictive cooperative agreements ever made by the NSK membership to limit the flow of news to the public was "broken" not by one of its own members but by the "noncartelized" foreign press in Japan. Several years later, in noting a number of "positive" attributes of the original agreement, the NSK suggested that they were thankful that they had been able to achieve their goal of providing an environment within which the crown prince could select a suitable marriage partner. Curiously, however, they also noted that because the abrogation of the agreement had been carried out *freely*, "the Japanese public was able to learn of the selection of the crown princess through reporting by domestic media organizations and not the foreign press." The Japanese media, the NSK concluded, had been able "to avoid the confusion that would have resulted had this announcement been made known to the Japanese public through foreign wires and broadcasts."[24]

To summarize, the key function of the NSK is to promote the interests of the newspaper industry and regulate its relations with other groups. How that role has been operationalized varies according to the situation in which the association finds itself. In the case of the *kisha* club system, the NSK has promoted industry interests by serving as a key source of support for its maintenance. As we examine the fifty-year history of the NSK's handling of the "*kisha* club problem," one thing that becomes apparent is the association's extreme reluctance to alter the club system in any substantive way, particularly if it might jeopardize its own position in controlling access to the clubs, or alter the fundamental character of the cartel arrangement.

A somewhat different role is apparent in the agreement with the IHA "voluntarily" to limit news reporting in the crown prince's marriage search. Here the NSK gets involved in a more microlevel managing of the news reporting process. No doubt there were honorable intentions involved in trying to preserve the privacy of the principals in this case. But the willingness of the NSK to acquiesce to the censorship request also reflects the benefits to its members of ensuring that none of them would get scooped by another member company. Once the agreement was in place, neither the news companies nor the IHA had to be bothered by the encumbrances and irritations that might be imposed in an open reporting relationship. This becomes truly problematic, of course, when official sources can hide behind the same kind of cloak of secrecy, shielded from public scrutiny.

Media *Keiretsu*

Keiretsu relationships have received considerable attention over the past decade in the context of the competitive performance and trade policies of Japan's major financial and manufacturing industries.[25] While the significance of these "enterprise groupings" in Japan's media industry is not nearly as well known, it is no less central to understanding this sector. Contemporary Japan provides a variety of outlets other than newspapers for disseminating information to the public. Yet what might appear to be real alternatives in the news reporting process prove on closer inspection to be less than meets the eye. The reason is that national newspapers have limited the spread of alternative media—and thereby competition within the larger media industry—by gaining control of these media as they developed through direct and indirect ownership, personnel, and programming ties.

Consider, first, ownership and control of the national newspapers themselves. Most newspapers in Japan are incorporated as joint-stock companies, but in reality they are something much closer to employee-controlled organizations. A special provision of the Japanese Commercial Code allows newspaper companies to impose restrictions on the sale or transfer of their shares.[26] Most newspaper companies, including all five national newspapers, are not listed on a stock exchange, and their shares are controlled primarily by associations managed for the benefit of their workers—reporters, editors, and staff—with some residual shares held by the founding families.[27]

The industry itself convinced the government to pass this ownership exemption in 1951, arguing that it would free them from external control by outsiders and better allow them to perform their mission as public organs. It also, of course, protected the newspapers and their employees from the possibility of being taken over, especially by foreigners. As the newspapers extended their influence to other media, this rule effectively protected the entire media industry from outside influence.

Once the basic ownership and control of the national newspapers was established, the next step was to extend their influence to other media, especially the emerging broadcast industry. Newspapers first became involved in radio broadcasting in 1924. The initial hope was that they could use this new medium to increase sales of their newspapers. (In contrast, radio broadcasting in the United States was promoted primarily by radio manufacturers, who wanted to increase their hardware sales.) At first there was considerable competition among the newspapers as each tried to establish its market position. Only a year and a half after radio broadcasting began in Japan, however, the government stepped in and put the three existing radio stations under the control of the precursors to NHK and the Ministry of Posts and Telecommunications. While the newspapers still seconded directors to these stations, this move greatly reduced their power. By the mid-1930s even this limited influence was eliminated as radio became completely controlled by the state.[28]

After the war, the Occupation broke up the state's broadcasting monopoly and the newspapers once again took the lead in establishing a commercial broadcast structure in Japan. These papers wanted to ensure that broadcasting stations would serve as auxiliary businesses, not as competitors, and staked out ownership positions in the fledgling industry as a way to make this happen.[29] A telling statistic: of the first sixteen companies to apply for commercial radio licenses in 1951, fifteen were newspaper companies.[30] Within a decade, both the radio and television portions of the broadcasting industry were already becoming organized around an inchoate *keiretsu* structure, or what one expert on Japanese broadcasting describes as "information conglomerates." His explanation of the strategic rationale of the newspapers is interesting, for it captures a way of thinking about market competition heard frequently in Japanese industry: "In effect newspaper publishers were eager to subsidize and affiliate with broadcasting stations so that printed pages, radio, and television could *coexist harmoniously*. A newspaper concerned itself with programmes from the affiliated station and the TV station relied on its mother newspaper for news and commentaries. This was so not only in Tokyo. Local papers mimicked the pattern. The result was a unique information network."[31]

An important juncture for television broadcasting occurred in 1957, when then minister of post and telecommunications, Tanaka Kakuei, licensed thirty-four new television broadcasting companies.[32] Tanaka used this opportunity to strengthen state control over this rapidly growing medium by restricting the number of entrants into the market through an allocation system similar to that imposed on newspapers during the war. Just as Japan's wartime government, with the cooperation of the national newspapers, had enforced a one-newspaper-per-prefecture rule (see chapter 2), so too did Tanaka work to limit commercial broadcast stations to something approaching one station per prefecture, with exceptions for large metropolitan areas. This limitation was later relaxed, allowing several newspaper-affiliated stations per prefecture, but even today no *keiretsu* controls more than one station in a prefecture, as we shall see shortly.

When Tanaka later became prime minister, in the early 1970s, he continued to encourage "rationalization" in the industry, with the (not unintended) effect of strengthening *keiretsu* relations. He was especially interested in gaining influence over the Tokyo broadcasting stations, which provided programming to the rest of the country. Up to that point, some of these stations were jointly owned by several national newspapers.[33] In

1973 and 1974, Tanaka helped the national newspapers eliminate these crossholdings, making each central broadcasting station the domain of a single newspaper. As part of this "*keiretsu* unification" (*keiretsu ippon-ka*) process, each national newspaper mandated that its affiliated television station use the parent newspaper as the primary source of its own news. They also required that the station's newscasters come from the newspaper company's editorial affairs board—a feature that can still be found today even on such prominent news shows as *Asahi*'s "News Station."[34]

Legal restrictions on ownership of broadcast companies prevented the complete integration of these two types of media. Until recently, newspapers were limited to holding no more than 10 percent of the shares of any single station. But the national newspapers have regularly circumvented this rule by getting other companies in their group to invest in stations as well.[35] They have further extended their influence by sending key management people to the station to work in top-level executive positions and by helping to direct working capital to the stations by arranging for loans from their own banks.[36] In early 1995 the ownership limit was raised from 10 percent to 20 percent. This change recognizes contemporary reality: that the parent newspaper companies exercise de facto control over their affiliated broadcasting stations. But by actually loosening ownership limits, this "reform" will obviously do nothing to weaken these relationships.

Two other players also factor into the broadcasting picture: local television stations and local newspapers. The number of broadcasting stations across Japan has increased substantially since the 1950s, meaning that the original limit of one station per prefecture no longer holds. But the importance of *keiretsu* affiliation continues, as nearly all local stations in Japan are directly affiliated with one of the national newspaper-broadcasting groups. In most cases the parent newspaper owns shares in the station, and in some cases so too does the newspaper's metropolitan broadcasting affiliate. Personnel and other capital connections from the national newspaper and the metropolitan broadcaster, as well as the local station's dependence on the nationals for news and programming, further consolidate their clear identity as a member of the group.

Local broadcasting stations have also become linked to local newspapers in ways that provide an interesting mirror of what happened nationally. Just as national newspapers were originally concerned about losing market share to broadcasting in the early years, so too were local newspapers. To protect their interests, the local papers mimicked their national counterparts by becoming co-investors in and sending top executives to the local stations. They also reproduced the news reporting relationships established by the national papers, by providing local and regional news to the station, in much the same way that the national newspaper-broadcasting group provides national and international news reporting.

As a result of this ongoing process of organizing and reorganizing the Japanese broadcasting industry, one finds today not only strong financial, personnel, and news reporting ties between the five national newspapers and their Tokyo broadcast stations, but also between these metropolitan affiliates and the remaining commercial stations throughout the country. Figure 11 shows the *keiretsu* affiliations of Japan's VHF and UHF broadcasting stations as of 1994, broken down by prefecture. The five national networks are Tokyo Hōsō (JNN), Nippon Terebi (NNN), Fuji (FNN), Terebi Asahi (ANN), and Terebi Tokyo (TXN). At the apex of each network is a national newspaper—*Mainichi, Yomiuri, Sankei, Asahi,* and *Nikkei,* respectively. And within each network is a Tokyo-area-based station, known as the "key" or "parent" station (*kiikyoku* or *oyakyoku*). The key stations are critical to the network in part because they are responsible for the majority of programming. In addition, these five stations represent the largest share of Japan's (geographically concentrated) viewership, accounting for 44 percent of the total broadcasting market in Japan in 1989.[37]

Local stations that receive more than half of their news and other programming from the network are referred to as "full network" stations, and those that do not are called "cross-network" stations. As of 1995 only 15 of the 123 commercial stations in Japan (and only 3 of the primary-signal VHF stations) had cross-network programming. The remaining 108 local stations had clear affiliations with network *keiretsu,* with the key stations providing as much as 90 percent of a local station's programming.[38] Even the stations located in Japan's second-largest metropolitan area, the Kansai region of Osaka-Kyoto-Kobe, get most of their programming from the national network. Mainichi Hōsō, for example, receives 82 percent of its prime-time programming from the JNN network headed by TBS. TBS provides Mainichi Hōsō with a full 23 of the 28 hours of prime-time programming available in any given week, leaving it with just 3.5 hours to fill with its own programming, allowing for a half-hour of programming provided by the affiliated station in nearby Nagoya, CBC, and one hour for the local station.[39]

Television broadcasting is not the only alternative medium in Japan that is organized within newspaper-led *keiretsu.*[40] But it is the national newspapers' control over television broadcasting that is most important. Television plays a central role in the mass-media-based "teledemocracies" that are emerging in many countries. It is a "hot" medium that can convey news events in ways that are more immediate and emotionally powerful than the daily newspaper. And it is a daily part of many people's lives in Japan, as it is in other advanced industrial societies. Despite this potential power, the influence of this medium in Japan has never been fully developed. Virtually all Japanese television viewers are exposed to one or more of the same five national networks, and these networks are themselves controlled by the national newspapers and dependent on them and their affiliated key stations for news and programming. In this way, media groups have effectively limited the number of participants in Japan's marketplace of ideas, thereby leading to a homogenization of views across different types of media.

Conclusion

Japan's media industry—and its impact on the Japanese political process—must be understood in a total institutional context. The central players in the industry, of course, are the national newspapers. Not only have these been the primary source of news and opinion in Japan, they have become, as Eleanor Westney aptly puts it, the "key nodes of interconnection" among various parts of Japan's overall media industry.[41] This central role is represented by their position at the apex of the threefold system of news management introduced in chapter 1. The main components of the system, as discussed earlier, are the *kisha* clubs themselves, to which the national papers have privileged access. But the impact of the clubs has been greatly magnified by two other institutional components of the system: the industry *kyōkai* (NSK), which has been instrumental, as the representative of the newspapers, in maintaining the clubs' special prerogatives and coordinating other political and economic interests; and media *keiretsu*, which have extended newspaper control of news reporting to broadcasting and other outlets in Japan and effectively preempted the rise of alternative media.

The fact that the NSK has spent half a century working to preserve exclusive access for its members to the clubs should not surprise us. Nor should the aggressive way in which newspapers moved into the broadcasting industry when it emerged as a new medium in Japan. Preventing the rise of alternative producers, after all, is a central goal in any cartel. Outsiders cannot be expected to play by the same rules as the cartel's members, and this exposes insiders to the risks of genuine competition and the need to change their ways of doing things. The greatest of all monopoly rents, as Sir John Hicks once put it, is "the quiet life." As long as the foreign and nonmainstream press are denied access to the clubs, as the NSK has insisted, and as long as alternatives to the printed press itself are kept under control of the mainstream papers, as the media *keiretsu* have ensured, Japan's major newspapers continue to enjoy a life far quieter than it otherwise would be. But it also means that Japan's "information marketplace" remains anything but marketlike.

Prefecture	Mainichi Shimbun / Tokyo Hoso Network (JNN)	Yomiuri Shimbun / Nippon Terebi Network (NNN)	Sankei Shimbun / Fuji Network (FNN)	Asahi Shimbun / Terebi Asahi Network (ANN)	Nikkei Shimbun / Terebi Tokyo Network (TXN)	Independent Channels
Hokkaido	Hokkaido Hoso (HBC)	Sapporo Terebi (STV)	Hokkaido Bunka Hoso (UHB)	Hokkaido Terebi (HTB)	Terebi Hokkaido (HTB)	
Aomori	Aomori Terebi (ATV)	Aomori Hoso (RAB)		Aomori Asahi Hoso (ABA)		
Iwate	Iwate Hoso (IBC)	Terebi Iwate (TVI)	Iwate Menkoi Terebi (MIT)			
Miyagi	Tohoku Hoso (TBC)	Miyagi Terebi (MMT)	Sendai Hoso (OX)	Higashi Nippon Hoso (KHB)		
Akita		Akita Hoso (ABS)	Akita Terebi (AKT)	Akita Asahi Hoso (AAB)		
Yamagata	Terebyu Yamagata (TUY)	Yamagata Hoso (YBC)		Yamagata Terebi (YTS)		
Fukushima	Terebyu Fukushima (TUF)	Fukushima Chuo Terebi (FCT)	Fukushima Terebi (FTV)	Fukushima Hoso (KFB)		
Tokyo	Tokyo Hoso (TBS)	Nippon Terebi (NTV)	Fuji Terebi (CX)	Terebi Asahi (ANB)	Terebi Tokyo (TX)	
Gunma						Gunma Terebi (GTV)
Tochigi						
Ibaragi						
Saitama						Terebi Saitama (TVS)
Chiba						Chiba Terebi (CTC)
Kanagawa						Terebi Kanagawa (TVK)
Niigata	Niigata Hoso (BSN)	Terebi Niigata (TNN)	Niigata Sogo Terebi (NBT)	Niigata Terebi 21 (NT21)		
Nagano	Shintetsu Hoso (SBC)	Terebi Shinshu (TSB)	Nagano Hoso (NBS)	Nagano Asahi Hoso (ABN)		
Yamanashi	Terebi Yamanashi (UTY)	Yamanashi Hoso (YBS)				
Shizuoka	Shizuoka Hoso (SBS)	Shizuoka Daiichi Terebi (SDT)	Terebi Shizuoka (SUT)	Shizuoka Asahi Terebi (SATV)		
Toyama	Churippu Terebi (TUT)	Kita Nippon Hoso (KNB)	Toyama Terebi (T34)			
Ishikawa	Hokuritsu Hoso (MRO)	Terebi Kanazawa (KTK)	Ishikawa Terebi (ITC)	Hokkaku Asahi Hoso (HAB)		
Fukui		Fukui Hoso (FBC)	Fukui Terebi (FTB)	Fukui Hoso (FBC)		
Aichi	Chubu Nippon Hoso (CBC)	Chukyo Terebi (CTV)	Tokai Terebi (THK)	Nagoya Terebi (NBN)	Terebi Aichi (TVA)	
Gifu						Gifu Hoso (GBS)
Mie						Mie Terebi (MTV)

Figure 11. Network Ties Between National and Local Broadcast Stations.

Prefecture	Mainichi Hoso (MBS)	Yomiuri Terebi (YTV)	Kansai Terebi (TBK)	Asahi Hoso (ABC)	Terebi Osaka (TVO)	
Osaka	Mainichi Hoso (MBS)	Yomiuri Terebi (YTV)	Kansai Terebi (TBK)	Asahi Hoso (ABC)	Terebi Osaka (TVO)	
Shiga						Biwako Hoso (BBC)
Kyoto						Kinki Hoso (KBS)
Nara						Nara Terebi (TVN)
Hyogo						San Terebi (SUN)
Wakayama						Terebi Wakayama (WTV)
Tottori / Shimane	Sanin Hoso (BSS)	Nihonkai Terebi (NKT)	Sanyo Chuo Terebi (TSK)			
Okayama / Kagawa	Sanyo Hoso (RSK)	Nishi Nippon Terebi (RNC)	Okayama Hoso (OHK)	Setonaikai Hoso (KSB)	Terebi Setouchi (TSC)	
Tokushima		Shikoku Hoso (JRT)				
Ehime	Iyo Terebi (ITV)	Minamikai Hoso (BNB)	Ehime Hoso (EBC)			
Kochi	Terebi Kochi (KUTV)	Kochi Hoso (BKC)				
Hiroshima	Chugoku Hoso (BCC)	Hiroshima Terebi (HTV)	Terebi Shinhiroshima (TSS)	Hiroshima Homu Terebi (HOME)		
Yamaguchi	Terebi Yamaguchi (TYS)	Yamaguchi Hoso (KBY)		Yamaguchi Asahi Hoso (YAB)		
Fukuoka	RKB Mainichi Hoso (RKB)	Fukuoka Hoso (FBS)	Terebi Nishi Nippon (TNC)	Kyushu Asahi Hoso (KBC)	(TVQ)	
Saga			Saga Terebi (STS)			
Nagasaki	Nagasaki Hoso (NBC)	Nagasaki Terebi (NIB)	Terebi Nagasaki (KTN)	Nagasaki Bunka Hoso (NCC)		
Kumamoto	Kumamoto Hoso (RKK)	Kumamoto Kenmin Terebi (KKT)	Terebi Kumamoto (TKU)	Kumamoto Asahi Hoso (KAB)		
Oita	Oita Hoso (OBS)	Terebi Oita (TOS)	Terebi Oita (TOS)	Oita Asahi Hoso (OAB)		
Miyazaki	Miyazaki Hoso (MRT)	Terebi Miyazaki (UMK)	Terebi Miyazaki (UMK)	Terebi Miyazaki (UMK)		
Kagoshima	Minami Nippon Hoso (MBC)	Kagoshima Terebi (KTS)	Kagoshima Terebi (KTS)	Kagoshima Hoso (KKB)		
Okinawa	Ryuku Hoso (RBC)		Okinawa Terebi (OTV)			

Shaded Cells = VHF   Clear Cells = UHF Channels

Source: *Nihon minkan hoso renmei* (Association od Japanese Broadcasters), 1994.

Six

Why Information Cartels Matter

> If the press is not an independent institution, it is
> not of itself capable of remedying abuses of
> power. It can participate in the remedy, but can-
> not be the causal agent.
> (*Herbert J. Altschull,* Agents of Power)

THIS STUDY has addressed the institutional underpinnings of state-society relations through the analytic lens of the Japanese press. I have argued that Japanese politicians and bureaucrats, together with the mainstream media, have both promoted and benefited from what I call "information cartels": institutionalized rules and relationships guiding press relations with their sources and with each other that serve to limit the types of news that get reported and the number and makeup of those who do the reporting. Three specific institutions provide the underpinnings for this news management process: *kisha* clubs, the newspaper industry *kyōkai,* and media *keiretsu.*

The clubs themselves have been most important in the cartelization process by defining the basic relationship that exists between journalists and their news sources—bureaucrats, politicians, business leaders, the po-lice, interest groups, and consumer groups. The rigid rules of access and conduct established by the clubs impose powerful constraints on the im-pact, content, and slant of the media's messages. One of the things making the clubs so powerful is their very pervasiveness. In Tokyo alone they can be found in every ministry, in the party headquarters of all major political parties, in key peak economic organizations such as Keidanren, and in large corporations. From Tokyo they radiate throughout the rest of Japan in a web of regionalized clubs in prefectural parliaments, police headquar-ters, courts, and chambers of commerce. As a result, they cover virtually all major business, state, and political organizations in Japan.

Supporters of the club system, mostly Japanese journalists, editors, and newspaper managers, say that the clubs are beneficial because they create a stable, convenient environment within which to work; limit control by sources; reduce "excessive" competition; and provide a quick, efficient, and economical way to get information to the public.[1] Hara Toshio, though largely critical of the club system, notes an additional merit: that club journalists have more equal access to information within the club and among themselves, at least when compared to journalists in the United States, where members of an inner circle have better access than their colleagues from less prestigious papers.[2] Still, in spite of these ostensible benefits, there can be no denying the fundamental constraint the clubs place on competition, for both ideas and markets. As David Butts, the Tokyo bureau chief for Bloomberg Business News, noted in 1993, "This isn't a matter of government officials not inviting certain reporters to a briefing. . . . It's a matter of journalists deciding to exclude fellow journalists."[3]

Helping to ensure that the shop stays closed are the *kyōkai* and the *keiretsu*. Throughout its history, the NSK has worked to assert exclusive access for its members in the clubs, and thereby to the news itself. It has not only kept out the foreign press (with a few recent exceptions), but also excluded other media organizations from within Japan itself. Media groups organized around Japan's national newspapers ensure that alternative news outlets, especially television broadcasting, are brought into the club system and follow its newsgathering and reporting rules. In so doing, they amplify the impact of the relationships outlined earlier and, by limiting the number of participants in the marketplace of ideas, play an important role in the homogenization of views across media. In this final chapter, we step back from the mechanisms for managing the news to consider their broader implications for our understanding of media and politics and of the state-media-society relationship in contemporary Japan.

Metaphors for the Media

Just what role does the mainstream press in Japan play in the political process? And with what consequences? Much of political and media theory has offered an ideal type of the media's role in democratic society as one of a "watchdog"—working on behalf of the public to bring to light inconsistencies and irregularities in the activities and behavior of politicians, civil servants, business people, and other political actors. Whatever the merits of this metaphor for the media in other countries, it does not work for Japan. As Farley points out, the Japanese watchdog is one that rarely barks.[4] Frequently stories are not pursued, wayward politicians are not held accountable, and the public is left ignorant of fundamental incongruencies in its own political and economic system. Krauss notes the same for the one television network outside of the national newspapers' direct control, NHK: "If this [watchdog] view has any validity for television, one would expect to find patterns of television news that emphasize the conflicts of government, opposition parties and protest movements, and the failure of policy. But this is not the case."[5]

The mirror image of the watchdog metaphor is that of media as "lapdog"—a docile and obedient servant of the state, something akin to what one might expect to find in the "party journalism" of the former USSR or in China today.[6] This view has permeated some of the critical Western literature on Japan over the past decade, with van Wolferen a leading exemplar.[7] While this image may seem consistent with evidence presented earlier, it is insufficiently attentive to the *independent* interests of the mainstream media and the ways that they negotiate to improve their position vis-à-vis the government. Members of Japan's *kisha* clubs do not give up newsgathering autonomy for nothing. Autonomy is exchanged for the certainty that one will not easily be scooped and that all member news agencies will be given the same information in an equitable manner. Consistent with the relational approach introduced in chapter 1, this suggests something closer to dual interests and reciprocity. It is not that journalists blindly follow the dictates and wishes of state sources, or that they are subservient to the powers that be, but that the system for gathering and reporting news—a system designed to serve media companies' economic and other interests—has frequently led them to support state goals. It is in this sense that the media can be understood as collaborators with the state in the management of society.[8]

The pervasiveness of close, reciprocal interaction between news sources and journalists also makes clear the limitations of a third metaphor—the media as "spectator," or neutral conduit of information. This image, as Pharr points out, is implicit in much of the literature on Japanese political science, by virtue of the very lack of attention paid to the media as an active participant.[9] But it fails to capture the truly symbiotic nature of the journalist-source relationship in a closed shop. What distinguishes the information cartel from other types of cartels is the element of exchange, not between those making up the cartel, but between cartel members and their sources. The high degree of reciprocity is most striking when we consider that, although they are not directly party to the cartel, sources actively support it, abiding by and playing a role in the establishment of rules.

The limitations of each of these views have led Ellis Krauss, Susan Pharr, and other scholars of Japan to look for alternative metaphors to frame the basic relationship that exists between news sources and news reporters, and between each of these and society. Krauss plays off of earlier metaphors when he suggests that the Japanese media is less watchdog than "guard dog"—doing little initially to point attention against the wrongdoer, but pursuing the criminal once his or her existence is revealed.[10] This helps to explain the long periods of quiescence followed by short bursts of activity among the Japanese press in the reporting of scandals. But the metaphor is incomplete, since it ignores a key detail: a guard dog is unlikely to attack if the intruder is already well known.

Pharr introduces another provocative metaphor—that of the media as "trickster."[11] In this image, borrowed from symbolic anthropology, the mass media become less predictable and more difficult to manage than in other images. Though powerful, they do not try to serve their own interests.[12] In support of this view, Groth's study of the media and political protest suggests that "The mass media occupy an ambiguous insider-outsider role with regard to various political forces—politicians, bureaucrats, average citizens, and protest movements—and offer a mosaic of ideas and images. The media elude control by any group. The mass media encourage, support, applaud, and endorse, but they also badger, ridicule, embarrass, and challenge."[13]

While it is true that the media in Japan have varied at times in their relations with different political forces, this is frequently a function of their ties to these forces: where linkages are strong and institutionalized through club relations, the media play the role of insiders; where such ties are weak, they can become outsiders whose presentation of ideas and information is both less uniform and less predictable. It is only in the second role where the trickster image fits, and this is not a role generally played by the Japanese mainstream media.

Pharr also suggests that the trickster media are sufficiently independent of the state that they can transform it over time. But both the transformational and independent qualities of the mainstream media are hard to discern throughout much of Japanese political history. Even the widely reported role of the media, and especially television, in bringing about the downfall of the LDP in 1993 has yet to demonstrate any lasting impact, perhaps because such interpretations represent an oversimplification of a very complex and long-term process—the devolution of a political party. Finally, Pharr suggests that the trickster can play an important role in society by building "communitas"—presumably a reference to civil society. But it is hard to see how effective this community can be when it is being built without opening informational access to all parts of society.

The institutional mechanisms used to manage information flows and coordinate the news reporting process in Japan outlined in this book suggest the appropriateness of another metaphor, namely, that of the mainstream media as "coconspirator" in the managing of information. I use this term in the sense of an open collaboration between certain actors in society, who, in pursuing their own interests, intentionally or unintentionally harm other key segments of society. As Adam Smith famously observed, when members of the same trade are allowed to meet together and set the rules of the industry, the result is often some kind of "conspiracy against the public."[14] Smith included in this not only the raising of prices, but an assortment of self-interested mechanisms that put constraints on trade. While he had industrialists in mind when he wrote it, the warning applies no less well to any industry. In the case of Japan's mainstream media, the "conspiracy against the public" is a joint one with official news sources. The rules of trade have been written by the industry itself, backed up by its industry association, but they have also been sanctioned by state actors who understand their effectiveness in gaining support for state policies. The broad goal of the nation's key media players, like that of its government leaders, is to limit access to the central halls of power to a carefully chosen few.

The Outcomes of Japan's Information Cartels

The institutional arrangements discussed here—the *kisha* clubs, the newspaper *kyōkai*, and the media *keiretsu*—reinforce each other in ways that have profoundly altered the nature of news reporting in Japan and the role of the media in the political process. To understand just how, it is worth reviewing the purported functions played by the media in open societies and then considering the ways in which Japan's information cartels have altered these functions. As a comparison point, consider five basic functions of the democratic media, as derived by Graber from the writing of well-known American political leaders, Supreme Court opinions, and First Amendment scholars: as a marketplace of ideas, a source of political information, the voice of public opinion, a guardian of minority rights, and a policer of errant politicians.[15]

This is a set of ideals that the media in no country perhaps reaches on a consistent basis. As noted below, close relationships between journalists and news sources everywhere—including those involving reporters covering the White House and a few other key centers of power in Washington, as well as those involving British reporters covering the parliament at Westminster through the press "lobby"—no doubt shape and constrain what news gets reported.[16] Some critics, such as Noam Chomsky and Ben Bagdikian, have gone further in arguing that structural features of the contemporary mass media, including high levels of industry concentration and patterns of media cross-ownership, impose more basic constraints on the diversity and free flow of information and opinions.[17] So the criteria outlined by Graber represent an ideal rather than reality. Nevertheless, these criticisms apply with even greater force to Japan where institutionalized practices have led to a number of specific outcomes for the overall media industry.

Credentialing of Facts

One important consequence of the cartelization of information in Japan is the extreme reliance on what Bagdikian terms "credentialed facts." As Bagdikian explains, credentialed facts carry the imprimatur of authority that comes from the formal titles of official news sources. Because official statements are seen as "objective" facts, citing them has the advantage of making it difficult to "accuse the reporter, editor, or news organization of introducing personal judgments or bias into a news story." But this reliance also dissuades journalists from reporting "unofficial" facts or circumstances and presenting the voices of unestablished groups, leading to an overall conservative cast to the news. According to Bagdikian, "Where there are not genuinely diverse voices in the media the result inevitably is an overemphasis on a picture of the world as seen by the authorities, or as the authorities wish it to be."[18]

Credentialed facts constitute a large proportion of political news reporting in all democratic countries. In a study of the *New York Times* and the *Washington Post*, Leon Sigal found that public officials were the source of close to 80 percent of all political news stories reported in these two papers.[19] In Japan, as a result of the institutions under which information is cartelized, and especially the *kisha* clubs' binding official news sources together with mainstream reporters, this bias is even greater. According to Hara Toshio, former president of the Kyodo News Service, as much as 90 percent of all news in Japan comes from official sources.[20]

It is not just that Japanese journalists tend to rely heavily on official sources for information and on official versions of events. More importantly, they frequently limit themselves to a very small subset of the official sources available without attempting to provide alternative perspectives. Feldman quotes one reporter on why only the LDP leadership's views are reported as follows:

> Covering a certain event by obtaining information from two Diet members, each having basically different views, experiences, and ways of thinking, may result in different information and interpretation of the same phenomenon. To prevent such a complication, and avoid having to later verify the correct version from third, fourth, and fifth persons, a reporter prefers to meet the highest-ranking Diet member who participated in a given political event—this means a political party or party faction leader, or a chairman of an LDP's committee—and write a story based on their viewpoint.[21]

One could perhaps argue that the hierarchical character of the Japanese party system and the strong controls exercised by party leadership over back benchers make party leaders better positioned to convey prevailing views. But this does not explain the reporter's justification for ignoring what even he acknowledges are divergent views among others within the government. What he characterizes as the "complication" of differing viewpoints would be considered by many others as the essence of the journalist's responsibility!

So why does all this matter? As March and Olsen have pointed out, because so much of the information on which democratic polities act comes from official sources, "the way in which that information is generated and disseminated by and within the government affects the quality of democratic discourse."[22] We might add that the way the media select official information and filter it to the public also affects the quality of a nation's discourse and, ultimately the "quality" of its politics. In Japan, information—and therefore political choice—have been narrowly controlled for an especially long time.

Weakening of the Political Auditing Function

A second consequence of Japan's information cartels is the nearly wholesale elimination of what Graber refers to as "policing" and what March and Olsen have labeled the "political auditing" function of the mainstream media—the process of monitoring the powers that be against dishonesty and corruption. Auditors serve as the agents of those who cannot be as well informed, but they frequently have difficulty remaining independent of those they audit. According to March and Olsen, this is especially the case in countries like Norway, where from 1950 to 1980 legislators were organized into parties and journalists into clusters. A similar pattern exists in Japan, where journalists are organized into very tight-knit groups and ruling politicians have generally belonged to factions largely indistinguishable in terms of their policy orientation. In contrast, in countries where legislators and journalists operate relatively independently, such as the United States, it has been more difficult for government officials to co-opt them.[23]

Scholars of Japan have long noted the lack of a political auditing function among the Japanese media. In a detailed study of the politics of scandal in Japan, for example, Farley finds that scandals are rarely uncovered by the mainstream press and often not uncovered at all. She even goes so far as to suggest that the Recruit stock-for-favors scandal—one of the few true cases of investigative journalism in postwar Japan—almost did not break at all. In many cases, it is only after the process has already been started that the mainstream media pick up these stories and pursue them. Even then, they frequently focus on minutiae, following stories so closely that they miss policy implications and appropriate reforms altogether, thus reducing their potential impact.[24]

While there are a number of reasons why Japanese reporters do not exercise a political auditing function, loyalty bred by proximity to their sources is certainly one. Krauss takes this argument a step further in suggesting that rather than acting as auditors of the political system, the media have been a conservative force that has "contributed to the continuity of state, especially bureaucratic, power in postwar Japan." While many factors explain the close to four-decade reign by the LDP, the fact that journalists tended to avoid reporting scandals involving key LDP politicians was certainly one of them.[25] In the phrasing sometimes employed by press club reporters, "no scoop is everybody's happiness."[26]

Limiting the Agenda-Setting Process

A third consequence of Japan's information cartels is more subtle but at least as important. This is the fundamental shift in the relationship between news makers and news organizations in the overall "agenda-setting process" in Japan. Responding to earlier "minimal effects" literature, a variety of empirical studies have shown that the media (especially television) in North America at times play an important role in the setting of political and social agendas.[27] To be sure, this process is not perfect. Bagdikian and others have argued, for example, that structural features of the U.S. media have led to the selective pursuit of some stories while systematically ignoring others of equal or greater importance.[28] But the evidence in Japan suggests even more strongly that not only do the mainstream media not report important stories or important details related to such stories (such as the names of individuals or companies involved), they do not set political agendas nearly as often or as forcefully as elsewhere.

In an important empirical study, Ishikawa Masumi analyzed the *Asahi*'s reporting of the Structural Impediments Initiative, rice liberalization, and political ethics and compared it with the timing of external events.[29] What is striking in Ishikawa's results is that he found that news reporting of all three topics *follows* important public announcements rather than precedes them. This result contrasted with previous results for the United States, where researchers have found that maximum press coverage comes before political announcements are made. Ishikawa concludes that agenda-setting in Japan does not appear to be a result of independent press reporting prior to those announcements, and he offers an interesting explanation for this: in Japan, he claims, "the impact of government on the media is greater than the impact of the media on the government."[30]

The argument that the Japanese media have not played a significant role as agenda setters is supported by others, including the media historian Yamamoto Taketoshi, political scientists Ellis Krauss and Ofer Feldman, and journalist and media critic Ivan Hall. As elaborated in chapter 2, Yamamoto notes that this feature of the Japanese media is historically determined: the press's adoption of policies of "impartiality and nonpartisanship" (*fuhen futō*) in the late nineteenth century did not give it greater power vis-à-vis the state; nonpartisan meant progovernment in practice, then as it does today. It was a "nonpartisan" Japanese press, for example, that failed to write forcefully about LDP corruption, a vastly unfair electoral system, and organized crime, thereby making possible the perpetuation of almost four decades of LDP rule. Feldman also concurs with this description of a limited agenda-setting role played by the Japanese press, pointing out that Japanese journalists tended to focus on the dominant political party, the LDP, for most of the postwar era even during elections. Feldman found that although close to 40 percent of voters supported various opposition parties, the political coverage of these parties by the Japanese media was far below this proportion.[31]

The work of another astute observer of the Japanese media, Ivan Hall, suggests that the lack of an agenda-setting function in Japan results in part from the practice of suppressing reports about Japan's national problems. Hall notes that "where the Japanese differ from the other industrial democracies is not in the way they trumpet their national achievements, but in their strenuous effort to hide the darker side." This the Japanese do, he argues, by utilizing various approaches long used for managing the truth. Among these is "the sense in Japan—honed to a finer point than elsewhere—of information as a political resource to be guarded, exploited and distributed in general accordance with the national interest by those charged with the tending of that interest."[32] Thus, it is through their role in the management of (especially damaging or unfavorable) social, economic, and political information that journalists and news organizations in Japan frequently "set the agenda"; that is, by choosing not to put certain topics on the agenda for public discourse in the first place. How very different from the democratic functions outlined above by Graber.

This is not to say that the Japanese media never report or support social issues or protest movements. Reich, Campbell, Groth, and others have noted that the Japanese media vigorously reported key environmental and other social issues in the early 1970s and thereafter.[33] What is clear from these studies, however, is that while the media can play a role in campaigns for social reform, this is more often than not done within the context of the state and not against it. In a particularly revealing example, Groth shows how the mass media influenced the strategies of protest movements by showing institutionalized means of conflict resolution (court cases, meetings with bureaucrats, etc.) in a neutral light while casting opprobrium over more confrontational, grass-roots activities (human barricades, etc).[34] This is consistent with the view of the media as important "social managers" in Japan, a role quite different from that as agenda setters.

Marginalizing Alternative Media

A fourth consequence of cartelization is the marginalization of the outside or "alternative" media, which cannot be trusted because they are not living in the corridors of power and do not have direct access to the all-important "credentialed facts" discussed above. When we speak of the "alternative" press in Japan, we are referring to what Hall calls the "pariahs routinely excluded from the reporters' clubs," and not radical or leftist publications.[35] Among these are weekly magazines (both serious and scandalous); opinion monthlies; localized publications such as community papers, industry, and "sports" papers; and "mini media" (a term used to denote the "nonmass" media, including nonregularly published, issue-based broadsheets and pamphlets). Foreign correspondents and all Japanese freelance journalists are also included in this group.

Much of the aggressive and adversarial reporting found in Japan is found in these alternative media. Farley, for example, juxtaposes the suppressed stories in the mainstream press to the scandal-mongering of the outside press and suggests that without the outside press there would be fewer reported incidents and even greater corruption in Japan.[36] Likewise, Groth argues that the alternative media that were cultivated by protest groups in his study were in some ways more effective than the mainstream mass media in letting the public know about the movement's causes. Even so, these media are largely discounted in Japan, and, as Groth notes, their attempts to inform the citizenry have at times backfired.[37]

Perhaps the greatest hurdle faced by these media in terms of their credibility is their inability independently to obtain information from key sources. Although sources meet on occasion with outside journalists, the quid pro quo for access is that they cannot be cited. A considerable portion of the information of interest found in the outside media has been leaked by journalists in the clubs who, as a result of club rules, cannot use it themselves and consequently share it with (or sell it to) these other media. Sometimes these articles are actually written by *kisha* club journalists themselves, albeit pseudonymously. But in both of these instances, the information cannot be attributed and must be written in an unsubstantiated manner. This means that the alternative media are unable to show readers that their stories are based on the credentialed facts of reputable journalism. In addition, because their opportunities to meet with key sources are infrequent, the alternative media are rarely able to get multiple sources for a story, even without attribution. Often the precise details of a story are left not only to the reader's imagination (through nonattribution), but to the journalist's as well (through insufficient official contacts). If the problem of the mainstream media is an overreliance on credentialed sources, the problem of the alternative press is its insufficient access to the same.

Homogenization of the News and Opinion

One final consequence of Japan's information cartels is the homogenization of news and opinion in Japan. Observers of Japan's mainstream newspapers have frequently noted that they look pretty much the same, report pretty much the same stories, and offer up pretty much the same innocuous editorial opinions. As Krauss puts it, there is a high degree of "predictability" in reporting coming out of club-related media outlets, and this includes not only newspapers but television coverage as well.[38] Even Japan's Foreign Press Center, which provides information about Japan and other services to the foreign press, has noted in its publication *Japan's Mass Media* that Japan's "newspapers look so much alike and cover the same stories so intensively."[39] Hall supports the evaluation presented here, suggesting that the clubs are largely responsible for this homogeneity: "The collaboration (and mutual monitoring) among club members themselves contributes to that virtual identity of layout and that bland, noncontroversial conformity of reportage and interpretation so often noted among Japan's competing news organizations."[40]

The press clubs are not the sole cause of uniformity in Japan, however. The ownership and control structure of the Japanese media itself has helped this along through *keiretsu* linkages among the key players. As Westney notes, "Given the dominance of newspapers in the information-gathering process of commercial television, the lack of diversity among them has widespread effects throughout the media system. . . . The maxim of 'one source, many outlets' captures the strategy of the nationals, and while this makes good business sense it does little for the diversity of the media system."[41]

How Distinctive Is Japan?

No country has an entirely free and open "marketplace" for information, of course. Long-term relationships between journalists and official sources are a common feature of reporting in every country. So too is cooperation among journalists themselves (for example, in pool reporting). Sensitive information may become known by an individual journalist or small group of journalists but not get reported because of concerns over losing a source. And journalists may have to negotiate with their sources for the what, when, why, who, and how of its release. This is an inevitable part of news reporting, if for no other reason than the fact that official news sources always have access to privileged information that journalists want.

Having said this, however, it is equally important that we do not underestimate the significance of system differences for the political process across otherwise democratic societies. While it is true that the basic rules of conduct in the newsgathering and dissemination process help to open access to official information, the nature of these rules and their impact on news reporting can vary widely. Two features of the media environment in Japan are key to understanding its present form: blurred state-society boundaries and a cohesive but insular industry structure. While the liberal press of nineteenth-century Europe came into being as a result of the rise of liberal capitalism and the ending of formal censorship, in Japan it was introduced into a country with a limited civil society and a long history of strict controls on publishing. Meiji era journalists and oligarchs were both part of the same elite, and their close ties flowed in both directions: early newspapers were founded by former samurai, while journalists ran for public office and moved easily into and out of the state bureaucracies. This history shaped early journalists' view of the purpose of the printed press, as they saw themselves as *insiders* whose ultimate goal was to push for the modernization of Japan through the "enlightenment" of the masses.[42] Yet in adopting the corollary stance of an "impartial and nonpartisan" position toward political elites, the press became a de facto supporter of the state and its policies. This became even more significant, of course, when Japan began its wartime buildup, as the media came to be used as an important part of the state's propaganda machine. After Japan's defeat, its media industry never underwent significant reform at the hands of the Occupation authorities, unlike many other industries that had served the state.

At the same time, a cohesive but insular industry structure ensures that these close ties to the state are carefully managed among all major rivals in the industry. Information flows within the press club system take place not on an ad hoc, case-by-case, informal, or situational basis, but through the formal structures and institutionalized procedures of the newsgathering system itself. Insider journalists are provided the same information and make shared agreements about how to report it. Outside journalists are excluded from this information and left to fend for themselves. To make certain that they preserve this prerogative, cartel members have worked through their industry association to prevent reform.

How do these differences play out at the level of news reporting relationships? Consider, first, the press system in the United States, specifically in the context of the three defining characteristics of Japan's information cartels: limited access, strict rules of reporting, and enforced sanctions against rule-breakers. Regarding the first characteristic, it is clear that access to official sources is much more open in the United States. The Japanese Communist paper *Akahata* (Red flag), for example, in the past has been granted access to the White House and key American sources, while it has never had similar access in Japan. As a political organ, *Akahata* is expressly excluded from club membership. In the United States, in contrast, access to key government sources is allowed to anyone with a press badge. As Sigal suggests, American journalists are not "nearly as clubby as the groups on beats in London or Tokyo."[43]

Second, the newsgathering process itself is much less rule-bound in the United States. There is nothing comparable to the Japanese press's agreements to limit the news reporting of the entire industry and little that resembles the informal agreements at the club level to restrict the flow of news outlined in chapter 4. There is certainly nothing comparable to the policy of rival newspapers agreeing to share papers in advance of publication to ensure common reporting on an issue and to make sure no one gets scooped. The Canadian system is similarly open. As described by one observer (the chief editor for a major Canadian newspaper), at the end of parliamentary debate the prime minister and members of the cabinet allow the media to gather around them in a "scrum" and ask questions at will. But because they do not follow systematic rules, "the pack is there for the scrum but they don't all do the same story."[44]

Finally, sanctions are individual rather than group-based. While press-source relations in North America often involve tacit understandings, there are no groupwide obligations. It is true that reporters on political beats in the United States sometimes face complaints from journalistic rivals if tacit covenants governing background briefings are broken. It is also true that reporters may justifiably be excluded from future briefings for breaking an embargo. But this is done by the sources themselves, not by an organized set of industry rivals. A violator in this case harms only his or her own relationship with the source, and "sanctions" (such as they are) are enforced by the source, not by a group composed of his or her competitors. This difference is crucial because without systematic enforcement mechanisms, the ability of rivals to control what each other does is limited.

The institutional machinery for cartelizing official news is virtually absent in the United States, and as a result, each of these features cannot be systematically and effectively employed. It is at this fundamental level— the initial source—that the two systems vary so dramatically. While the

U.S. media industry shares common institutional features in the "downstream" stages of reporting—notably in the role of concentrated media groups in the dissemination of the news—there is nothing similar at the "upstream" stages.[45] And it is here that the two systems are sufficiently distinctive to represent not simply differences in degree but differences in kind.

Nevertheless, the United States is not entirely representative of the world of media, nor even of the Western media. Its strong protections of free-speech rights, fragmented state structure, orientation toward minimal regulation, and other features ensure distinctive processes and outcomes. Indeed, it is possible that it is the United States that is the outlier, not Japan. Certainly it is the case that other countries in Asia have picked up one important feature of the "Japanese model": soft censorship within the context of a weakly developed civil society. In Thailand, for example, competing reporters gather at the end of news conferences so that the most senior among them can help form a consensus on the slant and tone of the story. In some cases, even the specific mechanisms are the same: in Korea, the club system itself was introduced during Japanese colonization and continues today with many of the same consequences.

Research is only beginning on the media systems in these other Asian countries, so it is difficult to say where the overlaps and distinctive features occur. A better-studied system is the British press, which makes for an interesting point of comparison because the British press has also operated within a system of limited access. Specific details of this system, known as the "Lobby," are reserved for the appendix, but it is worth briefly reviewing the primary similarities and differences, since both are clearly differentiated from their American counterpart. In Britain, as in Japan, news access is limited to a select group of individuals and organizations— those journalists whose names are on the official "Lobby list." The Lobby also has a clearly defined set of rules intended to reduce competition among journalists who are on the list, and there are a set of sanctions to discipline journalists who break these basic rules of the organization.

Nevertheless, there are also significant differences between the two systems, as the appendix shows. First, the British Lobby system is limited to only one form of news reporting (political) and only a few locations, in contrast to the hundreds of clubs in Japan that infuse major organizations throughout society. Second, the Lobby is not as powerful or well organized as the *kisha* clubs. Whereas sanctions in Japan are frequently enforced, in Britain they remain more at the level of a threat. Indeed, there is no record that they have ever used this power, although the threat of enforcement is presumably real.[46] Third, journalistic breaches in the Lobby are dealt with by the news sources themselves, not by other journalists (i.e., rivals). Finally, the Lobby does not enjoy the same powerful set of institutional backups that the Japanese press clubs have in the industry association. British competition policy prevents the kind of micromanaging of the news that takes place within Japan's newspaper association, where special committees comprised of managerial and editorial representatives from all of the major rival news organizations gather on a regular basis to discuss ways to "improve" and fine-tune the newsgathering and reporting system, as well as other aspects of the news industry.

It is useful to remember that one finds a free-wheeling daily press in Britain in many arenas, able and willing to take on sensitive issues, such as political scandals and the royal family. This is something one rarely finds in Japan, and mainly in semilegitimate newsweeklies.[47] Consider once again the case of the news embargo on the crown prince's marriage search, discussed in chapter 5. It is difficult to imagine anything even remotely similar occurring within the British press, even given the public outcry following the death of Princess Diana in 1997. Among other things, news sources in Britain would not have access to a large-scale trade association with the ability to coordinate the behavior of all the major players in the industry. Sources would have to negotiate with individual newspapers, many of which are local rather than national in scope and influence, a very cumbersome alternative indeed. And even if one assumed that some kind of agreement to restrict reporting were made, it could not be readily enforced because there are no systematic mechanisms for imposing sanctions on rule-breakers.

In conclusion, it is clear that there are factors inherent to the newsgathering process itself that can affect the flows of official information and news reporting in any country. But it is also clear that a country's media system is very much a product of its own distinctive history and national institutions. Just as the institutions of democratic capitalism vary among the advanced industrialized societies, so too do the institutions governing the ways in which news organizations gather and report the news. Without a historical frame of reference, therefore, the media's function in society and their role in politics cannot be understood.

Retrospect and Prospect

In addressing any country's press system, it is important to keep in mind one's time frame. The relative openness of the contemporary American press reported by many media observers, for example, was not always in place. It was not so long ago that sexual and other peccadillos in the White House were widely known within the press corps but went entirely unreported. As Gopnik has argued, there was a prevailing "access culture" in pre-Watergate American journalism, in which discretion on the part of the journalist was exchanged for access. But this came at a cost: "For a journalist not to print what he or she knew to be true—whether it was that F.D.R. had to have help to take his pants off or that J.F.K. needed help to keep his on—was to enter into a conspiracy to suppress truth."[48] The explicit recognition here of the conspiratorial characteristics of this relationship is noteworthy, as is the conclusion that it is the truth that in the end suffers.

Watergate helped break down this code of discretion by journalists, of course, as have the various scandals initiated by the American mainstream media since then. In Japan as well, there have been discussions on reforming the media. The proprietary newsgathering practices of the *kisha* clubs, in particular, have engendered increasingly caustic criticism by domestic pundits and overseas journalists alike. Critics have pointed to the irony of a putatively "free" press having a hand in limiting the free flow of information to the public or seemingly acquiescing to information controls implemented by sources. After the LDP's electoral loss in 1993, there was renewed discussion of this as critics suggested that the media had been at least partially responsible for the long, corrupt reign of the LDP in the first place. This inchoate reform movement has come in response to these criticisms and has resulted in at least some small changes, especially with respect to improving the access granted to foreign journalists.

As with many potential reforms in Japan, foreign pressure (*gaiatsu*), has played an important role. Among those taking the lead in demanding changes in the club system have been the American embassy in Tokyo, which understood the role played by the clubs as information barriers to trade; Bloomberg Business News, which well understood the same; and the Foreign Press in Japan.[49] This pressure has been partially successful, in the sense that foreigners are now in principle allowed into most clubs, but the reality is that this is still ad hoc, and the small number of organizations that have gained access are generally considered "nonregular" members, with fewer benefits. More important, however, is the fact that domestic Japanese journalists are still excluded as a matter of course. There has been a long and continuing history of denial and delay in club reform going back to the early postwar period, both in terms of the access offered to the foreign media and certain elements of the Japanese press, as chapter 5 documents. As Ivan Hall has put it, foreign journalists in Japan hoping for access "have been subjected to the oriental torture of a thousand slices."[50]

Foreign reporters in the 1980s and early 1990s, for example, found themselves on the outside of leading economic stories in part because they were excluded from press conferences involving major Japanese corporations. This truly became a trade barrier, however, in the case of financial news, where receiving information as little as a minute later than one's competitors can mean a considerable financial loss to one's subscribers and oneself, a fact Bloomberg Business News was well aware of. After years of shuttling back and forth between the Kabuto club in the Tokyo Stock Exchange and the NSK in an effort to gain better access through club membership, Tokyo bureau chief David Butts finally decided to take matters into his own hands in the spring of 1993 by storming the club and demanding that he be given company reports at the same time that his Japanese competitors—including Nikkei Business News—were receiving them (rather than the standard five to fifteen minutes later). Japanese reporters criticized this tactic for creating "confusion" in the market but eventually relented.[51]

In the end, it may be unreasonable to expect dramatic change in a system in which beneficiaries are also making the rules. This means, however, that genuine reform in Japan's media industry requires something more fundamental: the *elimination* of the club system itself. To do so, the mainstream media, and its representative industry association, must first be stripped of the power to determine who gains access to formal and informal news settings. Anything short of this simply means that new entrants must also play by club rules, and a perpetuation of the century-old system of exclusive news management. In addition, the legitimate power to sanction must be given back to news sources, and any illegitimate role played by them (such as cases where sanctions are imposed by the public prosecutor's office or the police simply because they do not like a journalist's story) must be made illegal, as they violate the public's free access to information and its right to know. The understanding must be that briefings be as open as they are in other advanced democracies, that is, that all credentialed journalists enjoy equal access, and that information is not a political resource to be bartered back and forth by media, political and economic elites. It must be given to the public—its rightful owners.[52]

A second important area of reform in Japan's mass media system comes from the establishment of an independent role played by television. However, as noted earlier, when government officials were confronted with the reality that Japan's media industry was finding numerous ways to circumvent the decades-old ruling limiting the ownership of television stations by the newspaper press to 10 percent, a ruling intended to maintain a degree of diversity within the media industry and reduce concentration, the government rewrote the rule to make it conform to this reality. This regulatory shift from a 10 percent to 20 percent ownership by the newspaper press does not suggest a weakening of the traditional network links discussed here. If anything, it suggests not only a strengthening of such ties among industry leaders, but state sanctioning of that process. In Japan, legal restrictions have always been circumvented using sister companies and individuals "friendly" to the company anyway, and it is expected that this practice will continue given the weak structure and limited powers of the Japanese Fair Trade Commission. Finally, while it may be that the introduction of satellite broadcasting such as CNN may help the Japanese public gain a different interpretation of international affairs than that found in stories written or produced by club journalists affiliated with the MFA and other ministries, that, too, remains to be seen.

Will radical reform happen anytime soon? This is doubtful given that the current environment does not appear to be predisposed toward reform. In particular, with respect to reforming the media institutions described here, the blurred boundaries and strong industry features mean that this will be quite difficult to achieve. Reforms to date—such as the NSK's 1993 recommendation that greater access be given to foreign journalists—have yet to lead to dramatic changes, or an increase in the kind of investigative journalism by the mainstream press found in the United States. As others have noted, while some changes have occurred in the style of news reporting in recent years, the fundamental structure of the news reporting process, including the role played by the press clubs, remains intact.[53] It will be interesting to see just how far these reforms continue to go, and whether they are ultimately substantive or merely symbolic.[54] It also remains to be seen just what impact recent reform efforts elsewhere in Japan's political landscape will have on the press-politics relationship.

Who Sets the Media's Agenda?

The political science literature on Japan has frequently emphasized the considerable role played by the Japanese state, both in economic development and in the political process. But only rarely have the sources of state capacity in Japan been addressed. Phrased differently, we know considerably more about the political and bureaucratic processes operating within the Japanese state than we do about the broader state-society environment in which those processes operate. Yet this environment is fundamental in determining just how the Japanese state has been able to achieve its goals.

What lessons can comparative politics draw from this discussion? Certainly one implication is that there may be substantial, and so far largely unexplored, cross-national differences in the extent of involvement and the roles played by the press in the political agenda-setting process. Unlike in the United States and a number of other Western countries, where evidence suggests that the print and broadcast media do indeed serve to set the political agenda, this media function is much less pronounced in Japan. It is also likely to be reduced in other countries where effective information cartels exist. In addition, variations in press institutions may affect informational and intellectual access. Japan, for example, has been described as an informational "black hole"—a place where news flows in but does not flow back out. An important part of the reason for this may lie in the restrictions on access imposed on foreign and non-mainstream Japanese journalists, and sometimes scholars.

But perhaps most important is the observation that in the study of the media's role in the political process, the issue is not simply the extent to which the media define the agenda of society as a whole, but also how the state can, explicitly or implicitly, define the media's own agenda, and the institutional mechanisms through which this takes place. In the case of Japan, the press-based information cartels that limit competition to a select group of club members and extend these ties vertically to other media organizations also provide a formal structure that makes it easier for politicians and bureaucrats to assert control and define their own agendas. In this sense, differences in the role of the media in state-society relations may provide an important link in explaining the institutional sources of state power.

I have argued that the press and other media are far less important in independently defining an agenda for political discourse, serving neither as watchdog of the state nor as lapdog—neither "Fourth Estate" nor "for the state," to use the terminology of chapter 1. Rather, political news and information is conveyed to the public in Japan, but because of institutional constraints, it is conveyed in a highly delimited fashion that narrows the range of societal inquiry into the political process. What this means is that, together with the limited agenda-setting role played by the media in Japan, the selective reporting of the news results in the creation of an informationally inferior product where people do not get "all the news that's fit to print."

It is somewhat ironic that Japan's "information society," with its high levels of newspaper readership and television viewership, is so lacking in diverse viewpoints. This suggests the need to move beyond simple numbers to understanding the concrete relationships within which news is reported. The task in trying to understand the media's function in the political process is to determine the conditions under which they play one role rather than another by demarcating the boundaries and strengths of these institutional ties and by describing the rules and institutionalized practices that govern their behavior. Here we must answer such questions as: What actors have access to the media and on what terms? Whose view of the world ("reality") and events is presented? And what news stories are ignored or underreported?

I conclude with a conundrum: Some observers in North America have criticized the role of the media in the political process because of their power in setting the agenda of discourse. What Japan suggests, however, is a situation even more problematic: one in which the media do not set, but rather limit, the agenda, thereby letting others (notably political actors) set it instead.

Appendix A

Regulations for the Diet Press Club

1. Name

The name of this club is the "Kokkai kishakai" (Diet Press Club).

2. Location

The club is located at 1-6-2 Nagatacho, Chiyoda-ku, in the Diet Press Club Building.

3. Purpose

The purpose of this association is to attain mutual benefits for members in collecting and gathering news from the parliament, and to promote goodwill and betterment among members.

4. Composition

The members of this club are all newspapers, wire services, or broadcast companies belonging to the Japan Newspaper Publishers and Editors Association who have met the membership requirements outlined in section 13 of this agreement.

5. Duties

The following activities are carried out in order to fulfill the purposes of this association:

1. Activities to make possible the free and just collection and reporting of news concerning parliament
2. Management of the Diet Press Club building
3. Allocation and control of Diet Reporters' badges
4. Liaison and coordination with the House of Representatives and the House of Councilors as needed by this association
5. Any other activities necessary to fulfill the goals of this club

6. Boards

To manage this association, secretaries and permanent secretaries should be appointed based on the following regulations.

7. Secretaries

Secretaries and permanent secretaries will be selected according to the following rules.

Secretaries

Seventeen secretaries will be chosen. In addition to the members from Kyodo, *Mainichi, Asahi, Yomiuri, Nihon Keizai, Chunichi, Nishi Nihon, Hokkaido,* Jiji, *Sankei,* and NHK, five members will be chosen from among the member private broadcasting companies. One additional member will come from a company not listed above. The length of terms and selection procedures are explained in the detailed rules outlined below.

Permanent Secretaries

The permanent secretaries will be selected from the larger group according to the selection procedures explained in the detailed rules. Their term will last one year, and they will have the utmost responsibility.

8. Secretaries Group, Permanent Secretaries Group

The secretaries and permanent secretaries will each organize their own groups and will organize and run this association according to the following procedures.

Secretaries Group

The secretaries group will represent the association, make decisions, and carry out the duties listed in section 5. In addition, they will make decisions on memberships and withdrawals, the budget, the year-end balance, sanctions, approvals, rules, detailed rules, reorganization, and other concerns.

Permanent Secretaries Group

The permanent secretaries group will propose new measures for the secretaries group and carry out and supervise the club's daily activities. In emergency situations, the permanent secretaries will represent and run the entire association, but after this time, their actions must be approved by the secretaries group.

Decision Methods

For the secretaries group to make decisions, at least half of the secretaries must be present and two thirds must approve the decision. For the permanent secretaries group, all members must be present and must approve of a decision unanimously. In the case of both types of meetings, the director must be present but cannot be involved in decision making.

9. General Members Group

Every March, this association will hold a meeting for all members in order to discuss the year's activities. This members' meeting usually takes the place of the secretaries' meeting. However, when over three quarters of the members make a request, a meeting of all club members must be held.

10. Membership Dues

To maintain and operate this club, membership fees, registration fees, and fines must be collected from members. Refer to the detailed rules attached.

11. Fiscal Year

This association's fiscal year begins on April 1 and ends on March 31.

12. Executive Office

This association has an executive office consisting of one chief director and some staff members. The chief director is appointed by the secretaries.

13. Membership and Withdrawal

To join this association, at least two secretaries must recommend membership and the secretaries group must recognize and approve membership. When withdrawing from this association, members must notify the association. However, based on section 14, a member may be forced to resign from the club.

14. Sanctions

When members disregard the purpose of this association, or when they violate their responsibilities, they can be punished in the following manner as decided by the secretaries group:

1. Dismissal
2. Banishment from the Diet Press Club Building
3. Required to make an apology
4. Given a warning

For actions 1 and 2, at least two-thirds of the secretaries must be present and at least two-thirds of this number must agree on the decision.

15. Detailed Rules

The following rules are to be abided by in executing this agreement:

1. Detailed rules for the selection of secretaries and permanent secretaries
2. Detailed rules for membership fee collection
3. Detailed rules for control and supervision of Diet Reporters' badges
4. Detailed rules for the distribution of press releases

Additional Rules

1. Matters not regulated in this association agreement will be handled by the secretaries group.
2. This association agreement and its detailed rules will take effect on April 1, 1972.
3. After March 31, 1972, members of this association under the prior agreement will automatically become members under this association agreement.

Detailed Rules for Collection of Membership Dues

1. Membership Fees

1. The membership fee for this association is collected following figure 1.
2. The membership fee must be paid by the specified date.

2. Registration Fee

New members are required to pay a 200,000 yen registration fee.

3. Fines

There will be a 1,000 yen fine for lost Diet Reporters' badges.

Detailed Rules for the Selection of Secretaries and Permanent Secretaries

1. Secretaries

Selection of secretaries will be based on section 7 of the Diet Reporters Association agreement. In addition, the five secretaries that are selected from among the private broadcasting company members must be nominated by the Association of Private Broadcasting Company News Chiefs and must be approved by the secretary's group. In the case of the one member who is chosen from among the companies not listed in the sixteen above, the nomination must be approved by all eleven companies in the Diet Press Club association and approved by the secretaries group.

2. Permanent Secretaries

The permanent secretaries group will have four members. One member is always the chief political reporter from the Kyodo wire service. In alternation, one member will be the chief political reporter from either *Mainichi*, *Asahi*, or *Yomiuri*. One member will be selected from the private broadcast companies, and finally, in alternation, one member will be the chief reporter from either *Nippon Keizai*, *Chunichi*, *Nishi Nippon*, *Hokkaido*, Jiji, *Sankei*, or NHK.

Detailed Rules for Control and Supervision of Diet Reporters' Badges

1. Distribution

1. Refer to the next section for the allocation of Diet Reporters' badges.
2. The secretaries group will decide on the distribution of badges to new members.
3. The secretaries group must approve all requests by member companies to change the number of badges allocated to a given company.
4. In general, the furnishing of badges is carried out at the same time that renewals for badges are carried out.

2. Control

Members must be responsible for their own badges and the chief director must be responsible for the office's badges.

3. Replacement

1. When a member loses a badge, the member must tell the chief director and report it to the secretaries group immediately.

2. When a member wants to replace a lost badge, the member company must request it. In this case, the badge will usually be replaced on the date of the next session of parliament.

Detailed Rules for the Distribution of Materials for Reporting

1. Distribution

Members will receive official reports, bills, budgets, year-end balances, minutes, and other notices distributed by the House of Representatives and the House of Councilors.

2. Allocation

1. The number of allocations of reports and reporting materials for members will normally be as detailed above. However, in extraordinary situations, the allocation of materials will be decided by the permanent secretaries group.

2. If a change in allocation is requested, the member company requesting the change must ask the secretaries group who will make the decision.

Appendix B

Kitami Administration of Justice Press Club Agreement

General Agreement[1]

Section 1

This club is called the Kitami Administration of Justice Press Club and is located in the Hokkaido Police Department, Kitami District.

Section 2

This club generally consists of member companies of the Japan Newspaper Publishers and Editors Association.

Section 3

The purpose of this club is to promote friendship among its members. Another goal is to coordinate activites in order to make the collection of data easier.

Section 4

To handle the business of the club, alternating secretary companies are appointed.

General Meetings

Section 5

Important matters of this club will be decided at general meetings.

Section 6

In this club, upon request by member companies, the secretary company will call general meetings, with members of the secretary companies serving as chairpersons.

Section 7

For general meetings, at least half of the member companies must attend and a majority of those attending must agree on any decision. However, when amending this club agreement, or when disciplining a member company, at least two thirds of the members must agree.

Secretaries

Section 8

The secretary companies represent the club, negotiate with the outside when necessary, and distribute reports to the member companies.

Section 9

Secretary companies will have alternating three-month terms in the following order:

1. *Doshin Mainichi*, HBC
2. NHK, *Asahi*, STV, uhb
3. *Yomiuri, Hokkai Times*, HTB

News Agreements and Other Issues

Section 10

When it is necessary to conclude a news agreement between member companies, the regulations of the Japan Newspaper Editors and Publishers Association must be followed. However, with reference to section 3, secretary companies can negotiate with news sources with agreement of all member companies to formalize how to collect data, and to determine convenient times for member companies to collect data concerning personnel affairs, commendations, and justice.

Membership

Section 11

The member companies must notify this club when members join or leave.

Sanctions

Section 12

According to section 7, members can be expelled from the club for violating this agreement, tarnishing the image of the club, or breaking friendly relations with other member companies.

Finances

Section 13

All of the club's expenses are covered by membership and other fees.

Section 14

The membership fee per person is 500 yen per month. The fees for the spring and autumn general meetings held in April and October are 1,000 yen per person.

Section 15

The fiscal year is from April 1 to March 31.

Section 16

The incoming group of secretaries is responsible for auditing and reporting the year-end financial statement.

Congratulations and Condolences

Section 17

For congratulations and condolences of members, this club together with the Kitami Municipal Press Club will give the following:

1. Marriage	5,000 yen
2. Death	10,000 yen
3. Death (Spouse, child, parents)	5,000 yen
4. Transfer	5,000 yen
5. Hospitalization (at least one week)	5,000 yen
6. Birth of a child	5,000 yen

Section 18

For congratulations and condolences not mentioned, monetary gifts can be given if all members agree.

Other Issues

Section 19

The club will be managed together with the Kitami Municipal Government Press Club.

Section 20

Concerning the management of this club, any issues not mentioned in this agreement will be handled according to the the regulations of the Japan Newspaper Publishers and Editors Association.

Additions

This agreement is in effect from September 1987.

Member Companies

Hokkaido shimbunsha	Nippon Hōsō Kyōkai (NHK)
Hokkai Times	Hokkaido Hōsō (HBC)
Asahi shimbunsha	Sapporo Terebi Hōsō (STV)
Mainichi shimbunsha	Hokkaidō Bunka Hōsō (UHB)
Yomiuri shimbunsha	Hokkaido Terebi hōsō (HTB)

Appendix C

Chronology of Agreements between the Imperial Household Agency and the Magazine *Kisha* Club

Sept. 1960

The Imperial Household requests that magazines not use photographs of the royal family on their covers. The same applies for foreign magazines. If photos are used, privileges to cover the royal family will be lost. Permission to use such photos in human interest stories may be granted by the Imperial Household Agency. Photos cannot be used for newspaper advertisements or on posters.

Aug. 1962

Agreement prohibiting coverage or reports concerning the Princes's family stay at the Numazu residence. (*Shukan heibon* broke this rule and published a picture captioned, "Princess Michiko Swimming." They later made a formal written apology and disciplined themselves by promising not to cover any Imperial Household matters for two weeks.)

April 1963

Agreement not to cover Princess Michiko's stay at Hayama following her miscarriage. (Companies who broke this agreement would be expelled from the club. Due to a misunderstanding, *Shukan myojo* wrote an article that violated the agreement. As a consequence, they had to promise not to cover any Imperial Household matters for two weeks.)

Mar. 1964

Agreement concerning coverage and reports about Prince Hironomiya in Gakushuin pre-school. (Companies violating this agreement were to be disciplined by the club with the approval of the Imperial Household Agency's General Affairs Bureau.)

Mar. 1964

Reconfirmation of agreements concerning the use of photographs provided by the Imperial Household Agency, including the use of these photographs on magazine covers.

July 1965

Agreement concerning coverage or reports of the Princes's family stay at the Karuizawa residence. (Non-pool magazine *Shukan josei* violated the agreement by running their own article. The club destroyed the film and prevented the publication of the article in question.)

July 1965

Agreement concerning the use of the royal family symbol. In general, use of the symbol is strictly forbidden. If a company wants to use the symbol, they must get permission from the Imperial Household Agency's General Affairs Bureau. (In March 1965, the news gathering subcommittee of the Japan Magazine Publishers Association's editorial affairs committee and the club heads reported to the Imperial Household Agency about discussions to determine when the symbol could and could not be used independently.)

July 1965

Agreement concerning the coverage or reports of the Mikasonomiya family and the Konoe family. (*Jose jishin* broke this agreement, and as punishment the magazine was required to let the JMPA have control over its photographs for one year.)

Aug. 1965

Agreement stating that only after a magazine had used its own photographs for a period of a week could they run photographs purchased from newspapers or wire services.

April 1966

Agreement concerning the coverage or reports of Prince Hironomiya at Gakushuin elementary school.

April 1966

Club agreement that articles written about Prince Hironomiya for commercial reasons are prohibited. In August 1968, the agreement was extended to include articles about any royal family member.

Nov. 1966

Agreement prohibiting coverage of the Prince and Princess at Azabu Lawn Tennis Club. (This agreement applied to newspapers as well.)

June 1968

Confirmation of guidelines covering the fashion of royal family members. Articles should not be only about fashion, but must have another focus. When royal family members and a celebrity are portrayed on the same page, the layout must be edited in such a way that it does not give the impression that the royal family member is regarded as one would a celebrity.

April 1971

Agreement limiting the use of pictures of the Emperor and Empress visit to Europe on magazine covers. Cover photos can be used only twice until next January (1972). If a photo is used on the cover, the entire magazine must be devoted to the Emperor and Empress. If the photo is used for this purpose, the company must discuss their plans and show the photographs they will use to the Imperial Household Agency's General Affairs Bureau before the magazine is published. If the magazine's plans are approved, when advertising this edition, the company can advertise the cover photo in newspapers or on television. They cannot advertise the cover on trains, store posters, or on billboards. Television and/or newspaper ads must be run in appropriate spots and/or at the appropriate time.

April 1983

Agreement prohibiting coverage that reveals the directions to, or the location of, Prince Hironomiya's residence while studying in England.

(*Source*: Maruyama Noboru, *Hōdō kyōtei—nihon masukomi no kamman na jishi* [Tokyo: Daisan shokan, 1992], 24–25.)

Appendix D

A Comparison with the British Lobby

THE WESTMINSTER LOBBY correspondents get their name from a place: the lobby located at the main entrance to the Chamber of the House of Commons where they have exclusive access to members of Parliament, receive copies of documents embargoed for later release, and "have access to 'briefings'—by the Prime Minister's press staff twice a day, by the Leader of the House of Commons and the Leader of the Opposition once a week, and by other Ministers and politicians."[1] Their numbers are limited by the "authorities of Parliament," the sergeant-at-arms having a list with the names of those journalists permitted to enter. Instituted in 1885 when the once-open doors of the House of Commons were closed after several bombings (on one occasion by Irish Americans), the "Lobby list" effectively excluded what one of the privileged few described at the time as "the 'soi-disant leaders of opinion, the miscellaneous buttonholers, and the propagandist idlers who haunt the House on important occasions.' "[2] In short, excluded were those having alternative points of view.

Initially, provincial evening papers and Sunday papers were also excluded from the Lobby, but by 1960 both had been given access, and membership numbers jumped from around 30 in the prewar and wartime period to more than 120 in the late 1960s.[3] There are about 150 members today.[4] Those still excluded from this key center of political discourse include, however, such important weeklies as *The Economist*, the *New Statesman*, the *Spectator*, and the *Tribune*. Foreign correspondents as well as tabloids are also excluded.

Seymour-Ure, the author of a detailed analysis of Lobby history, suggests that the increase in the number of members in the interwar period and the institutionalization of other practices in the postwar period such as the "Lobby Meeting" has had the effect of reducing competition rather than increasing it. In 1910, for example, with only thirty members or so, the work of the Lobby journalist entailed "individual sleuthing" and "competition for early information"; but with the growth of government and the increase in membership, the task of the Lobby journalist "was much less adaptable to individual initiative and bred less scoops."[5] The introduction of the Lobby Meeting—"collective gatherings of Lobby men at which they put questions to a Minister or member of the opposition and hear expositions of Government or party policies"[6]—in the interwar period also served to limit competition, as more and more often journalists spent their time in group proceedings practicing "collective lobbying" and receiving identical information. One contemporary analysis of the Lobby system had this to say about its role: "The roots for the present twisted relationship between government and the press go deep. Even when the Lobby was formed, it was more than just a trade club for the journalists covering Westminster: already it was shaping up as an important conduit for official information, for news management by governments."[7]

In terms of its exclusivity, its codified rules, and the threat of sanctions, the British Lobby can be considered an information cartel, albeit a quasi-public one. As Seymour-Ure points out, "Lobby journalists operate under conditions which are ultimately under the control of the Commons. They are in practice self-governing; but rather in the sense of a self-governing colony, with a strictly limited area of discretion."[8] It was the government and not newspaper enterprises that first established the Lobby list as a means of controlling the numbers (and possibly the makeup) of the journalists entering the Lobby in the House of Commons in the first place. Moreover, it is the members of the House of Commons who have the power to enforce the paramount sanction—expulsion. Although there is no record that they have ever used this power, the threat of enforcement is presumably real. In one case in 1920, for example, when a newspaper published the details of a secret document, the speaker of the House later commented in his memoirs that he had warned the journalist involved that "in the event of a repetition of such an event as publishing a document headed "Private and Confidential," I should strike him off the list of those admitted under the Speaker's authority to the Press Gallery."[9]

While it has many "public" attributes, the Lobby is not solely a public arrangement: Lobby members make their own rules, even if sanctions for violating them and the means of enforcing them are relatively vague. In addition, although the Parliament limits their numbers, it does not have any say over which individual a news organization sends to the Lobby. Various rules have evolved to govern the relationship between sources and journalists, some of which have been codified and included in a pamphlet entitled *Notes on the Practice of Lobby Journalism*, which is handed to new members. These rules were established in order to "make the Lobby acceptable to the House."

Although the main function of the Lobby journalist is to gather behind-the-scenes information on policies and members of Parliament, and, as suggested earlier, to serve as a conduit for government information, the two most distinctive characteristics of this newsgathering system are its secrecy and its almost total reliance on the journalistic practice of nonattribution. With respect to secrecy, it has been argued that this is "inevitable

. . . because of the secretiveness of the political system" itself.[10] In other words, a secretive bureaucracy and secretive politicians require journalists to keep their own "brotherhood," as it were, secret. In fact, although the institution celebrated its 110th anniversary in 1994, it was not until the late 1960s that its existence was publicly recognized. Indeed, one of the Lobby rules (first made public in 1969) states that "It has become common practice for Ministers and others to meet the lobby collectively to give information and answer questions. Members are under an obligation to keep secret the fact that such meetings are held and to avoid revealing the sources of their information."[11]

But it is the practice of nonattribution, which has been fully institutionalized by Lobby journalists, that is most troubling to critics of the Lobby system. As one book noted, "All journalists accept that some people will talk more freely if their identity is concealed and they protect confidential sources. But most journalists outside the Lobby seek on-the-record statements whenever they can so that sources are identified and a person must stand by his or her own words. Lobby journalists prefer to work on off-the-record terms in a world of pretense. They depend on briefings that supposedly never take place with government spokesmen who do not officially exist."[12] By agreeing not to attribute their sources, they are subject to control; nonattribution, the key mechanism supporting the journalist-source relationship in the Lobby, serves as a primary means for sources to control the flow and content of information in important ways. Whether such control would exist in a noncartelized situation, however, is unclear.

In sum, then, what can we say about the Lobby–*kisha* club comparison? In Britain, as in Japan, the political information-gathering process takes place within a "closed shop" made up of journalists having proprietary access to information and sources. In the case of political information in Britain or, more specifically, news emanating from Westminster (and sometimes Whitehall), access is limited to those journalists whose names are on an official registry known as the "Lobby list." In Japan, access is limited not only to political news, but to *all* categories of news—political, economic, or "social"—by prior membership in a relevant club.

In both cases, those journalists given privileged access have established a clearly defined set of rules and practices. To take just one example, Lobby rules include the provision that, although Lobby members "have complete freedom to get [their] own stories in [their] own way . . . they should do nothing to prejudice the communal life of the Lobby, or the relations with the two Houses and the authorities." These rules are "risk-reducing" in the sense that they serve to limit the possibility that any member journalist or news organization will miss an important story or alternatively, obtain a scoop. They are "access-enhancing" in the sense that they establish a framework for the journalist-source relationship that makes it possible to build relations of mutual trust between an exclusive group of journalists and their sources. The effectiveness of these rules is reinforced by the threat of sanctions. In the case of Japan, these are frequently enforced, while in Britain this remains more often at the level of a threat—specifically, members of the House of Commons have the power to enforce the paramount sanction, expulsion.

It is no wonder that, just as critics of the Japanese press have frequently used the appellation "cartel" in describing the press club system there, so too have critics in Britain. One British author notes that, "practically speaking, it is an information cartel," while another describes the Lobby as a "cartel for the provision of political news and information."[13] Still, although certain features of the newsgathering and reporting process in Britain and Japan are similar, their pervasive and systemic character in Japan sets them apart from their Anglo (and American) counterparts.

Notes

Preface

1. In this book I use the Japanese term *kisha* to stress the distinctive element involved. Even though others use alternative translations, among them "reporters club" and "press clubs," the distinctiveness of the term is lost when it is rendered in English.

2. Chalmers Johnson, *Japan's Public Policy Companies* (Washington, D.C.: American Enterprise Institute for Public Policy Research, 1978), 9. Emphasis in original.

Chapter One
Bringing in the Media

1. See Robert M. Entman, *Democracy without Citizens: Media and the Decay of American Politics* (New York: Oxford University Press, 1989). Entman also argues that "the concept of a marketplace of ideas does more to mystify than to clarify journalism's influence in politics and contributions to democracy" (29).

2. The terms "press" and "media" are used interchangeably throughout this chapter and unless otherwise noted refer to both broadcast and print media.

3. Gladys Engel Lang and Kurt Lang, "Mass Communications and Public Opinion: Strategies for Research," in *Social Psychology: Sociological Perspectives* ed. Morris Rosenberg and Ralph H. Turner (New York: Basic Books, 1981), 653.

4. Ibid., 655.

5. Ibid., 654. In fact, one of Lazarsfeld's colleagues went so far as to declare the field dead (660).

6. The two works that had the greatest impact were Joseph T. Klapper, *The Effects of Mass Media* (New York: Columbia University, Bureau of Applied Social Research, 1949), and Elihu Katz and Paul F. Lazarsfeld, *Personal Influence: The Part Played by People in the Flow of Mass Communications* (Glencoe, Ill.: Free Press, 1955). Lang and Lang offer an interesting analysis of this period and suggest that these two works had considerably more influence than they warranted. See Lang and Lang, "Mass Communications," 661.

7. Ibid.

8. The statement that there were "Three Estates in Parliament; but, in the Reporters' Gallery yonder, there sat a Fourth Estate more important far than they all" is attributed to Edmund Burke, in Lucas A. Powe, *The Fourth Estate and the Constitution: Freedom of the Press in America* (Berkeley: University of California Press, 1991), 261. Among those emphasizing the fourth estate role of the press are Shanto Iyengar, Mark D. Peters, and Donald R. Kinder, "Experimental Demonstrations of the 'Not-So-Minimal' Consequences of Television News Pro-

grams," *American Political Science Review* 76, 4 (December 1982): 848–58, and Doris A. Graber, *Mass Media and American Politics* (Washington, D.C.: Congressional Quarterly Press, 1980).

9. Many Marxist scholars are among those who argue that the media act as the mouthpiece of the capitalist state, including Ralph Miliband, *The State in Capitalist Society* (London: Weidenfeld & Nicolson, 1969). Also see Todd Gitlin, *The Whole World Is Watching: Mass Media in the Making and Unmaking of the New Left* (Berkeley: University of California Press, 1980).

10. This is a slight alteration of the original phrase "bringing the state back in," which was the title of a book and an argument calling on political and social scientists to return to an earlier theoretical framework that gave greater consideration to the role played by the state in the formation and implementation of policy. See Peter B. Evans, Dietrich Rueschemeyer, and Theda Skocpol, eds., *Bringing the State Back In* (New York: Cambridge University Press, 1985). In the sense that Max Weber first noted the importance of studying the press, we can suggest bringing it *back* in. In fact, however, the media have long been neglected in political and social science research.

11. In a similar vein, Entman argues that the interaction between journalism and democracy is "a product of a process, of a close and indissoluble interrelationship among the media, their messages, their elite news sources, and the mass audience." Entman, *Democracy without Citizens*, 10.

12. Ben H. Bagdikian, *The Media Monopoly*, 3d ed. (Boston: Beacon Press, 1987), xxiii.

13. Max Weber, *The Theory of Social and Economic Organization*, trans. A. M. Henderson and Talcott Parsons, ed. Talcott Parsons (New York: Free Press, 1964), 152.

14. This is also the subject of a book by Peter L. Berger and Thomas Luckmann, *The Social Construction of Reality: A Treatise in the Sociology of Knowledge* (Garden City, N.Y.: Doubleday, 1966).815. Denis McQuail *Mass Communication Theory: An Introduction*, 2d ed. (London: Sage Publications, 1987), 51.

15. Denis McQuial *Mas Communication Theory: An Introduction*, 2d. ed. (London: Sage Publications, 1987), 51.

16. Gitlin, *The Whole World Is Watching*, 1.

17. Sidney Verba et al., *Elites and the Idea of Equality: A Comparison of Japan, Sweden and the United States* (Cambridge: Harvard University Press, 1987), 161–65. See also Ikuo Kabashima and Jeffrey Broadbent, "Referent Pluralism: Mass Media and Politics in Japan," *Journal of Japanese Studies* 12 (Summer 1986): 335.

18. Verba, *Elites and the Idea of Equality*, 161.

19. Theda Skocpol, "Bringing the State Back In: Strategies of Analysis in Current Research," in *Bringing the State Back In*, ed. Evans, Rueschemeyer, and Skocpol, 19–21; emphasis in original. Skocpol uses this term to describe the theoretical framework employed by Stephen D. Krasner, *Defending the National Interest: Raw Material Investments and U.S. Foreign Policy* (Princeton: Princeton University Press, 1978); Alfred C. Stepan, *The State and Society: Peru in Comparative Perspective* (Princeton: Princeton University Press, 1978); Peter J. Katzenstein, ed., *Between Power and Plenty: Foreign Economic Policies of Advanced Industrial States* (Madison: University of Wisconsin Press, 1978); and others.

20. Skocpol, "Bringing the State Back In," 20. For a reference to the notion of policy networks, see also Peter J. Katzenstein, "Conclusion: Domestic Structures and Strategies of Foreign Economic Policy," *International Organization* 31, 4 (Autumn 1977): 879–920.

21. Krasner, *Defending the National Interest*, 17.

22. Peter A. Gourevitch, *Politics in Hard Times: Comparative Responses to International Economic Crises* (Ithaca: Cornell University Press, 1986), 227, 230.

23. Ibid., 230.

24. Roger Friedland and Robert D. Alford, "Bringing Society Back In: Symbols, Practices and Institutional Contradictions" in *The New Institutionalism in Organizational Analysis*, ed. Walter W. Powell and Paul J. DiMaggio (Chicago: University of Chicago Press, 1991), 237.

25. Ibid., 236.

26. Others contend that Skocpol misrepresents studies she claims are societally reductionist. See Gabriel A. Almond, "The Return to the State," *American Political Science Review* 83, 3 (September 1988): 853–901.

27. Skocpol, "Bringing the State Back In," 20.

28. Friedland and Alford, "Bringing Society Back In," 237.

29. Ibid., 238.

30. Gourevitch, *Politics in Hard Times*, 230.

31. Paul Weaver suggests that one of the "tensions" inherent in liberal journalism is "the tension between access and autonomy, between the effort of the press to get as much unambiguous true information about as many events as possible—which requires a maximum of access to the actors of these events, which in turn entails a maximum of dependency on these actors—and its efforts to preserve its capacity for independent judgment." Weaver, "The New Journalism and the Old—Thoughts after Watergate," *Public Interest*, 35 (Spring 1974): 70.

32. Skocpol, "Bringing the State Back In," 21.

33. See, for example, Ronald Philip Dore, *Flexible Rigidities: Industrial Policy and Structural Adjustment in the Japanese Economy, 1970–80* (Stanford: Stanford University Press, 1986); Mark W. Fruin, *The Japanese Enterprise System: Competitive Strategies and Cooperative Structures* (New York: Oxford University Press, 1992); Michael L. Gerlach, *Alliance Capitalism: The Social Organization of Japanese Business* (Berkeley: University of California Press, 1992); and Michael L. Gerlach and James R. Lincoln, *The Organization of Japanese Business Networks* (Cambridge: Cambridge University Press, forthcoming).

34. Richard J. Samuels, *The Business of the Japanese State: Energy Markets in Comparative and Historical Perspective* (Ithaca: Cornell University Press, 1987), 8.

35. Chalmers A. Johnson, *MITI and the Japanese Miracle: The Growth of Industrial Policy, 1925–1975* (Stanford: Stanford University Press, 1982), 273. *Amakudari* refers to the practice whereby elite bureaucrats obtain lucrative positions in either public corporations or private industry upon retirement. Administrative guidance, on the other hand, is offered as an example of how bureaucrats bring business on board when traditional control mechanisms are no longer available.

36. Daniel I. Okimoto, *Between MITI and the Market: Japanese Industrial Policy for High Technology* (Stanford: Stanford University Press, 1989), 144–45.

37. See, for example, Patricia Boling, "Private Interest and the Public Good in Japan," *The Pacific Review* 3, 2 (1990).

38. Johnson, *MITI and the Japanese Miracle*, 273.

39. Katzenstein, "Conclusion," 899.

40. Mark Tilton, *Restrained Trade: Cartels in Japan's Basic Materials Industries* (Ithaca: Cornell University Press, 1996).

41. Sheldon Garon, *Molding Japanese Minds: The State in Everyday Life* (Princeton: Princeton University Press, 1997), 236.

42. In a book of the same title, Ben Bagdikian argues that the number of competing media organizations is rapidly diminishing.

43. Foreign Press Center Japan, *Japan's Mass Media*, "About Japan Series," no.7 (1994): 18.

44. *Tokyo* and *Chunichi* are managed by the same company and are often counted as a single bloc paper. The major difference between the national papers and the bloc papers is that the latter publish and distribute within a single large geographical area. To compete with the national papers, these papers have agreed not to compete in each others' respective circulation areas. They also share articles, features, serialized short stories, and other columns.

45. The circulations of the bloc papers fall in the 800,000 to 2,000,000 range, and those of the prefectural papers in the 100,000 to 550,000 range. Kawai Ryosuke, *Yoron to masu komyunikēshiyon* (Public opinion and the mass media) (Tokyo: Bureen Shuppan, 1989), 59.

46. Foreign Press Center Japan, *Japan's Mass Media*, 73. The weeklies and monthlies come in a number of different genres. There are "general interest" magazines such as the newspaper-affiliated weeklies *Shukan asahi, Sunday mainichi,* and *Shukan yomiuri,* and publication company weeklies such as *Shukan bunshun, Shukan post,* and *Shukan hoseki.* Monthly general interest magazines include *Views, Bart,* and *Marco Polo.* There are also weekly women's magazines, including *Josei jisshin, Shukan josei,* and *Josei seven,* and the women's monthly *Shufu no tomo.* Economic and business weeklies include *Shukan economisto, Shukan tokyo keizei,* and *Shukan daimondo,* among others.

47. Ivan P. Hall, *Cartels of the Mind: Japan's Intellectual Closed Shop* (New York: W.W. Norton, 1998), 50.

48. Amano Katsufumi, Matsuoka Yukio, and Ueda Yasuo, eds., *Genba kara mita masu komi gaku II* (The mass media experience II) (Tokyo: Gakubunsha, 1996), 179. The article in question was a forty-page report entitled "*Tanaka kakuei no kenkyū—sono kinmyaku to jinmyaku*" (A study of Tanaka Kakuei—His financial and personal ties).

49. Foreign Press Center Japan, *Japan's Mass Media*, 55.

50. Ibid., "Introduction."

51. Susan J. Pharr and Ellis S. Krauss, *Media and Politics in Japan* (Honolulu: University of Hawaii Press, 1996), 92. Krauss describes the NHK evening news as it was in 1983; changes have occurred in format and style since then.

52. Ibid., 117.

53. Ellis S. Krauss, "Changing Television News in Japan," *Journal of Asian Studies* 57, 3 (August 1998): 689–90.

54. The quote comes from Hall, *Cartels of the Mind*, 49. For a detailed study of NHK, see Krauss, "Portraying the State: NHK Television News and Politics," *Media and Politics in Japan*, ed. Pharr and Krauss, 89–129.

55. Circulations figures are from 1995. See Inaba Michio and Arai Naoyuki, eds., *Shimbungaku* (Newspaper studies), 3d ed. (Tokyo: Nihon Hyōronsha, 1995), 304.

56. Kawai points out that in Britain the largest-selling paper is not the quality paper, *The Times*, but the popular paper, *The Sun*. Newspapers with the largest circulations in Germany, France, and Italy are also popular as opposed to quality papers. See Kawai, *Yoron to masu komyunikēshiyon*, 64.

57. Although it is sometimes suggested (more frequently in the 1960s than now) that Japanese newspapers can be categorized according to political ideology, with *Asahi* the most progressive, *Mainichi* in between, and *Yomiuri* and then *Sankei* on the right, at least in comparison with the partisan papers in Europe, the Japanese press does not generally exhibit clear political views in terms of their editorial policies. Indeed, a very rigidly defined notion of "objectivity" prevails in Japan today, much as it did in the late nineteenth century. See chapter 2.

58. Amano Katsufumi, Matsuoka Yukio, and Murakami Takashi, eds., *Genba kara mita masu komi gaku* (The mass media experience) (Tokyo: Gakubunsha, 1996), 7.

59. Ibid., 12–13.

60. Foreign Press Center Japan, *Japan's Mass Media*, 35.

61. Young C. Kim, *Japanese Journalists and Their World* (Charlottesville: University Press of Virginia, 1981).

62. Taketoshi Yamamoto, "The Press Clubs of Japan," *Journal of Japanese Studies* 15, 2 (Summer 1989): 371–88; the quotation is from 375.

63. Nihon Shimbun Kyōkai Kenkyūjo, *2000-nen no shimbun: Shimbun medea no chūchōki bijyon sōgo kenkyū hōkokushō* (Newspapers in the year 2000: The final report on the mid- to long-term vision for the newspaper media) (Tokyo: Nihon Shimbun Kyōkai Kenkyūjo, 1989), 241. This survey of editors belonging to the association was conducted in June 1989.

64. Ofer Feldman, *Politics and the News Media in Japan* (Ann Arbor: University of Michigan Press, 1993), 16.

65. Foreign Press Center Japan, *Japan's Mass Media*, 30.

66. See Krasner, *Defending the National Interest*; Kabashima and Broadbent, "Referent Pluralism"; and Karel van Wolferen, *The Enigma of Japanese Power: People and Politics in a Stateless Nation* (London: Macmillan, 1989), for respective examples of these views.

67. For a thorough explanation of these differing perspectives, see Krauss and Pharr, *Media and Politics in Japan*. In addition to these three perspectives, Pharr offers an intriguing alternative—the media as "trickster," marked by a dual insider-outsider status and eluding control by any single group in Japanese society. In the trickster image, the mass media is seen as less predictable than in the other images. We return to this discussion in chapter 6.

68. We return to a more detailed discussion of the coconspirator role in the final chapter.

Chapter Two
Press, Politics, and the Public in Historical Perspective

1. Stephen E. Koss, *The Nineteenth Century,* vol. 1 of *The Rise and Fall of the Political Press in Britain* (London: Hamish Hamilton, 1981), 2.

2. Michael Schudson, *Discovering the News: A Social History of American Newspapers* (New York: Basic Books, 1978), 30. Also see Craig J. Calhoun, ed., *Habermas and the Public Sphere* (Cambridge: MIT Press, 1992).

3. Yamamoto, "The Press Clubs of Japan." These restrictions were so severe that until 1841 one could not even mention the Tokugawa family name in a publication without threat of punishment.

4. James L. Huffman, *Politics of the Meiji Press: The Life of Fukuchi Gen'ichiro* (Honolulu: University of Hawaii Press, 1980), 15.

5. Inaba Michio and Arai Naohiro, eds., *Shimbungaku* (Newspaper studies) (Tokyo: Nihon Hyōronsha, 1988), 27.

6. Albert A. Altman, "Shimbunshi: The Early Meiji Adaptation of the Western-Style Newspaper," in *Modern Japan: Aspects of History, Literature and Society* (Berkeley: University of California Press, 1975), 52.

7. Ibid.; emphasis added.

8. Peter Duus, *The Rise of Modern Japan* (Boston: Houghton Mifflin, 1976), 55, 73.

9. Huffman, *Politics of the Meiji Press,* 48. This newspaper was not an indigenous paper but was merely a translation of the Dutch *Javansche Courant* published in Batavia (modern-day Jakarta). It was in circulation for less than two months.

10. Schudson, *Discovering the News,* 30.

11. Albert A. Altman, "The Press and Social Cohesion during a Period of Change: The Case of Early Meiji Japan," *Modern Asian Studies* 15, 4 (1981): 866.

12. Duus, *The Rise of Modern Japan,* 55.

13. Toward the end of the Tokugawa period, Japan had been forced to sign a number of treaties with the Western powers that forced open several ports to foreign trade. These treaties had also given foreigners residing in Japan extraterritorial rights. At the same time China was rapidly being carved up into Western spheres of influence.

14. Altman, "The Press and Social Cohesion," 866.

15. Gregory J. Kasza, *The State and the Mass Media in Japan, 1918–1945* (Berkeley: University of California Press, 1988), 4.

16. Governor Iseki of Kanagawa Prefecture, for example, served as the patron of the *Yokohama mainichi shimbun,* Japan's first daily, while Kido Kōin (a prominent Meiji leader and member of the Iwakura mission) provided the funding for Yamagata Tokuzō to start the *Shimbun zasshi.* Likewise, Maejima Hisoka, the head of the newly established postal service and later Japan's first postal minister, financially supported the *Yūbin hōchi shimbun.*

17. It is worth quoting in full Black's rationale for publishing this paper: "Neither [the *Yokohama mainichi* nor the *Tokyo nichi nichi*] dared to write leading articles nor to comment seriously on the occurrences of the day; and their columns were always defaced with such filthy paragraphs as to render them worse than

contemptible in the eyes of foreigners; though they appeared to be enjoyed by the Japanese, who, for the most part, had no conception of what a newspaper was, nor what were its uses." Black would later be tricked into giving the paper up when in 1874 the government established a decree forbidding foreigners from owning, publishing, or editing Japanese-language newspapers. In Harry Emerson Wildes, *Social Currents in Japan, with Special Reference to the Press* (Chicago: University of Chicago Press, 1927), 21, 23. See also Kanesada Hanazono, *The Development of Japanese Journalism* (Tokyo: Tokyo Nichi Nichi, 1934), 23.

18. James L. Huffman, "The Meiji Roots and Contemporary Practices of the Japanese Press," *The Japan Interpreter* 11, 4 (Spring 1977): 459.

19. Peter Figdor, "Newspapers and Their Regulation in Early Meiji Japan: 1868–1883," in *Papers on Japan*, vol. 6 (Cambridge: East Asian Research Center, Harvard University, 1972): 8–9.

20. Richard H. Mitchell, *Censorship in Imperial Japan* (Princeton: Princeton University Press, 1983), 41; emphasis added. Naturally, the four papers receiving this preferential treatment—the *Tokyo nichi nichi shimbun, Shimbun zasshi, Yokohama mainichi shimbun,* and *Nisshin shinjishi*—were all those listed earlier as having close ties to influential government leaders through their financial sponsorship.

21. Ibid., 41–42.

22. Figdor, "Newspapers," 9.

23. Wildes suggests, for example, that not only was the *Yokohama mainichi* "openly assisted by the Yokohama district governor Iseki, but it was also allotted use of the *Motogi* steel type." Wildes, *Social Currents*, 20.

24. Takashi Itō and George Akita, "The Yamagata-Tokutomi Correspondence: Press and Politics in Meiji-Taishō Japan," *Monumenta Nipponica* 36, 4 (1981): 391–423; the quotation is from 400.

25. Ibid., 401; emphasis added.

26. Ibid., 402. Additionally, Huffman notes that during the popular rights movement the government sought unsuccessfully to buy off a number of papers. In Huffman, *Politics of the Meiji Press*, 147.

27. Ariyama Teruo, *Kindai Nihon jaanarizumu no kōzō: Osaka asahi shimbun shironiji jiken zengo* (The structure of modern Japanese journalism: Before and after the White Rainbow Incident) (Tokyo: Tokyo Shuppan, 1995), 135.

28. Itō and Akita, "Yamagata-Tokutomi Correspondence."

29. Wildes, *Social Currents*, 56.

30. Yamamoto Taketoshi, *Shimbun kisha no tanjō: Nihon no medea o tsukutta hitobito* (The birth of newspaper journalists: The people who created the Japanese media) (Tokyo: Shinyosha, 1990).

31. Wildes, *Social Currents*, 56.

32. Wildes also notes that a "Mr. Matsui declares that it is quite a common matter for newspapermen assigned to political headquarters, government offices, large corporations and similar news centers to receive allowances from such places." Ibid.

33. Mitchell, *Censorship*, 3.

34. Figdor, "Newspapers," 3.

35. Ibid.

36. Kasza, *State and the Mass Media in Japan*, 4.

37. Inaba and Arai, *Shimbungaku*, 47.

38. Mitchell, *Censorship*, 26.

39. Harry Emerson Wildes, "Press Freedom in Japan," *American Journal of Sociology* 32, 4 (January 1927): 603.

40. Figdor, "Newspapers," 8.

41. Katsura Keiichi, *Iwanami bukkuretto no.15: Meiji-Taishō no jaanarizumu* (Iwanami booklet no. 15: Journalism in the Meiji-Taishō period) (Tokyo: Iwanami Shoten. 1992), 12.

42. Wildes, "Press Freedom in Japan," 603.

43. Kasza, *State and the Mass Media in Japan*, 7.

44. Ibid. Duus also notes that these "jail editors" were "nominally in charge of the paper, but in fact hired to suffer imprisonment if the paper infringed the libel laws." Duus, *Rise of Modern Japan*, 99.

45. Kasza, *State and the Mass Media in Japan*, 8.

46. Mitchell, *Censorship*, 151, x.

47. Ibid., 234–35.

48. Ibid., 236.

49. Kasza, *State and the Mass Media*, 169.

50. Ibid., 123.

51. Mitchell, *Censorship*, x.

52. Kasza, *State and the Mass Media*, 172–73.

53. Wildes, *Social Currents*, 105, 113.

54. Mitchell, *Censorship*, 199, 240. *Fuseji* means literally to "suppress a passage."

55. Ibid., 126.

56. Andrew E. Barshay, *State and Intellectual in Imperial Japan: The Public Man in Crisis* (Berkeley: University of California Press, 1988), 16.

57. Huffman, "Meiji Roots," 460.

58. Duus, *Rise of Modern Japan*, 99.

59. Huffman, "Meiji Roots," 460.

60. Yamamoto Taketoshi, *Shimbun to minshū* (Newspapers and democracy) (Tokyo: Kinokuniya Shinsho, 1994), 8–9.

61. See Itō and Akita, "Yamagata-Tokutomi Correspondence"; John D. Pierson, *Tokutomi Sohō, 1893–1957: A Journalist for Modern Japan* (Princeton: Princeton University Press, 1980); and Huffman, *Politics of the Meiji Press*.

62. See Huffman, *Politics of the Meiji Press*, 147–48.

63. In the end, however, political crises prevented the publication of that paper. See Yamamoto, *Shimbun to minshū*, 14; see also Huffman, *Politics of the Meiji Press*, 131.

64. Kisaburo Kawabe, *The Press and Politics in Japan: A Study of the Relation between the Newspaper and the Political Development of Modern Japan* (Chicago: University of Chicago Press, 1921). Kawabe notes, for example, that Ki Inukai (leader of the Kokumintō or Nationalist party and a former minister of education), Katsundo Minoura, and Yukio Ozaki (leaders of the *Kenseikai* who also held ministerial posts) all worked for the *Yūbin hōchi*, while Viscount Takaaki Kato (leader of the Kenseikai, an ambassador, and member of the imperial cabinet) was presi-

dent of the *Tokyo nichi nichi*. Others who worked for important papers included Gijin Okuta (mayor of Tokyo, vice-minister, and president of the Bureau of Legislation), who wrote for the *Meiji shimpō*, and Saburo Shimada (a member of the Kenseikai and ex-speaker of the House of Representatives), who was editor-in-chief of the *Nichi nichi* for a number of years. Seiji Hayakawa (ex-vice-speaker of the House of Representatives) and Tokitoshi Takemori (ex-minister of finance) were also former journalists, as were the Marquis Saionji (twice premier and the chief delegate to the Paris Peace Conference), Masahisa Matsuda, late Viscount Munemitsu Mutsu, Viscount Miyoji Itō, and many other distinguished statesmen. Additionally, Takashi Hara (leader of the Seiyukai and premier) first wrote for the *Hōchi* and later became editor-in-chief of the *Osaka mainichi* and *Osaka shimpō*.

65. Wildes, *Social Currents*, 46.

66. Yamamoto, *Shimbun kisha no tanjō*, 286. When officials were unable to control the press at this level, they would move a stage up and utilize the institutional links between editors and high-ranking officials. In 1918, for example, when a dispute broke out between government bureaucrats and the members of one of the *kisha* clubs, the government turned to the newspapers' own association, the Shunjū-kai, to mediate the dispute. Ultimately, the editors sided with the government officials and not their own journalists.

67. Yamamoto, "The Press Clubs of Japan," 383.

68. Ibid. Also see Ariyama Teruo, *Kindai Nihon jaanarizumu no kōzō*, 124, 131. Ariyama notes that in 1916 the Shunjū-kai invited Prime Minister Terauchi and Home Minister Goto to their fall meeting. Two years later, Terauchi invited the members of this association to the prime minister's official residence, hoping to use the association as his "pipe" to the newspaper world.

69. Nor was this pattern of political patronage and allegiance to the state limited to the Tokyo papers. As Mitchell has pointed out, "Local officials, too, adopted the official patronage pattern. While the relationship between newspapers and authorities varied in each area, in many cases it was so intimate that it is impossible to disentangle the private from the official." Mitchell, *Censorship*, 40.

70. Figdor, "Newspapers," 9; emphasis added.

71. Thomas C. Leonard, *The Power of the Press: The Birth of American Political Reporting* (New York: Oxford University Press, 1986), 57.

72. Yamamoto, *Shimbun kisha no tanjō*, 90.

73. Ibid., 30. Yamamoto notes that "at best the period in which the *minken-ha* papers were prominent lasted a decade, and possibly only 2–3 years, depending how you measure their period of ascendancy."

74. Mitchell, *Censorship*, 33.

75. Yamamoto, *Shimbun kisha no tanjō*, 9.

76. Kawabe, *Press and Politics*, 65; and Mitchell, *Censorship*, 44.

77. Mitchell, *Censorship*, 45.

78. Yamamoto, *Shimbun to minshū*, 8–9; and Yamamoto, *Shimbun kisha no tanjō*, 92.

79. Fukuchi Genichirō had petitioned his friend Itō Hirobumi in order to obtain patronage status.

80. Inaba and Arai, *Shimbungaku*, 29.

81. I adopt Carol Gluck's translation here. See Carol Gluck, *Japan's Modern Myths: Ideology in the Late Meiji Period* (Princeton: Princeton University Press, 1985), 58–59.

82. Inaba and Arai, *Shimbungaku*, 28–29.

83. Katsura, *Iwanami bukkuretto* no. 15, 13–14.

84. Duus, *Rise of Modern Japan*, 114, 101.

85. Mitchell, *Censorship*, 68.

86. Kasza, *State and the Mass Media*, 5–6.

87. Kawabe, *Press and Politics*, 75. See also Katsura, *Iwanami bukkuretto* no. 15, 19.

88. Inaba and Arai, *Shimbungaku*, 30. In 1882 thirty-four papers nationwide were allied with the "progressive" Kaishintō (headed by Okuma Shigenobu and including the *Yūbin hōchi shimbun* and *Yokohama mainichi*); twenty-one with the "liberal" Jiyūtō (headed by Itagake and including *Jiyū shimbun* and *Chōya shimbun*), and twenty with the government-backed Teishintō (*Nichi nichi* and *Meiji nippō*).

89. Katsura, *Iwanami bukkuretto* no. 15, 13–14.

90. Inaba and Arai, *Shimbungaku*, 30–31.

91. Yamamoto, *Shimbun kisha no tanjō*, 18. See also Katsura, *Iwanami bukkuretto* no. 15, 15.

92. See Yamamoto, *Shimbun kisha no tanjō*, 188. *Hanbatsu* or "clique" government refers to the fact that only members of the oligarchy were allowed to hold such important posts as prime minister or minister. As Duus notes, "Down until 1901 all of the premiers were drawn from the ranks of the oligarchy and so were most key ministerial posts. The only junior figures admitted to the cabinet were senior bureaucrats, like Katsura Tarō or Saionji Kimmochi, who enjoyed the special trust of one or the other of the oligarchic leaders. In popular parlance this cozy political cronyism was known as *hanbatsu seiji* or 'clique government.' " Duus, *Rise of Modern Japan*, 155.

93. Yamamoto, *Shimbun to minshū*, 69. Duus also suggests that the establishment of the Diet was one of the factors in the decline of these papers, having provided an alternative locus for the discussion of political issues that was "free from police harassment and unhindered by press laws." Duus, *Rise of Modern Japan*, 156.

94. Yamamoto, *Shimbun kisha no tanjō*, 32. He also suggests that in taking positions in the government these journalists gave a bad image to the antigovernment faction and its papers. Ibid., 156.

95. Gluck, *Japan's Modern Myths*, 66.

96. Ironically, in 1909, in a period of Diet ascendancy, party politicians, in an unintentionally vengeful act, voted "to restrict media autonomy rather than to enhance it" by passing the landmark "Newspaper Law," which would remain in effect until the end of the war. See Kasza, *State and the Mass Media*, 15.

97. Yamamoto, *Shimbun kisha no tanjō*, 188.

98. Gluck, *Japan's Modern Myths*, 50.

99. Inaba and Arai, *Shimbungaku*, 31.

100. Koichi Saburo, "Masu media to ideorogii: 'Chūritsusei,' 'tōhasei' no rekishiteki keifu" (Mass media and ideology: The historical lineage of words such

as "neutrality" and "partisanship"), *Shisō*, no. 403 (January 1958): 96–113. The quotation is from 97.

101. Katsura, *Iwanami bukkuretto* no. 15.
102. Yamamoto, *Shimbun to minshū*, 30.
103. Ibid., 33.
104. Wildes, *Social Currents*, 39, 45.
105. Ibid, 32–33.
106. Huffman, *Politics of the Meiji Press*, 156.
107. Katsura, *Iwanami bukkuretto* no. 15, 20.
108. Leonard, *Power of the Press*, 36, 9, 5.
109. Yamamoto, *Shimbun to minshū*, 31.
110. Gluck, *Japan's Modern Myths*, 50.
111. Katsura, *Iwanami bukkuretto* no. 15, 20.
112. Figdor, "Newspapers," 21.
113. Inaba and Arai, *Shimbungaku*, 29.
114. Ariyama, *Kindai Nihon jaanarizumu no kōzō*, 135.
115. Yamamoto, *Shimbun kisha no tanjō*, 297. See also Ariyama, *Kindai Nihon jaanarizumu no kōzō*, 136.
116. Ariyama, *Kindai Nihon jaanarizumu no kōzō*, 136.
117. Yamamoto, *Shimbun to minshū*, 35.
118. Ariyama, *Kindai Nihon jaanarizumu no kōzō*, 136.
119. Mitchell, *Censorship*, 96.
120. Ibid., 96–97.
121. Ibid., 97–99.
122. Ariyama, *Kindai Nihon jaanarizumu no kōzō*, 138.
123. Yamamoto, *Shimbun to minshū*, 35.
124. Ariyama, *Kindai Nihon jaanarizumu no kōzō*, 136.
125. Mitchell, *Censorship*, 99.
126. Yamamoto, *Shimbun kisha no tanjō*, 34.
127. Inaba and Arai, *Shimbungaku*, 31.
128. Yamamoto, *Shimbun kisha no tanjō*, 137.
129. Katsura, *Iwanami bukkuretto* no. 15, 22.
130. Wildes, *Social Currents*, 36.
131. Ibid., 28.
132. Inaba and Arai, *Shimbungaku*, 35.
133. Wildes notes of the *Yūbin hōchi* that "in 1882 it was bought by Fumio Yano, formerly a secretary in the treasury and a close friend of Marquis Okuma. For over forty years the paper was regarded as the special spokesman of that statesman, and it was the administration mouthpiece whenever Okuma or his supporters were in power. Yano sold the paper at about the time of the Sino-Japanese war to other friends of Okuma, but the journal has never quite won independence from official sources. In 1910 its president was Katsundo Minoura, a veteran politician and a former Cabinet Minister. Minoura was succeeded by Dr. Juichi Soyeda, the first president of the Bank of Formosa and of the Japan Industrial Bank, former head of the Imperial Railways and a vice minister. When Soyoda retired, in 1923, when Hochi passed out from Okuma influence, Chuji Machida, formerly of the

Bank of Japan and an under-secretary of the Department of Communications, became its president." Wildes, *Social Currents*, 31.

134. Inaba and Arai, *Shimbungaku*, 36.

135. Wildes notes that the *Yomiuri*'s first editor's early "detachment from the openly propagandist press and his retention of Yukio Ozaki (formerly of *Hōchi*, and a famous liberal) on his staff gave to *Yomiuri* a reputation for radicalism and for 'yellowness' which was wholly undeserved." Wildes, *Social Currents*, 33.

136. Ibid., 33, 35.

137. Inaba and Arai, *Shimbungaku*, 36. See also Wildes, *Social Currents*, 33.

138. Inaba and Arai, *Shimbungaku*, 34.

139. Itō Hirobumi first used the term only a few days after the inauguration of the constitution when he explained the theory of "transcendental cabinets" (*chō-zen naikaku*), or "nonpartisan cabinets responsible to the emperor and not to the Diet." See Duus, *Rise of Modern Japan*, 155; and Gluck, *Japan's Modern Myths*, 58–59.

140. Yamamoto, *Shimbun to minshū*, 188.

141. Gluck, *Japan's Modern Myths*, 58.

142. Yamamoto, *Shimbun to minshū*, 199.

143. As Yamamoto notes, "it was precisely at that point in time when the government maintained its greatest ability to suppress the parties and the public . . . that the news-oriented papers (*hōdō shimbun*) had become the popular form in the industry and adopted the standardized editorial policy of 'impartiality and nonpartisanship.' " Ibid., 188.

144. Ibid.

145. The White Rainbow Incident resulted from an article published in 1918 by the *Osaka asahi shimbun* in which the paper made reference to a phrase from the Chinese classics—"the white rainbow pierced the sun" (*hakkō hi o tsura-nuku*)—that government officials understood to be an assassination threat against the emperor. For a detailed explanation of this incident and its aftermath, see Barshay, *State and Intellectual*, 152–55.

146. *Sōgō janarizumu kenkyū*, no. 116, special edition: "Kisha kurabu no kōzai" (The merits and demerits of the press clubs) (Tokyo: Tokyosha, 1986): 5–35.

147. These included the *Jiji shimpō*, *Yomiuri shimbun*, *Tokyo nichi nichi shimbun*, *Yūbin hōchi*, *Asano shimbun*, *Mainichi shimbun*, *Yamato shimbun*, *Tokyo asahi shimbun*, *Miyako shimbun*, and *Nihon shimbun*. See Nihon Shimbun Kyōkai, ed., *Shimbun no shuzai* (Newspaper reporting), vol. 2 (Tokyo: Nihon Shimbun Kyōkai, 1968), 270. This book is extremely hard to obtain, having been removed from public circulation by the NSK after pressure from the Burakumin, a group of historical outcasts in Japan who were offended by a passage in the book. I was able to obtain only the section on the *kisha* clubs from a source in the NSK who kindly copied it for me, but who shall remain anonymous.

148. Later the name was changed again to the Dōmei Shimbun Kisha Kurabu. The *Shimbun kenkyū* article of 1965 cites a *Nihon shimbun nenkan* of 1925 as saying that the Domei Kisha Kurabu was "composed of those nationwide daily papers and news agencies which had obtained authorization from the government and which had published continuously for two years or more." Today it is known as the Kokkai Kisha Kai. Nihon Shimbun Kyōkai, ed., *Shimbun kenkyū* (April 1965): 44.

149. Yamamoto, "The Press Clubs of Japan," 379.

150. Included among these were the Gaikō Kenkyūkai (later known as the Kasumi club), established in the Ministry of Foreign Affairs shortly after the end of the Sino-Japanese War. Other early press clubs included those established in the Ministry of Commerce and Industry (the Uneme club, founded in 1902), the War Ministry (the *Hokutokai* or Big Dipper club, established in 1904), party headquarters of the Seiyukai (the Tokkakai or Tenth Day Club), and another established in the Ministry of Justice in 1905. Other places that established clubs in this early period were the Home Affairs Ministry (the Ote club, established in 1907) and the club founded in 1910 in the Tokyo Stock Exchange (the Kabuto club). Nihon Shimbun Kyōkai, ed., *Shimbun kenkyū*.

151. Yamamoto, "The Press Clubs of Japan," 381.

152. Duus notes that the Japanese public was angry that the government had not forced the Russians to pay an indemnity to defray war costs. Because the Japanese press had only reported Japan's victories and not "how tightly pressed the government had been in the last months of the war," the public had felt humiliated by the Portsmouth settlement. See Duus, *Rise of Modern Japan*, 134.

153. Yamamoto, "The Press Clubs of Japan," 371–88.

154. Ibid., 382.

155. Nihon Shimbun Kyōkai, ed., *Shimbun no shuzai* (Newspaper reporting) (Tokyo: Nihon Shimbun Kyōkai, 1968), 279.

156. Yamamoto, "The Press Clubs of Japan," 385.

157. William J. Coughlin, *Conquered Press: The MacArthur Era in Japanese Journalism* (Palo Alto: Pacific Books, 1952), 9. Coughlin also notes that by this time "provincial papers, incidentally, often complained bitterly of exclusion from these clubs." Ibid.

158. *Sōgo janarizumu kenkyū*, no. 116, 17.

159. Nihon Shimbun Kyōkai, *Shimbun no shuzai*, 284. See also *Sōgo jaanarizumu kenkyū*, vol. 116, 17.

160. Yamamoto, "The Press Clubs of Japan," 387, n. 37.

161. Mainichi Shimbun Shakaibu, *Jōhō demokurashii* (Information democracy) (Tokyo: Mainichi Shimbunsha, 1992), 212.

162. Ariyama, *Kindai Nihon jaanarizumu no kōzō*, 141.

163. Nihon Shimbun Kyōkai, *Shimbun no shuzai*, 91.

164. Ibid.

165. In 1943 this association was abolished and replaced with the government-backed Japan Newspaper Association (Nihon Shimbunkai), which included the managers and editors of key newspapers as well as a number of government bureaucrats hoping to "guide" the newspaper industry as it pursued its national mission.

166. Nihon Shimbun Kyōkai, *Shimbun no shuzai*, 288.

167. Arai Naohiro, *Jaanarizumu* (Journalism) (Tokyo: Toyo Keizai Shimposha, 1977), 20.

168. Nihon Shimbun Kyōkai, ed., *Nihon Shimbun Kyōkai 10-nen shi* (A ten-year history of the NSK) (Tokyo: Nihon Shimbun Kyōkai, 1955), 19.

169. Prior to the introduction of this reform, many of the clubs had rather distinctive names. The reform introduced a standard formula for deriving the name of a club: each club name was to begin with the name of the ministry or

organization to which it was affiliated, followed by the word "*kai*" (club or association).

170. Ibid., 17.

171. Nihon Shimbun Kyōkai, *Shimbun no shuzai*, 286, 287; emphasis added.

172. Kazue Suzuki, "The Press Club System in Japan," M.S. thesis, Iowa State University, 1982, 120.

173. Nihon Shimbun Kyōkai, *Nihon Shimbun Kyōkai 10-nen shi*, 19, 20; emphasis added.

174. Ibid.

175. Suzuki, *Press Club System*, 237.

176. Coughlin, *Conquered Press*, 11.

177. Ibid., 20.

178. Edward S. Herman and Noam Chomsky, *Manufacturing Consent: The Political Economy of the Mass Media* (New York: Random House, 1988), 43.

179. Ibid., 23.

180. Coughlin, *Conquered Press*, 67.

181. Ibid., 67, 23.

182. Ibid., 66.

183. Ibid., 86; emphasis added. It is assumed that this referred to the Press and Publications Division itself.

184. Ibid., 87.

185. Ibid., 165.

186. Nihon Shimbun Kyōkai, *Nihon Shimbun Kyōkai 10-nen shi*, 165.

187. Ibid.

188. Nihon Shimbun Kyōkai, *Shimbun no shuzai*, 164.

189. See, for example, D. Eleanor Westney, *Imitation and Innovation: The Transfer of Western Organizational Patterns to Meiji Japan* (Cambridge: Harvard University Press, 1987).

190. Herbert Passin, "Writer and Journalist in the Transitional Society," in *Communications and Political Development*, ed. Lucian W. Pye (Princeton: Princeton University Press, 1963), 8.

191. Sven Steinmo, Kathlen Thelen, and Frank Longstreth, eds., *Structuring Politics: Historical Institutionalism in Comparative Analysis* (Cambridge: Cambridge University Press, 1992), 3.

192. Calhoun, *Habermas and the Public Sphere*, 153.

193. Schudson, *Discovering the News*, 4.

194. Barshay, *State and Intellectual*, 8.

195. Robert D. Putnam, *Making Democracy Work: Civic Traditions in Modern Italy* (Princeton: Princeton University Press, 1993), 179.

Chapter Three
Japan's Information Cartels
Part I. Competition and the Closed Shop

1. Leon V. Sigal, *Reporters and Officials: The Organization and Politics of Newsmaking* (Lexington, Mass.: D. C. Heath, 1973), xv.

2. Anthony Smith, ed., *Newspapers and Democracy: International Essays on a Changing Medium* (Cambridge: MIT Press, 1980), x.

3. Sigal, *Reporters and Officials*, 124.

4. Hara Toshio, "Happyō jaanarizumu jidai e no teikō" (Resisting announcement journalism) *Shimbun kenkyū* (December 1979): 21.

5. John Eatwell, Murray Milgate, and Peter Newman, eds., *The New Palgrave: A Dictionary of Economics*, vol. 1 (London: Macmillan; New York: Stockton Press; Tokyo: Maruzen, 1987), 531.

6. Powe, *The Fourth Estate and the Constitution*.

7. Robert Entman and Steven Wildman, "Reconciling Economic and Non-Economic Perspectives on Media Policy: Transcending the 'Marketplace of Ideas,' " *Journal of Communication* 42, 1 (Winter 1992): 5–19; the quotation is from p. 7.

8. James Curran and Michael Gurevitch, eds., *Mass Media and Society* (London: Edward Arnold, 1991), 84.

9. According to Martin Linsky, "In 1923, 795 communities in the United States had only a single newspaper or two newspapers with single ownership. There were 1,362 such communities in 1953 and over 1,500 by 1978." Linsky, "The Media and Public Deliberation," in *The Power of Public Ideas*, ed. Robert B. Reich (Cambridge, Mass.: Ballinger, 1988), 208.

10. Entman and Wildman, "Reconciling," 12.

11. Curran and Gurevitch, *Mass Media and Society*, 84.

12. Smith, *Newspapers and Democracy*, xi.

13. John A. Lent, *The Asian Newspapers' Reluctant Revolution* (Ames: Iowa State University Press, 1971), 121–24.

14. Sigal, *Reporters and Officials*, 5, 53.

15. Ibid., 38, 52–53.

16. For a fascinating account of pool reporting during the Gulf War and the media's reaction to it, see Hedrick Smith, ed., *The Media and the Gulf War: The Press and Democracy in Wartime* (Washington, D.C.: Seven Locks Press, 1992).

17. Jeremy Tunstall, *The Westminster Lobby Correspondents: A Sociological Study of National Political Journalism* (London: Routledge & Kegan Paul, 1970), 12.

18. Ibid., 52.

19. Anthony Smith suggests that the newspaper "continues to see its role within society as a mediator of public opinion, as a broker of information between authority and society, and as an inciter of public sentiment when governmental action appears misjudged." See his *Newspapers and Democracy*, xiii.

20. Entman and Wildman also suggest that there are "limitations in the constructs implied by the 'marketplace of ideas' metaphor." See their "Reconciling," 5.

21. Japanese call the clubs *kisha kurabu* (*kisha* meaning one who records or writes, and *kurabu* being the Japanese rendering of the English word "club").

22. Inaba Yutaka, *Kisha kurabu o kiru* (Criticizing the press clubs) (Tokyo: Nisshin Hōdō Shuppanbu, 1978), 14.

23. In fact, there are two *kisha* clubs in NHK. Although NHK does not receive direct funding from the government and gets its revenue from subscription fees, its Board of Governors, which makes all major budgetary and programming decisions, is appointed by the prime minister with Diet approval.

24. Kawai, *Yoron to masu komyunikēshiyon*, 137.

25. Nishiyama Takesuke, *Za riiku: Shimbun hōdō no ura-omote* (Both sides of news report leaks) (Tokyo: Kodansha, 1992), 123.

26. *Asahi shimbun*, February 2, 1993, morning edition.

27. Nishiyama, *Za riiku*, 151.

28. The local papers have extremely limited access to official government sources in Tokyo.

29. The latter club is comprised of social affairs journalists from ten different media outlets and was apparently formed when these companies broke off from the larger Tsūsan Kishakai in 1970. Noted in Kyodo Tsushin Shakaibu, ed., *Kyodo Tsūshin shakaibu* (The Kyodo Wire Service social affairs desk) (Tokyo: Kyodo Tsu-shinsha, 1992), 177.

30. Nihon Zasshi Kishakai, *Nihon Zasshi Kishakai 25-nenshi* (Twenty-five-year history of the Japan Magazine Publishers Association) (Tokyo: Nihon Zasshi Ki-shakai, 1985). This association also functions as a kind of media cartel for the magazine press.

31. According to one report, a journalist's influence is based on a 1–4 ranking depending on what happens once inside a politician's house. At the first and lowest level, the journalist is allowed to stay in a 4.5-mat tatami room at the entrance and is greeted by the politician with a "good morning." Coffee is served. At the second level, he or she is allowed to enter the living room. Japanese sake is served. The third level can be reached only if one has graduated from the same university as the politician or is related to someone powerful. Here, one is allowed to enter the politician's study and, even if the politician is not there, can help oneself to Remy Martin. It is said that the highest class of journalists can nap in the politician's bedroom. Naminorisha, ed., *Yajiuma masu komi kōza* (Yajiuma mass media semi-nar) (Tokyo: Kōshobo, 1987), 51.

32. Kido Mataichi et al., eds., *Kōzō gendai jānarizumu II: Shimbun* (The struc-ture of modern journalism II: Newspapers) (Tokyo: Jiji Tsushinsha, 1973), 85.

33. Nihon Shimbun Kyōkai, ed., *Nihon Shimbun Kyōkai Kenkyūjo nenpō*, no. 12 (1994), 32.

34. The Prime Minister's Office PR room (*kōhōshitsu*) was established in July 1960 at the same time the Ikeda cabinet was established. Kido et al., eds., *Kōzō gendai jānarizumu II*, 153–54.

35. Nishiyama, *Za riiku*, 133.

36. Kawai, *Yoron to masu komyunikēshiyon*, 198. In terms of the extent of gov-ernment PR activities, there are those of the Prime Minister's Office (which in-cludes two PR offices—the cabinet chief secretary's PR room and the cabinet prime minister's secretary's PR room) as well as those in each of the major minis-tries and government offices. In 1985 the amount for the Prime Minister's Office was twelve billion yen, and it is thought that each ministry has about the same amount.

37. Kawai Masayoshi, *Nyūsu hōdō shuzai no shikumi ga wakaru hon* (Under-standing news reports and newsgathering) (Tokyo: Asuka, 1992), 183.

38. Nishiyama, *Za riiku*, 132.

39. Discussed in Kyodo Tsūshin Shakaibu, *Kyodo Tsūshin Shakaibu*, 177.

40. Mainichi Shimbun Shakaibu, *Jōhō demokurashii*, 132–33.

41. Amano Katsufumi, "Torikomareru jaanarizumu" (Co-opted journalists), *Sōgo jaanarizumu kenkyū* (1989): 46–52.

42. Nishiyama, *Za riiku*, 129–30.

43. Elizabeth Roy, *Look Japan* (September 1991): 13.

44. Yamamoto, "The Press Clubs of Japan," 371–88; esp. 378.

45. With respect to the payment of bills for outside phone lines, 63.6 percent of the clubs in special government agencies reported that their phone bills were paid by the source, and 62.8 percent of the city hall clubs, 62.5 percent of the clubs in general companies, and 61.7 percent of clubs in urban and rural prefectures experienced the same. Thirty percent of the sports clubs and 6.7 percent of those in central government agencies said that they received this benefit. Data are from the organ of the *Mainichi shimbun* labor union, *Honryū*, August 26, 1993.

46. Journalists have adopted a slightly different set of rules for mah-jongg to allow for the fact that frequently at least one of the players may have to leave without concluding the game.

47. *Honryū*, August 26, 1993.

48. Naminorisha, *Yajiuma masu komi kōza*, 90.

49. Ibid., 91.

50. Unpublished documents from the Kanto branch of the labor union for Kyodo Tsūshin, one dated February 1992 and the other an undated outline of results from a survey of clubs for the period April 1991–January 1992.

51. Thomas W. Lippman, *The Washington Post Deskbook On Style*, 2d ed. (New York: McGraw-Hill, 1989); telephone interview with *Washington Post* spokesperson, September 18, 1994.

52. Telephone interview with *New York Times* spokesperson, September 18, 1994.

53. "Japan's Press Clubs—No Foreigners Need Apply," *Asian Wall Street Journal*, June 19, 1992 (originally published in *Tokyo shimbun*); emphasis added.

54. *Shimbun kenkyū* (April 1992).

55. *Honryū*, August 26, 1993.

56. Ibid.

57. Not-for-attribution comment by Kyodo journalist, January 1992.

58. Not-for-attribution interviews with high-ranking former employee of the LDP PR section, May 1994.

59. See *Asahi shimbun*, December 21, 1991, morning edition, pp. 23 and 31. Also: *Asahi shimbun*, February 11, 1992, p. 2 (Editorial) and p. 31.

60. Telephone interview with Joel Becchione, *New York Times*, September 18, 1994.

61. Emphasis added. Cited in Nishiyama, *Za riiku*, 125. William Nestor also refers to the clubs as "information cartels," without explicating the term. See Nestor, "Japan's Mainstream Press: Freedom to Conform?," *Pacific Affairs* 62, 1 (Spring 1989): 29–39, esp. p. 30.

62. Tilton, *Restrained Trade*.

63. *Herald Tribune*, June 16, 1993.

64. Hall, *Cartels of the Mind*.

65. Cartels may also require the intermediation of a trade association to guarantee their smooth functioning. The trade association can take on certain functions, which, although illegal, are difficult to detect. As Scherer points out, "Trade associations have often performed functions which ran afoul of the antitrust laws. Their meetings are superb vehicles for getting together and agreeing on prices, outputs,

market shares, etc." F. M. Scherer, *Industrial Market Structure and Economic Performance* (Chicago: Rand McNally, 1970), 449.

66. Philip Babcock Gove, ed. *Webster's Third New International Dictionary of the English Language*, unabridged; (Springfield, Mass.: G.&C. Merriam Co., 1981); emphasis added.

67. Eatwell, Milgate, and Newman, *The New Palgrave*, 372–74; emphasis added.

68. Ibid., 373.

69. Elaine Kurtenback, AP dispatch, January 25, 1990.

70. Interview with James Sterngold, *New York Times* Tokyo correspondent, May 1994.

71. In July 1993 the NSK recommended that the clubs begin to allow access to foreigners. Japanese journalists who are not members of the NSK have yet to be given access, and most foreigners are non-regular members.

72. Although figures are not available, local newspapers or broadcast companies do not have regular memberships in a sizable portion of the clubs in Tokyo's major government agencies.

73. Kawai, *Yoron to masu komyunikēshiyon*, 153 (1985 data).

74. Inaba, *Kisha kurabu o kiru*, 177. One might add *Nikkei* to this list.

75. It is important to keep in mind, too, that there are close business ties (or *keiretsu* linkages) between the five major national newspapers and the five national television stations. These relationships have been indicated with arrows in figure 7 and underscore the high degree of concentration among the Japanese media and firms belonging to the clubs. See chapter 5 for a more detailed discussion.

76. Regulations for the Nagata club dated July 1, 1984. These regulations also provide for membership by those foreign newspapers, news agencies, and broadcast companies that "carry out news activities similar to those of the members of the NSK."

77. Not-for-attribution interview with a "veteran Japanese journalist" on May 23, 1994.

78. NSK, "A New Guideline of the *Nihon Shimbun Kyōkai*'s Editorial Affairs Committee regarding the Kisha Club," June 10, 1993.

79. Not-for-attribution interview, May 1994. NSK's Tadokoro Izumi made the same comment on record.

80. Jung Bock Lee, *The Political Character of the Japanese Press* (Seoul: Seoul National University Press, 1985), 67.

81. Not-for-attribution interview with a "veteran Japanese journalist," May 23, 1994.

82. Interview with officials from the Zasshi Kyōkai (JMPA), May 23, 1994.

83. Smith, *Media and the Gulf War*, xi; emphasis added.

Chapter Four
Japan's Information Cartels
Part II. Structuring Relations through Rules and Sanctions

1. These agreements are also referred to as "gentlemen's agreements" (*shinshi kyōtei*), agreements made on the beat (*desaki kyōtei*), and embargoes (*shibari*).

2. Kawai, *Yoron to masu komyunikēshiyon*, 140.

3. In the case of broadcast stations, the time of broadcast is specified; in the case of newspapers, the agreement states whether the item is to appear in the morning or evening edition.

4. Nishiyama, *Za riiku*, 135.

5. Ibid., 136.

6. Oyama Ryosuke (pseudonym for a journalist in the judicial club), "Bunya 'deiri kinshi' no fushigi," in *Za shimbun* (The newspaper), ed. Ishii Masao (Tokyo: JICC Shuppankyoku, 1989), 173.

7. Data are from *Honryū*, August 26, 1993.

8. Inaba, *Kisha kurabu o kiru*, 125–26.

9. *Honryū*, August 26, 1993.

10. The Ministry of Foreign Affairs and other ministries have also been known to make formal agreements with the press to withhold stories. A recent case involved a MFA request for restraint during the Gulf War. Although the press abided by this request, later both the mainstream and nonmainstream press widely criticized the agreement.

11. These were particularly widespread during the illness and after the death of Emperor Hirohito.

12. Inaba, *Kisha kurabu o kiru*, 120.

13. Helen Hardacre, *Aum Shinrikyō and the Japanese Media: The Pied Piper Meets the Lamb of God* (New York: East Asian Institute, Columbia University, 1995), 18.

14. See, for example, Asano Kenichi, *Kagekiha hōdō no hanzai* (Reporting radicals unfairly) (Tokyo: Sanichi Shobo, 1990), and *Kyakkan hōdō* (Objective news reporting) (Tokyo: Chikuma Shobo, 1993).

15. The first comes from a personal interview with Hara Toshio, former president of Kyodo Tsushin, May 1994. The second comes from an unpublished paper by Maruyama Noboru, a media critic and author of a book on press agreements.

16. Other press agreements concluded in recent years between the mainstream media and government sources have also been widely criticized—most notably, the agreement between journalists in the MFA club and sources in the MFA not to report the movement of Japanese citizens in Kuwait during the Gulf War.

17. This is not to say that sources do not leak information to "trusted" journalists. But often when they do so they have to do it in such a manner that the other club members will not be able to detect it.

18. "Anything to Miss the Scoop," *The Economist*, July 27, 1991, 24.

19. Tarō Yayama, "The Newspapers Conduct a Mad Rhapsody over the Textbook Issue," *Journal of Japanese Studies* 9, 2 (Spring 1983): 304, 305.

20. Nishiyama describes conditions in most clubs as follows: "Usually *kisha* club journalists are able to conduct newsgathering while walking freely around the inside of the government ministries. The objects of their newsgathering (sources) cooperate with the members of the *kisha* club, and when a journalist from the same company who does not belong to the club comes to them, they keep their distance. . . . The club and the official agency become as one." Nishiyama, *Za riiku*, 93.

21. Asano Kenichi, *Hanzai hōdō to keisatsu* (Criminal reporting and the police) (Tokyo: Sanichi Shōbō, 1987), 111–34.

22. Nishiyama, *Za riiku*, 254–55.

23. Oyama, "Bunya 'deiri kinshi' no fushigi," 173.

24. Feldman, *Politics and the News Media in Japan*, 87. See also 82–93 for a useful description of *ban* and faction journalists.

25. Political journalists are said to feel greater affinity for other political journalists in the same club who come from competing news organizations than they do for a social affairs journalist from their own paper. Any sharing of information is much more likely to go on between rival political journalists than between a political and *shakaibu* journalists from the same company. Of course, in cases where journalists from the same newspaper but different bureaus are assigned to the same club, the outcome would be different. In such cases, these journalists are part of a team reporting the same beat or story, and they are expected to cooperate.

26. Mori Kyozo, "Questionable Attitude of News Reporters," *Japan Echo* 2, 1 (Spring 1975). Originally published in *Chuō Kōron* (January 1975).

27. Ibid.

28. Inaba, *Kisha kurabu o kiru*, 50–51.

29. Asano Kenichi, "Mainichi no 'satsumawari nyūmon' ni kaiteiru koto," *Za shimbun*, ed. Ishii Masao, 255.

30. This story is from Asano, *Kyakkan hōdō*, 177, 178.

31. Tase Yasuhiro, a twenty-year veteran political reporter and currently an editor of the *Nihon keizai shimbun* (Japan's *Wall Street Journal*), has argued that political journalists frequently confuse information about the political world (*seikai*) with information about politics (*seiji*). Tase Yasuhiro, *Seiji jaanarizumu no tsumi to batsu* (The crimes and punishments of political journalism) (Tokyo: Shinchosha, 1994), 7.

32. The social affairs section is also the most widely read section of the newspaper, with more than 50 percent of readers saying they read social affairs articles. Shimbun Kenkyū Dojinkai, *Shimbun handobukku* (Newspaper handbook) (Tokyo: Dabiddosha, 1990), 125.

33. They are not, however, necessarily the first to uncover these scandals. Frequently it is the magazine press that takes on this investigative role, in part because they are not constrained by the rules and obligations that press club membership entails. Although they have limited financial resources and small staffs, their major constraint is a lack of access due to their exclusion from the press clubs.

34. Honzawa Jiro, *Seiji kiji wa ura ga wakaru to omoshiroi* (The underside of political stories is interesting) (Tokyo: Yell Books, 1992), 55.

35. Journalists are assigned to one of these bureaus after an initial training period in the field and usually remain there for the duration of their careers as reporters, spending time in a number of bureau-related clubs. The club structure often closely follows this functional differentiation, with *shakaibu* journalists assigned to certain types of clubs and political and economic journalists dispatched to others. Naturally, some clubs include journalists from several bureaus.

36. In the Recruit case, once the story was broken by *Asahi*, each company formed its own news team. The members of these teams came mostly from the *shakaibu*, particularly from the press club in the prosecutor's office, though a num-

ber of *yūgun* (roving reporters) and a few political journalists were included among them.

37. The account here is taken from an article originally published in *Chūō kōron* and translated in the *Journal of Japanese Studies* 9, 2 (1983). See esp. 301, 304, 306–8, 311. Yayama describes the *sōkai* as follows: "These gatherings are basically friendly, and the more agreements are made at such gatherings, the less work each reporter has to do. In extreme cases, reporters can do their job just by sitting in the reporters' lounge all day." According to Yayama, the result of the vote was as follows: "Five were in favor, three opposed, five abstained (three of which were the three major dailies), and one did not vote." Ibid., 311.

38. *Shūkan hōseki*, November 1982, 44.

39. Another rule prohibits individual member organizations and nonclub members from obtaining exclusive interviews with the prime minister, a rule the Prime Minister's Office generally follows. A journalist or company that breaks this rule is kicked out of the club. Kawai, *Yoron to masu komyunikēshiyon*, 153.

40. Ibid., 153. This practice is also mentioned in Honzawa, *Seiji kiji wa ura ga wakaru to omoshiroi*, 21, and is relatively common. When journalists interview senior-level bureaucrats they also frequently submit questions in advance.

41. Ibid.

42. As detailed in chapter 2, the term *kondan* was originally used in reference to the informal mechanisms used for newspaper control and censorship during the wartime period. Nishiyama, *Za riiku*, 130.

43. Suzuki Kenji. "Nihon no shimbun: Aimai hyōgen jijō" (Japanese newspapers: A case of vague phrasing) *Shimbun kenkyū* (May 1990): 75.

44. While it has been argued that this means that the information gets out, the magazines often must write it as rumor, having gotten it secondhand. Consequently, readers never know what is unfounded gossip and what is true. In short, the magazine press does not have the aura of legitimacy that the newspaper press has, in part as a result of the system of journalism described here. They especially lack the legitimacy that comes with access to official sources. Ironically, as described earlier, such legitimacy also brings with it a heavy responsibility not to report what one knows. As a veteran journalist and editorial adviser of the *Asahi* once commented, "So far, the press has maintained the attitude of knowingly letting weeklies write everything their own way, on the ground that such magazines *do not command public trust.*" Kyozo, "Questionable Attitude," 40; emphasis added.

45. Kawakami Sumie, *Shimbun no himitsu* (Newspaper secrets) (Tokyo: JICC, 1990), 5–6.

46. Suzuki, "Nihon no shimbun," 76.

47. Interview with Mr. Tase Yasuhiro on November 30, 1994.

48. Suzuki, "Nihon no shimbun," 73.

49. Ibid., 76, 75.

50. Samuels, *The Business of the Japanese State*.

51. Eatwell, Milgate, and Newman, eds., *The New Palgrave*, 372–74.

52. Naturally, the phrase "harming the honor of the club" and related phrases are merely euphemisms for breaking club rules.

53. Regulations for the *Nagata* club, dated July 1, 1984.

54. This list was leaked to me by a journalist in the club, who shall remain anonymous.

55. This survey was conducted from May to June 1993. The questionnaire was sent to those clubs in which *Mainichi* journalists are present at least once a week. There were 444 responses, a response rate of about 80 percent.

56. *Honryū*, August 26, 1993, 2.

57. Ibid.

58. Club members also use this sanction to punish violators.

59. He also points out that one of the longest *deiri kinshi* on record was a four-month expulsion. The punishment is not always applied uniformly: sometimes a club member is excluded for only a week, and on other occasions exile lasts much longer. Ishii, *Za shimbun*, 168, 159.

60. The Tokyo prosecutor's office was founded in 1946. Throughout the post-war period it has been responsible for breaking, pursuing, and prosecuting some of Japan's most notorious political and economic scandals. Press conferences in the prosecutor's office are held twice daily and last anywhere from thirty minutes to an hour. *Kondan* are often held at the prosecutor's home and are referred to as the "xx school," with the name of the prosecutor replaced with the x. Ibid., 168. See also Kawai, *Nyūsu hōdō shuzai no shikumi ga wakaru hon*, 50.

61. This club has the following sixteen regular members: *Yomiuri*, *Mainichi*, *Asahi*, *Tokyo*, *Sankei*, *Nikkei*, *Hokkaido*, Kyodo, Jiji, NHK, Nihon Terebi, TBS, Fuji Terebi, Terebi Asahi, Terebi Tokyo, and Bunka Hōsō (radio). Most journalists in this club have from ten to twenty years of experience, having previously spent time in the Osaka prosecutor's office, the metropolitan police headquarters, or the national tax agency. The journalists in this club are divided into two categories: those who cover the supreme court, the high court, and the regional courts (the *saiban tantō*), and those who cover the prosecutors in each of these (the *kensatsu tantō*). Ishii, *Za shimbun*, 170.

62. Journalists are prohibited from talking with the frontline prosecutors, their assistants, or what are known as the "Tokusa G-men" (the prosecutor's undersecretaries). If they are caught so much as saying good morning to these individuals, they may be denied access (*deiri kinshi*) or given a strict warning (*genjō chūi*). One might wonder why journalists abide by this rule. Again, the cartel relations go far in explaining this. One journalist pointed out that some reporters do not want to be able to interview the lower-down prosecutors because the companies with the largest number of journalists would be at an advantage. Kawai Masayoshi, *Nyūsu hōdō shuzai no shikumi ga wakaru hon*, 50.

63. Ishii, *Za shimbun*, 177.

64. Nishiyama, *Za riiku*, 94.

65. Ishii, *Za shimbun*, 166–81.

66. Ibid., 166–88.

67. Nishiyama, *Za riiku*, 167–81.

68. This tactic has been used often by Ozawa Ichiro, who at one point refused to meet with journalists for about a month.

69. *Mainichi shimbun* labor union, unpublished booklet, 58.

70. A third type of sanction is that imposed by the *club* on a source. Though this is an extremely rare type of sanction, a few cases have been documented. In

one incident described in the weekly magazine *Shūkan hōseki*, economic journalists from the Tōshō club (which is responsible for covering news about the distribution industry) expelled the Tobu department store for not following a club "rule." Apparently, when companies elect during their shareholders' meetings to change the company president, it is customary for the retiring president and the new president to hold a press conference. But in this case, the company had merely had its PR section send a written notice to the club. In *Shūkan hōseki*, June 21, 1990, 210. In another case detailed in *Shūkan gendai*, former minister of the Environment Agency Ishikawa Shintaro suggested that some of the members of the club in that agency had written articles for *Akahata*, the organ of the Communist party. Club members were incensed at the allegation and boycotted the regularly scheduled briefings with Mr. Ishihara for more than a month. It is not clear in this case, however, who such "sanctions" hurt more—the club or the source. *Shūkan gendai*, November 10, 1978, 26–32, and November 24, 1978, 30–35.

71. These cases involve both situations where the source has given information to journalists on the condition that they do not publish it, and also those where the journalists have independently obtained information.

72. In one documented case in which journalists complained to the source when they were refused access to official press conferences, the source merely responded that "we do not think that these conferences are public. We consider that we are independently cooperating with the press." Ishii, *Za shimbun*.

73. "Anything to Miss the Scoop," *The Economist*, July 27, 1991, 24.

Chapter Five
Expanding the Web: The Role of *Kyōkai* and *Keiretsu*

1. The finest English-language account of the role of industry associations in promoting cartels in Japan is found in Tilton, *Restrained Trade*.

2. Coughlin, *Conquered Press*, 60.

3. Ibid., 64. The association's own history of its first ten years concurs, stating that "were you to compare the Japanese code with the canon written by the American Newspaper Editors Association, it would become clear that they resemble each other very closely. This code is not Japanese." In Nihon Shimbun Kyōkai, ed., *Nihon Shimbun Kyōkai 10-nen shi*, 95.

4. Pressnet: What's NSK, May 25,1998 [Internet]. Available: NSK Web page. URL: http://www.pressnet.org.jp. Emphasis added.

5. NSK membership list, published by the Nihon Shimbun Kyōkai, September 1, 1996.

6. Pressnet: What's NSK.

7. Nihon Shimbun Kyōkai, ed., *Nihon Shimbun Kyōkai 10-nen shi*, 165. This association history notes that SCAP was dissatisfied with the clubs and had said that their principal role should be for socializing, not newsgathering. It is not always clear how serious SCAP was in bringing about the abolition or reform of the system, particularly given that the number of press clubs had grown exponentially under the allied occupation of Japan. Suzuki notes that although there were only eighteen in 1945, by 1949 there were already sixty clubs in Tokyo, and the number continued to grow. Notably, one of the clubs established during this pe-

riod was the press club in the GHQ itself. Suzuki Kazue, "The Press Club System in Japan," 54.

8. Translations of the guideline are my own.

9. Each club has its own regulations (the *kurabu kiyaku*, referred to in chapter 3), and all such regulations uniformly state that membership in the club is determined first and foremost by whether the individual journalist's company is a member of the NSK.

10. Hall, *Cartels of the Mind*, 55. When Bloomberg's Tokyo bureau chief, David Butts, tried to gain access to the press club in the Tokyo Stock Exchange in 1991, he was turned down because he was not a member of the NSK. When he tried to gain membership for his organization in the NSK, he was told by the association that they did not have a category for foreign members.

11. Indeed, a spirited farmer from Kyoto, Takao Fujita, took the unusual step of filing a class-action suit with the Kyoto District Court in 1991, alleging unlawful use of public funds to support the press club in the Kyoto city hall. Though the court rejected his argument, he succeeded in getting at least a few journalists to think twice about the arrangement. The NSK included a detailed analysis of the case in its monthly magazine, but the Japanese public learned little about the issue as none of the major national newspapers reported it.

12. Nihon Shimbun Kyōkai, ed., *Nihon Shimbun Kyōkai 50-nen shi* (A fifty-year history of the NSK) (Tokyo: Nihon Shimbun Kyōkai, 1996), 122.

13. In responding to a request from the American National Press Club in 1992 that the Ministry of Foreign Affairs take the initiative in opening up the Japanese press clubs to foreign correspondents, then director of the International Press Division Seiji Morimoto noted, "I hope you appreciate that *kisha* clubs are private organizations and are not always susceptible to any influence or control which this ministry or any other government office may try to exert over them."

14. The NSK issued guidelines on the press clubs in 1957, 1962, 1966, 1972, 1978, 1985, and 1993.

15. Leslie Helm, "All on Board for Miyazawa," *Los Angeles Times*, April 27, 1993. Helm, who joined a group of Japanese political reporters on one such trip to the United States to follow then prime minister Miyazawa Kiichi, noted that shortly before the plane landed, and after the prime minister thanked reporters for their "accurate reporting of the situation," the crew delivered a bottle of seventeen-year-old Scotch to each reporter as a personal gift from the prime minister himself.

16. Hall, *Cartels of the Mind*, 66.

17. Ibid., 67.

18. It is worth noting that the EAC has also been responsible for handling issues arising from the *kisha* club system, setting up ad hoc committees on club reform whenever the pressure for change gets too great to ignore. Recent examples of committee activities include discussions with the public prosecutor's office about its sanctioning of journalists who file stories it does not approve of and negotiations with officials from government agencies that had begun to charge for information.

19. This account is taken from the NSK's recent fifty-year history, *Nihon Shimbun Kyōkai 50-nen shi*, 167–72.

20. The IHA is one of the key official bureaucracies covered by the social affairs desks of major Japanese news organizations.

21. The regular members of this press club include the big five newspapers, *Tokyo shimbun, Hokkaido shimbun,* the five major private broadcast stations, NHK, and the two news agencies.

22. These details have never been made public.

23. In the end, some NSK members were dissatisfied with the IHA's handling of information related to the process and progress of the search and began to refer cynically to their monthly meeting with the IHA representative as their monthly "Zen catechism" (*Zen mondō*).

24. Nihon Shimbun Kyōkai, ed., *Nihon Shimbun Kyōkai 50-nen shi,* 171, 172.

25. Gerlach, *Alliance Capitalism,* Gerlach and Lincoln, *The Organization of Japanese Business Networks.*

26. See Foreign Press Center Japan, *Japan's Mass Media,* 23; and Kim, *Japanese Journalists and Their World,* 13.

27. Feldman reports that as of 1993, fourteen newspaper companies offered stock exclusively to employees while twenty-three had over 50 percent held by their employees. Feldman, *Politics and the News Media in Japan,* 15.

28. Minotani Kazunari, *Hōsō-ron* (Broadcast studies) (Tokyo: Gakuyo Shobo, 1992), 17–18. See also Amano Katsufumi and Murakami Takashi, eds., *Genba kara mita shimbungaku* (The newspaper experience) (Tokyo: Gakubunsha, 1996), 138.

29. Westney, "Mass Media as Business Organizations: A US-Japan Comparison," in *Media and Politics in Japan,* ed. Susan Pharr and Ellis Krauss (Honolulu: University of Hawaii Press, 1996), 61.

30. Amano and Murakami, eds., *Genba kara mita shimbungaku,* 139.

31. Hidetoshi Kato, "Japan," chapter 13 in *Television: An International History,* ed. Anthony Smith, 2d. ed. (New York: Oxford University Press, 1998), 178; emphasis added.

32. Amano and Murakami, eds., *Genba kara mita shimbungaku,* 139.

33. Nihon Terebi, for example, was considered a part of the *Yomiuri* group but had some additional capital from *Mainichi* and *Asahi.*

34. Amano and Murakami, eds., *Genba kara mita shimbungaku,* 145.

35. *Yomiuri shimbun,* for example, used two affiliated companies, Yomiuri Telecasting and Yomiuri Land, to extend its control over its national broadcast station, NTN, raising its effective control position to nearly 20 percent.

36. Again focusing on *Yomiuri,* the chairman of NTN's board of directors and two other directors come from the *Yomiuri shimbun,* and NTN relies on the same banks for borrowing as its parent company.

37. Kawai, *Yoron to masu komyunikēshiyon,* 51. This figure rises to 57 percent when the five stations from the Osaka area are added.

38. Foreign Press Center Japan, *Japan's Mass Media,* 55.

39. Amano, Matsuoka, and Ueda, eds., *Genba kara mita masu komigaku II,* 41.

40. Ivan Hall, *Cartels of the Mind,* 50, for example, estimates that about one-half of Japan's weeklies are owned by the five national dailies. See also Westney, "Mass Media as Business Organizations," 59–63, on the linkages between publishing and magazine companies.

41. Westney, "Mass Media as Business Organizations," 59.

Chapter Six
Why Information Cartels Matter

1. Inaba and Arai, eds., *Shimbungaku*, 3d ed., 117.

2. Hara Toshio, *Jaanarizumu wa kawaru* (Journalism is changing) (Tokyo: Bansei-sha, 1994), 53.

3. "US Reporters Demand Access to Tokyo Results," *International Herald Tribune*, May 22–23, 1993.

4. Maggie Farley, "Japan's Press and the Politics of Scandal," in *Media and Politics in Japan*, ed. Pharr and Krauss, 133–63.

5. Ellis Krauss, "Portraying the State: NHK Television News and Politics," in ibid., 117.

6. For an interesting study of Chinese journalists' relations with the Chinese Communist party, see: Yuezhi Xhao, *Media, Market and Democracy in China: Between the Party Line and the Bottom Line* (Chicago: University of Illinois Press, 1998).

7. van Wolferen, *The Enigma of Japanese Power*.

8. See Garon, *Molding Japanese Minds*, 3–22, for a useful definition of social management.

9. Pharr, "Media and Politics in Japan: Historical and Contemporary Perspectives," in *Media and Politics in Japan*, ed. Pharr and Krauss, 7.

10. Cited in Maggie Farley, "Japan's Press and the Politics of Scandal," in ibid., 159.

11. Susan Pharr, "Media as Trickster in Japan: A Comparative Perspective," in ibid, 19–43.

12. Ibid. See Pharr's diagram on page 34 comparing this model to the other three.

13. David Earl Groth, "Media and Political Protest: The Bullet Train Movements," in ibid, 235. While Groth interprets his study of media coverage of political protests as evidence in favor of the trickster image, his focus is exclusively on reporting about marginalized groups. These groups are well outside of Japan's mainstream, have little privileged information to share, and have never utilized the cartel-like mechanisms of official news sources.

14. Adam Smith, *The Wealth of Nations* (Middlesex: Penguin Books, 1985), 232.

15. Doris A. Graber, "Press Freedom and the General Welfare," *Political Science Quarterly* 101, 2 (Centennial Year 1886–1986), 258. Graber herself is skeptical about how effectively the U.S. media play each of these roles.

16. For an analysis of press-source relations in the United States, see Sigal, *Reporters and Officials*; Stephen Hess, *Live from Capital Hill: Studies of Congress and the Media* (Washington, D.C.: Brookings Institution, 1991); and Timothy Crouse, *The Boys on the Bus* (New York: Random House, 1973). For the British case, see Tunstall, *The Westminster Lobby Correspondents*; and Peter Hennessy and David Walker, "The Lobby," in *The Media in British Politics* ed. Jean Seaton and Ben Pimlott (Aldershot: Avebury, 1987), 110–30.

17. Bagdikian, *The Media Monopoly*; Herman and Chomsky, *Manufacturing Consent*.

18. Bagdikian, *The Media Monopoly,* 213, 214.

19. Sigal, *Reporters and Officials,* 124.

20. Hara, "Happyō jaanarizumu jidai e no teikō," 21.

21. Feldman, *Politics and the News Media in Japan,* 65.

22. James G. March and Johan P. Olsen, *Democratic Governance* (New York: Free Press, 1995), 83.

23. Ibid, 164. March and Olsen note (without explication, however) that while co-optation is a greater danger in the Norwegian case, intermediary groups are still more likely to shape political discourse in a meaningful way.

24. Farley, "Japan's Press and the Politics of Scandal," 133–63.

25. Krauss, "The Mass Media and Japanese Politics," 361.

26. Farley, "Japan's Press and the Politics of Scandal," 137.

27. See Shanto Iyengar, Mark D. Peters, and Donald R. Kinder, "Experimental Demonstrations of the 'Not-So-Minimal' Consequences of Television News Programs," *American Political Science Review* 76, 4 (December 1982): 848–58.

28. Bagdikian, *The Media Monopoly,* 213.

29. Ishikawa Masumi, "Medea—kenryoku e no eikyōryoku to kenryoku kara no eikyōryoku" (Media's impact—"To the Powers that be" to 'From the powers that be), in *Leviathan, Tokushu: Masu medea to seiji* (Special issue: Mass media and politics) (Tokyo: Kitakusha, October 15, 1990), 30–48.

30. It would be of great interest to see if this pattern of limited and reactive coverage of political issues held up prior to the elections that saw the LDP removed from power in 1993 for the first time in nearly forty years.

31. Feldman, *Politics and the News Media in Japan,* 81.

32. Hall, *Cartels of the Mind,* 152.

33. See Campbell and Groth in *Media and Politics in Japan,* ed. Pharr and Krauss, chapters 6 and 7, respectively; Michael R. Reich, "Crisis and Routine: Pollution Reporting by the Japanese Press," in *Institutions for Change in Japanese Society,* ed. George DeVos (Berkeley: Institute of East Asian Studies, 1984), 148–65.

34. Groth, "Media and Political Protest," in *Media and Politics in Japan,* ed. Pharr and Krauss, 233–34.

35. Hall, *Cartels of the Mind,* 50.

36. Farley, "Japan's Press and the Politics of Scandal," 141.

37. Groth, "Media and Political Protest," 235.

38. Krauss, "Portraying the State," 110.

39. Foreign Press Center Japan, *Japan's Mass Media,* 30.

40. Hall, *Cartels of the Mind,* 8.

41. Westney, "Mass Media as Business Organizations," 79.

42. James L. Huffman, "The Meiji Roots and Contemporary Practices of the Japanese Press," 460.

43. Sigal, *Reporters and Officials,* 53.

44. Interview with Ian Haysom, editor of the *Vancouver Sun,* February 1994.

45. Bagdikian, *The Media Monopoly,* and Herman and Chomsky, *Manufacturing Consent.*

46. Tunstall, *The Westminster Lobby Correspondents.*

47. Ibid., 213. At least one British observer has argued that, despite the existence of the Lobby, newsgathering practices in London and Washington are more similar than different. Although more has been written about the norms for gathering news in the White House than those of the Lobby (in part because the latter has remained cloaked in secrecy), Tunstall argues that "it does not follow that many of the mechanisms known in Washington do not exist in London." Specifically, he notes that political reporting in the two capitals does not differ in respect to the actual access journalists have to politicians or in the frequent use of the political leak.

48. Adam Gopnik, "Read All about It," *New Yorker* (December 12, 1994): 84, 88.

49. It is ironic, of course, that the American Occupation had the power to do the same thing decades earlier but never exercised it.

50. Hall, *Cartels of the Mind*, 72.

51. Ibid., 46

52. Hall argues something similar in ibid., 52 and 66.

53. Krauss, "Portraying the State," 117.

54. Leslie Helm from the *Los Angeles Times*, who has written insightfully about the *kisha* clubs and other Japan-related issues, relayed in an interview in 1993 that he believed the changes so far to be primarily cosmetic.

Appendix B
Kitami Administration of Justice Press Club Agreement

1. This is a draft by *Asahi*, September 1987.

Appendix D
A Comparison with the British Lobby

1. Tunstall, *The Westminster Lobby Correspondents*, 4.

2. Ibid., 201. For a history of the Lobby system and its evolution beginning in the 1880s, see Colin Seymour-Ure, *The Press, Politics and the Public: An Essay on the Role of the National Press in the British Political System* (London: Methuen, 1968).

3. Once an organization has a lobby ticket it keeps it. When the Telegraph amalgamated with the Post in 1937, the former retained two lobby tickets. As Seymour-Ure notes, "the Post died but its Lobby rights went marching on." Ibid., 208.

4. However, as Seymour-Ure points out, only half of the people on the Lobby list have the right to attend the Lobby Meeting. Ibid., 209.

5. Ibid., 201, 204.

6. Ibid., 205.

7. Henessy and Walker, "The Lobby," in *The Media in British Politics*, ed. Seaton and Pimlott, 34.

8. Seymour-Ure, *The Press, Politics and the Public*, 197.

9. Ibid., 197–98.
10. Ibid., 196.
11. Tunstall, *The Westminster Lobby Correspondents*, 125.
12. Henessy and Walker, "The Lobby," 10.
13. Ibid., 41; also see 113.

Bibliography

Adler, Renata. *Reckless Disregard: Westmoreland v. CBS et al.; Sharon v. Time.* New York: Vintage Books, 1986.

Aera Mook 2. *Masu komi gaku ga wakaru* (Understanding journalism). Tokyo: Asahi Shimbunsha, 1996.

Almond, Gabriel A. "The Return to the State." *American Political Science Review* 83, 3 (September 1988): 853–901.

Altman, Albert A. "The Press and Social Cohesion during a Period of Change: The Case of Early Meiji Japan." *Modern Asian Studies* 15, 4 (1981): 865–76.

———. "Shimbunshi: The Early Meiji Adaptation of the Western-Style Newspaper." In *Modern Japan: Aspects of History, Literature and Society.* Edited by W. G. Beasley. Berkeley: University of California Press, 1975.

Amano Katsufumi. "Torikomareru jaanarizumu" (Co-opted journalists). *Sōgo jaanarizumu kenkyū* (1989): 46–52.

Amano Katsufumi and Murakami Takashi, eds. *Genba kara mita shimbun gaku* (The newspaper experience). Tokyo: Gakubunsha, 1996.

Amano Katsufumi, Matsuoka Yukio, and Murakami Takashi, eds. *Genba kara mita masu komi gaku* (The mass media experience). Tokyo: Gakubunsha, 1996.

Amano Katsufumi, Matsuoka Yukio, and Ueda Yasuo, eds. *Genba kara mita masu komi gaku II* (The mass media experience II). Tokyo: Gakubunsha, 1996.

Ando Hiroshi. *Nichibei jōhō masatsu* (U.S.-Japan information friction). Tokyo: Iwanami Shoten, 1991.

Apter, David E., and Sawa Nagayo. *Against the State: Politics and Social Protest in Japan.* Cambridge: Harvard University Press, 1984.

Arai Naohiro. *Jaanarizumu* (Journalism). Tokyo: Toyo Keizai Shimposha, 1977.

Ariyama Teruo. *Kindai Nihon jaanarizumu no kōzō: Osaka asahi shimbun shironiji jiken zengo* (The structure of modern Japanese journalism: Before and after the White Rainbow Incident). Tokyo: Tokyo Shuppan, 1995.

Asahi shimbun, December 21, 1991, morning edition pp. 23 and 31; February 11, 1992, morning edition, p. 2 and p. 31.

Asahi Shimbun Nagoya Shakaibu. *Dokyumento kan-kan settai* (Documenting meetings between public officials). Nagoya: Fubaisha, 1996.

Asahi Shimbun Shakaibu. *Kenryoku hōdō* (Reporting on the powerful). Tokyo: Asahi Shimbunsha, 1993.

Asahi Shimbun Shakaibu Ichikawa Hayami. *Kōshitsu hōdō* (Covering the court). Tokyo: Asahi Shimbunsha, 1993.

Asahi Shimbun Shakaibu Medea Han. *Iwanami bukkuretto no. 404: Jōhō o shimin ni!* (Iwanami booklet no. 404: Information to the citizens!). Tokyo: Iwanami Shoten, 1996.

Asahi Shimbun Tokyo Shakaibu OB-kai. *Sensō to shakaibu kisha* (War and the beat journalist). Tokyo: Sojin-sha, 1990.

Asahi Shimbunsha, ed. *Asahi kii waado '96–'97* (Asahi keywords for 1996–1997). Tokyo: Asahi Shimbunsha, 1996.

Asahi Shimbunsha Kokokukyoku, ed., *Shimbun kōkoku dokuhon* (A Guide to Newspaper Advertisements) Tokyo: Asahi Shimbunsha, 1991.

Asahi Shimbunsha Shakaibu. *Vs. asahi shimbun* (Voices against Asahi shimbun). Tokyo: Asahi Shimbunsha, 1993.

Asano Kenichi. *Hanzai hōdō to keisatsu* (Criminal reporting and the police). Tokyo: Sanichi Shōbō, 1987.

———. *Kagekiha hōdō no hanzai* (Reporting radicals unfairly). Tokyo: Sanichi Shobo, 1990.

———. *Kyakkan hōdō* (Objective news reporting). Tokyo: Chikuma Shobo, 1993.

Asano Kenichi and Kōno Yoshiyuki. *Matsumoto sarin jiken hōdō no tsumi to batsu* (Erroneous reporting in the Matsumoto sarin case). Tokyo: Daisan Bunmeisha, 1996.

Asano Kenichi and Yamaguchi Masanori. *Musekinin na masu medea: Kenryoku kainyū no kiki to hōdō higai* (Irresponsible mass media: Dangers of official meddling and damage caused by the mass media). Tokyo: Gendai Jinbunsha, 1996.

Aso Iku. *Jōhō kantei ni tassezu "jōhō kōshinkoku" Nihon no higeki* (Information doesn't reach the prime minister: The tragedy of Japan "a backward nation in information management"). Tokyo: Bungei Shunju, 1996.

Baba Koichi. *Iwanami bukkuretto no. 407 Shichōritsu kyōsō -sono omote to ura-* (Iwanami booklet no. 407: Competition for audience rating). Tokyo: Iwanami Shoten, 1996.

Bagdikian, Ben H. *The Media Monopoly*, 3d ed. Boston: Beacon Press, 1987.

Barshay, Andrew E. *State and Intellectual in Imperial Japan: The Public Man in Crisis*. Berkeley: University of California Press, 1988.

Beasley, W. G. *Modern Japan: Aspects of History, Literature and Society*. Berkeley: University of California Press, 1975.

Beer, Lawrence Ward. *Freedom of Expression in Japan: A Study in Comparative Law, Politics, and Society*. Tokyo: Kodansha, 1984.

Berger, Peter L., and Thomas Luckmann. *The Social Construction of Reality: A Treatise in the Sociology of Knowledge*. Garden City, N.Y.: Doubleday, 1966.

Bessatsu Takarajima, no. 72, 1989. Tokyo: JICC Shuppankyoku, 1989.

Bessatsu Takarajima, no. 237, 1995. Tokyo: Takarajimasha, 1995.

Bessatsu Takarajima, no. 244, 1996. Tokyo: Takarajimasha, 1996.

Bessatsu Takarajima, ed. *Kanryō gokuhi jinji roku* (Top secret reports on bureaucrats). Tokyo: Takarajimasha, 1996.

Bungei Shunju, June 1996. Tokyo: Bungei shunju, 1996.

Boling, Patricia. "Private Interest and the Public Good in Japan." *Pacific Review* 3, 2, (1990).

Bowen, Roger W. *Rebellion and Democracy in Meiji Japan*. Berkeley: University of California Press, 1980.

Calhoun, Craig J., ed. *Habermas and the Public Sphere*. Cambridge: MIT Press, 1992.

Chamoto Shigemasa. *Masukomi wa tatakatteiru ka* (Is the press actively fighting?). Tokyo: Outsuki Shoten, 1991.

———. *Sensō to jaanarizumu* (War and journalism). Tokyo: Sanichi Shobo, 1986.

Cook, Timothy J. *Making Laws and Making News: Media Strategies in the U.S. House of Representatives*. Washington, D.C.: Brookings Institution, 1989.

Coughlin, William J. *Conquered Press: The MacArthur Era in Japanese Journalism.* Palo Alto: Pacific Books, 1952.

Cranfield, G. A. *The Press and Society: From Caxton to Northcliffe.* London: Longman, 1978.

Crouse, Timothy. *The Boys on the Bus.* New York: Random House, 1973.

Curran, James, and Michael Gurevitch, eds. *Mass Media and Society.* London: Edward Arnold, 1991.

Daba Hiroshi. *Dai shimbunsha sono jinmyaku kinmyaku no kenkyū* (The major mass media: Its personal and financial ties). Tokyo: Hamano Shuppan, 1996.

Dacapo, no. 207, June 20, 1990. Tokyo: Magajin Hausu, 1990.

Dacapo, no. 265, November 18, 1992. Tokyo: Magajin Hausu, 1992.

Dore, Ronald Philip. *Flexible Rigidities: Industrial Policy and Structural Adjustment in the Japanese Economy, 1970–80.* Stanford: Stanford University Press, 1986.

Duus, Peter. *The Rise of Modern Japan.* Boston: Houghton Mifflin, 1976.

Eatwell, John, Murray Milgate, and Peter Newman, eds. *The New Palgrave: A Dictionary of Economics.* Vol. 1. London: Macmillan; New York: Stockton Press; Tokyo: Maruzen, 1987.

Ejiri, Susumu. *Characteristics of the Japanese Press.* Tokyo: Nihon Shimbun Kyokai, 1972.

Entman, Robert M. *Democracy without Citizens: Media and the Decay of American Politics.* New York: Oxford University Press, 1989.

Entman, Robert, and Steven Wildman. "Reconciling Economic and Non-Economic Perspectives on Media Policy: Transcending the 'Marketplace of Ideas.' " *Journal of Communication* 42, 1 (Winter 1992): 5–19.

Evans, Peter B., Dietrich Rueschemeyer, and Theda Skocpol, eds. *Bringing the State Back In.* New York: Cambridge University Press, 1985.

Feldman, Ofer. *Politics and the News Media in Japan.* Ann Arbor: University of Michigan Press, 1993.

Figdor, Peter. "Newspapers and Their Regulation in Early Meiji Japan: 1868–1883." In *Papers on Japan,* vol. 6. Cambridge: East Asian Research Center, Harvard University, 1972.

Foreign Press Center Japan. Japan's Mass Media. "About Japan" series, no. 7, 3d rev. ed. Tokyo: Foreign Press Center, 1994.

Friedland, Roger, and Robert D. Alford. "Bringing Society Back In: Symbols, Practices and Institutional Contradictions" in *The New Institutionalism in Organizational Analysis.* Edited by Walter W. Powell and Paul J. DiMaggio. Chicago: University of Chicago Press, 1991.

Fruin, W. Mark. *The Japanese Enterprise System: Competitive Strategies and Cooperative Structures.* New York: Oxford University Press, 1992.

Fujioka Shinichiro. *Shuzai kyohi* (Interview denied). Tokyo: Sofusha Shuppan, 1990.

Fujita Hiroshi. *Amerika no jaanarizumu* (American journalism). Tokyo: Iwanami Shoten, 1991.

Fukuoka Masayuki. *Te ni toru yōni seiji no koto ga wakaru hon* (A guide to the political system). Tokyo: Kanki Shuppan, 1995.

Furuno. Inosuke, *A Short History of the News Agency in Japan*. Tokyo: Shimbun Tsushin Chosa Kai, 1963.

Gans, Herbert J. *Deciding What's News: A Study of CBS Evening News, NBC Nightly News, Newsweek and Time*. New York: Vintage Books, 1979.

Garon, Sheldon. *Molding Japanese Minds: The State in Everyday Life*. Princeton: Princeton University Press, 1997.

Gendai, January 1990. Tokyo: Kodansha, 1990.

Gendai Janarizumu Kenkyukai, ed. *Kisha kurabu* (Press clubs). Tokyo: Kashiwa Shobo, 1996.

Gendai Jinbunsha Henshubu, ed. *Kensho! Aum hōdō* (An analysis of news coverage of the Aum Cult). Tokyo: Gendai Jinbunsha, 1995.

Gerlach, Michael L. *Alliance Capitalism: The Social Organization of Japanese Business*. Berkeley: University of California Press, 1992.

Gerlach, Michael L., and James R. Lincoln, *The Organization of Japanese Business Networks*. Cambridge: Cambridge University Press, forthcoming.

Gillmor, Donald M. *Power, Publicity and the Abuse of Libel Law*. New York: Oxford University Press, 1992.

Gitlin, Todd. *The Whole World Is Watching: Mass Media in the Making and Unmaking of the New Left*. Berkeley: University of California Press, 1980.

Gluck, Carol. *Japan's Modern Myths: Ideology in the Late Meiji Period*. Princeton: Princeton University Press, 1985.

Goto Fumiyasu. *Gohō* (Erroneous reports). Tokyo: Iwanami Shoten, 1996.

———. *Gohō to kyohō: Maboroshi no tokudane wa naze, Iwanami bukkuretto no. 154* (Erroneous reports and false alarms: Why are scoops fabricated?). Tokyo: Iwanami Shoten, 1990.

Goto Takao. *Kisha: Chōmin* (Journalist Chōmin). Tokyo: Misuzu Shobo, 1990.

Gourevitch, Peter A. *Politics in Hard Times: Comparative Responses to International Economic Crises*. Ithaca: Cornell University Press, 1986.

Graber, Doris A. *Mass Media and American Politics*. Washington, D.C.: Congressional Quarterly Press, 1980.

———. "Press Freedom and the General Welfare." *Political Science Quarterly* 101, 2 (Centennial Year 1886–1986).

Habermas, Jurgen. *The Structural Transformation of the Public Sphere*. Translated by T. Burger and F. Lawrence. Cambridge: MIT Press, 1989.

Hagiwara Yukio. *Jiken kisha 30-nen* (Thirty years of beat journalism). Tokyo: Tosho Shuppansha, 1991.

Hall, Ivan P. *Cartels of the Mind: Japan's Intellectual Closed Shop*. New York: W. W. Norton, 1998.

Hallin, Daniel C. *The "Uncensored War": The Media and Vietnam*. New York: Oxford University Press, 1986.

Halloran, Richard. *Japan: Images and Realities*. New York: Alfred A. Knopf, 1969.

Hamada Junichi. *Jōhō hō* (Mass communications law). Tokyo: Yubikaku, 1994.

Hanazono, Kanesada. *The Development of Japanese Journalism*. Tokyo: Tokyo Nichi Nichi, 1934.

Hara Toshio. *Atarashii jaanarisutotachi e* (For new journalists). Tokyo: Banseisha, 1992.

———. "Happyō jaanarizumu jidai e no teikō" (Resisting announcement journalism). *Shimbun kenkyū* (December 1979).

———. *Jaanarizumu wa kawaru* (Journalism is changing). Tokyo: Bansei-sha, 1994.

———. *Sore demo kimi wa jaanarisuto ni naruka* (And you still want to become a journalist?). Tokyo: Bansei-sha, 1990.

Hara Toshio, Uchihashi Katsuto, Aimono Fumio, and Yasue Ryosuke, *Iwanami bukkuretto No. 384 Hon to shimbun saihan seido o kangaeru* (Iwanami Booklet No. 384: Study on the Resale System for Books and Newspapers). Tokyo: Iwanami Shoten, 1995.

Hardacre, Helen. *Aum Shinrikyō and the Japanese Media: The Pied Piper Meets the Lamb of God*. New York: East Asian Institute, Columbia University, 1995.

Haruhara Akihito. *Nihon shimbun tsūshi* (A history of Japan's newspaper communications). Tokyo: Shinsensha, 1990.

Hatanaka Shigeo. *Nihon fashizumu no genron danatsu* (The suppression of free speech under Japanese fascism). Tokyo: Kobunken, 1986.

Hayashigatani Shotaro. *Nihon no shimbun hōdō* (Japan's press reporting). Tokyo: Ikeda Shoten, 1990.

Herman, Edward S., and Noam Chomsky. *Manufacturing Consent: The Political Economy of the Mass Media*. New York: Random House, 1988.

Hertsgaard, Mark. *On Bended Knee: The Press and the Reagan Presidency.* New York: Schocken Books, 1988.

Hess, Stephen. *Live from Capital Hill: Studies of Congress and the Media.* Washington, D.C.: Brookings Institution, 1991.

Hidaka Ichiro. *Nihon no hōsō no ayumi* (A history of Japanese broadcasting). Tokyo: Ningen no Kagakusha, 1991.

Higuchi Michiko, Suematsu Yoshinori, and Tanaka Kiyoyuki. *Seiji no shikumi* (Mechanisms of politics). Tokyo: Asuka Shuppansha, 1994.

Hogaku Seminaru Sogo Tokushu Shirizu 35. *Masu medea no genzai* (Mass media today). Tokyo: Nihon Hyoronsha, 1986.

Hogaku Seminaru Sogo Tokushu Shirizu 39. *Jinken to hōdō o kangaeru* (Human rights and criminal reporting). Tokyo: Nihon Hyoronsha, January 1988.

Hogaku Seminaru Sogo Tokushu Shirizu 45. *Hanzai hōdō no genzai* (The current status of criminal reporting). Tokyo: Nihon Hyoronsha, January 1990.

Hokkaido Shimbun Rodo Kumiai. *Kishatachi no sensō* (The journalists' war). Tokyo: Komichishobo, 1990.

Honda Katsuichi. *Hinkon naru seishin: Jijitsu to wa nanika II* (What is truth II). Tokyo: Miraisha, 1977.

———. *Hinkon naru seishin: C* (The impoverished spirit: C). Tokyo: Asahi Shimbunsha, 1989.

———. *Hinkon naru seishin: I* (The impoverished spirit: I). Tokyo: Suzuwa Shoten, 1992.

———. *Hinkon naru seishin: 22* (The impoverished spirit: 22). Tokyo: Suzuwa Shoten, 1992.

Honda Yasuharu. *Futo taiho* (False arrest) Tokyo: Kodansha, 1983.

Honzawa Jiro. *Seiji kiji wa ura ga wakaru to omoshiroi* (The underside of political stories is interesting). Tokyo: Yell Books, 1992.

Hōsō Bunka, October 1996. Tokyo: Nippon Hōsō Kyōkai, 1996.

Hoston, Germaine. *Marxism and the Crisis of Development in Prewar Japan.* Princeton: Princeton University Press, 1986.

Huddle, Norie, and Michael Reich, with Stiskin Nahum. *Island of Dreams: Environmental Crisis in Japan.* New York: Autumn Press, 1975.

Huffman, James L. "Freedom and the Press in Meiji-Taisho Japan." *Transactions of the Asiatic Society of Japan* (Third series, volume 19, Tokyo, 1984): 137–71.

———. "The Meiji Roots and Contemporary Practices of the Japanese Press." *The Japan Interpreter* 11 (Spring 1977): 448–66.

———. *Politics of the Meiji Press: The Life of Fukuchi Gen'ichiro.* Honolulu: University of Hawaii Press, 1980.

Igarashi Futaba. *Iwanami bukkuretto no. 192: Hanzai Hōdō* (Iwanami booklet no. 192: Criminal reporting). Tokyo: Iwanami Shoten, 1991.

Iimuro Katsuhiko. *Medea to kenryoku ni tsuite kataro* (Let's talk about media and authority). Tokyo: Riyonsha, 1995.

Ike, Nobutaka. *The Beginnings of Political Democracy in Japan.* Baltimore: The Johns Hopkins Press, 1950.

Inaba Michio and Arai Naoyuki, eds. *Shimbungaku* (Newspaper studies). Tokyo: Nihon Hyōronsha, 1988.

———. *Shimbungaku* (Newspaper studies), 3d ed. Tokyo: Nihon Hyōronsha, 1995.

Inaba Yutaka. *Kisha kurabu o kiru* (Criticizing the press clubs). Tokyo: Nisshin Hōdō Shuppanbu, 1978.

Inagaki Takeshi. *Shimbun ura yomi, sakasa yomi* (How to read newspapers: Don't be deceived by the press). Tokyo: Soshisha, 1996.

Inose Naoki. *Hinshi no jaanarizumu* (The death of journalism). Tokyo: Bungei shunju, 1996.

———. *Nyūsu no kokogaku* (News archaeology). Tokyo: Bungei shunju, 1992.

Inoue Yasumasa. *Keisatsu kisha* (Police journalist). Tokyo: Takarajimasha, 1993.

IPMS Group. *Kasumigaseki deta handobukku* (Handbook about the Japanese bureaucracy). Tokyo: The Japan Times, 1994.

Ishida Osamu. *Shimbun ga nihon o dame ni shita* (How the press ruined Japan). Tokyo: Gendaishorin, 1995.

Ishida Takeshi. *Nihon no seiji to kotoba: I* (Japanese politics and language: Part one). Tokyo: Tokyo Daigaku Shuppankai, 1989.

Ishii Kouki. *Kanryō tengoku nippon hasan* (The bankruptcy of Japan, a bureacratic heaven). Tokyo: Michi Shuppan, 1996.

Ishii Masao, ed. *Za shimbun* (The newspaper). Tokyo: JICC Shuppankyoku, 1989.

Itagaki Hidenori. *Shimbun kiji no ō uso o abaku* (Exposing newspaper lies). Tokyo: Nisshin Hodo, 1990.

Itō, Takashi, and George Akita. "The Yamagata-Tokutomi Correspondence: Press and Politics in Meiji-Taishō Japan." *Monumenta Nipponica* 36, 4 (1981): 391–423.

Iyengar, Shanto, Mark D. Peters, and Donald R. Kinder, "Experimental Demonstrations of the 'Not-So-Minimal' Consequences of Television News Programs." *American Political Science Review* 76, 4 (December 1982): 848–58.

Jinno Takeyoshi. *Jōhō kōkai kuni to jichitai no genba kara* (Freedom of information: Nationally and locally). Tokyo: Kadensha, 1996.

Johnson, Chalmers A. *Japan's Public Policy Companies.* Washington, D.C.: American Enterprise Institute for Public Policy Research, 1978.

———. *MITI and the Japanese Miracle: The Growth of Industrial Policy, 1925–1975.* Stanford: Stanford University Press, 1982.

Journalism Quarterly. "Special Issue: The First Amendment—The Third Century" 69, 1 (Spring 1992).

Juichinin no Kokuhatsu. *Hōdō higai* (Harmful reporting). Tokyo: Tsukuru Shuppan, 1991.

Kabashima, Ikuo, and Jeffrey Broadbent, "Referent Pluralism: Mass Media and Politics in Japan." *Journal of Japanese Studies* 12 (Summer 1986).

Kajiwara Hozumi. *Dosamawari kisha no nakiwarai nikki* (Diary of the ups and downs of an itinerant journalist). Tokyo: Koyu Shuppan, 1994.

Kamei Jun. *Shūkanshi no yomikata* (How to read weekly magazines). Tokyo: Hanashinotokushu, 1985.

Kamei Jun, Tsukamoto Mitsuo, and Fuwa Tetsuzo. *Terebi hōdō wa senkyo de yoron yūdō o yurusareru ka?* (Can we let TV broadcasts lead public opinion during elections?). Tokyo: Zenkoku Kakushinkon, 1993.

Kamiyama Sae and the "Special Report Group" (Kenshō tokubetsu shuzai han). *TBS za kenshō* (Scrutinizing TBS). Tokyo: Rokusaisha, 1996.

Kan Donjin. *Nihon genronkai to chōsen: 1910–1945* (The Japanese press and Korea: 1910–1945). Tokyo: Hosei Daigaku Shuppankyoku, 1987.

Kan Takayuki. *Tennōsei* (The emperor system). Tokyo: Gendaishokan, 1993.

Kanamitsu Kei. *Masu komi wa naze kenryoku ni yowai ka* (Why is the mass media weak against the powerful?). Tokyo: Shinnippon Shuppansha, 1994.

Kasuya Kazuki, ed. *Medea no tōsō* (Mass media struggle). Tokyo: PHP Kenkyusho, 1994.

Kasza, Gregory J. *The State and the Mass Media in Japan, 1918–1945.* Berkeley: University of California Press, 1988.

Kato Shuichi. *Iwanami bukkuretto No. 410: Nihon wa doko e yuku no ka* (Iwanami booklet no. 410: Where is Japan going?). Tokyo: Iwanami Shoten, 1996.

Kato Shujiro and Hashimoto Goro. *Nihon wa kō natte iru: seiji no shikumi* (Japan's political system). Tokyo: PHP Kenkyusho, 1995.

Katsura Keiichi. *Gendai no shimbun* (Modern newspapers). Tokyo: Iwanami Shoten, 1990.

———. *Iwanami bukkuretto no. 15: Meiji-Taishō no jaanarizumu* (Iwanami booklet no. 15: Journalism in the Meiji-Taishō period). Tokyo: Iwanami Shoten, 1992.

———. *Nihon no jōhōka to jaanarizumu* (Information-oriented Japan and its journalism). Tokyo: Nihonhyoronsha, 1995.

Katz, Elihu, and Paul F. Lazarsfeld. *Personal Influence: The Part Played by People in the Flow of Mass Communications.* Glencoe, Ill.: Free Press, 1955.

Katzenstein, Peter J., "Conclusion: Domestic Structures and Strategies of Foreign Economic Policy." *International Organization* 31, 4 (Autumn 1977): 879–920.

———, ed. *Between Power and Plenty: Foreign Economic Policies of Advanced Industrial States.* Madison: University of Wisconsin Press, 1978.

Kawabe, Kisaburo. *The Press and Politics in Japan: A Study of the Relation between the Newspaper and the Political Development of Modern Japan.* Chicago: University of Chicago Press, 1921.

Kawai Masayoshi. *Nyūsu hōdō shuzai no shikumi ga wakaru hon* (Understanding news reports and newsgathering). Tokyo: Asuka, 1992.

Kawai Ryosuke. *Yoron to masu komyunikēshiyon* (Public opinion and the mass media). Tokyo: Bureen Shuppan, 1989.

Kawakami Sumie. *Shimbun no himitsu* (Newspaper secrets). Tokyo: JICC, 1990.

Kawasaki Yasushi and Shibata Tetsuji. *Jaanarizumu no genten* (The essence of journalism). Tokyo: Iwanami Shoten, 1996.

Keizai Koho Centaa. *Kigyō to shakai no komyunikēshiyon* (Communication between business and society) (July 1991).

Kenkyu Shudan Komyunikeshon '90. *Masu komi no ashita o tō: hōsō* (Considering the future of the mass media: The broadcast media). Tokyo: Ohtsuki Shoten, 1993.

————. *Masu komi no ashita o tō: shuppan* (Considering the future of the mass media: Publishing). Tokyo: Otsuki Shoten, 1989.

Kenkyu Shudan 21. *Kore de iinoka tennō hōdō* (Reporting the emperor). Tokyo: Riberuta Shuppan, 1989.

Kensho Shimbun Hodo Henshu Iinkai. *Kensho nikkan hōdō: Pen no kake hashi* (Review of reports on the relationship between Korea and Japan). Tokyo: Omura Shoten, 1995.

Kido Mataichi et al., eds. *Kōzō gendai jaanarizumu II: Shimbun.* (The structure of modern journalism II: Newspapers). Tokyo: Jiji Tsushinsha, 1973.

Kim, Young C.. *Japanese Journalists and Their World.* Charlottesville: University Press of Virginia, 1981.

Kimura Aiji. *Masukomi daisensō: Yomiuri vs. TBS* (Mass communications war: Yomiuri vs. TBS). Tokyo: Sekibunsha, 1992.

————. *Yomiuri shimbun rekishi kenshō* (Reviewing the history of the Yomiuri shimbun). Tokyo: Sekibunsha, 1996.

Kitamura Hajime. *Fuhai shita medea shimbun ni saisei no michi wa arunoka* (Newspapers, corrupted media: Is there any way to regenerate them?). Tokyo: Gendai Jimbunsha, 1996.

Klapper, Joseph T. *The Effects of Mass Media.* New York: Columbia University, Bureau of Applied Social Research, 1949.

Kobayashi Hirotada. *Masu komi vs. aum shinrikyo* (The mass media vs. the Aum Cult). Tokyo: Sanichi Shobo, 1995.

————. *Shimbun kiji zappingu dokkaihō* (How to read newspaper articles critically). Tokyo: Jiyu Kokuminsha, 1993.

Koito Chugo. *Shimbun no rekishi: kenryoku to no tatakai* (Newspaper history: Fighting against authority). Tokyo: Shinchosha, 1992.

Koichi Saburo. "Masu media to ideorogii: 'Chūritsusei,' 'tōhasei' no rekishiteki keifu" (Mass media and ideology: The historical lineage of words such as "neutrality" and "partisanship"). *Shisō,* no. 403 (January 1958): 96–113.

Kondo Seiichi. *Beikoku hōdō ni miru Nihon* (Images of Japan in the American media). Tokyo: Simul Shuppankai, 1994.

Kōichi Saburo et al. *Medea no genzai kei* (The Current Status of the Mass Media) Tokyo: Shinyosha, 1995.

Koss, Stephen E. *The Nineteenth Century.* Vol. 1 of *The Rise and Fall of the Political Press in Britain.* London: Hamish Hamilton, 1981.

Koyama Fumio. *Kuga Katsunan "Kokumin" no sosshutsu* (Kuga Katsunan: the creator of "Kokumin"). Tokyo: Misuzu Shobo, 1990.

Krasner, Stephen D. *Defending the National Interest: Raw Material Investments and U.S. Foreign Policy.* Princeton: University of Princeton Press, 1978.

Krauss, Ellis S. "Changing Television News in Japan." *Journal of Asian Studies* 57, 3 (August 1998): 689–90.

Kumon Shunpei. *Nechizen no jidai* (The age of netizens). Tokyo: NTT Shuppan, 1996.

Kuroda Hidetoshi. *Mono ienu jidai* (A time when words could not be spoken). Tokyo: Tosho shuppansha, 1986.

Kuroda Kiyoshi. *Iwanami bukuretto no. 406: TBS jiken to jaanarizumu* (Iwanami booklet no. 406: The TBS case and journalism). Tokyo: Iwanami Shoten, 1996.

Kurume Kaoru. *Shimbun no ura ga wakaru hon* (The underside of newspapers). Tokyo: Piipurusha, 1990.

Kyodo Tsūshin Shakaibu, ed. *Kyodo Tsūshin Shakaibu* (The Kyodo Wire Service Social Affairs Desk). Tokyo: Kyodo Tsushinsha, 1992.

Kyozo, Mori. "Questionable Attitude of News Reporters." *Japan Echo* 2, 1 (Spring 1975). Originally published in *Chuō kōrōn* (January 1975).

Lang, Gladys Engel, and Kurt Lang, "Mass Communications and Public Opinion: Strategies for Research," in *Social Psychology: Sociological Perspectives*, ed. Morris Rosenberg and Ralph H. Turner. New York: Basic Books, 1981.

Lee, Jung Bock. *The Political Character of the Japanese Press.* Seoul: Seoul National University Press, 1985.

Lee, Martin A., and Norman Solomon. *Unreliable Sources: A Guide to Detecting Bias in News Media.* New York: Carol Publishing Group, 1990.

Lent, John A. *The Asian Newspapers' Reluctant Revolution.* Ames: Iowa State University Press, 1971.

Leonard, Thomas C. *The Power of the Press: The Birth of American Political Reporting.* New York: Oxford University Press, 1986.

Leviathan. "Tokushu: Masu medea to seiji" (Special issue: Mass media and politics) 7. Tokyo: Bokutakusha, October 15, 1990.

Lincoln, James R. "Japanese Organization and Organization Theory." In Staw, Barry M., and L. L. Cummings, eds., *Research in Organizational Behaviour: An Annual Series of Analytical Essays and Critical Reviews*, vol. 12. Edited by Barry M. Staw and L.L. Cummings. Greenwich, Conn.: JAI Press, 1989.

Linsky, Martin. "The Media and Public Deliberation." In *The Power of Public Ideas.* Edited by Robert B. Reich. Cambridge, Mass.: Ballinger, 1988.

Lippman, Thomas W. *The Washington Post Deskbook on Style*, 2d ed. New York: McGraw-Hill, 1989.

McCormack, Gavan, and Yoshio Sugimoto, eds. *Democracy in Contemporary Japan.* Armonk, N.Y.: M. E. Sharpe, 1986.

McQuail, Denis. *Mass Communication Theory: An Introduction*, 2d ed. London: Sage Publications, 1987.

Maesaka Toshiyuki. *Sensō to shimbun 1926–1935* (War and the newspaper: 1926–1935). Tokyo: Shakai Shisosha, 1989.

———. *Sensō to shimbun: 1936–1945* (War and the newspaper: 1936–1945). Tokyo: Shakai Shisosha, 1991.

Maezawa Takeshi. *Nihon jaanarizumu no kenshō* (Review of Japanese journalism). Tokyo: Sanshodo, 1993.

Mainichi Shimbun Osaka Iryo Shuzaihan. *Yakugai o ō kisha tachi* (Journalists investigating pharmacology). Tokyo: Sanichi Shobo, 1996.

Mainichi Shimbun Shakaibu. *Jōhō demokurashii* (Information democracy). Tokyo: Mainichi Shimbunsha, 1992.

March, James G., and Johan P. Olsen. *Democratic Governance*, New York: Free Press, 1995.

———. "The New Institutionalism: Organizational Factors in Political Life." *American Political Science Review* 78: 734–49.

Maruyama Noboru. *Hōdō kyōtei—Nihon masukomi no kamman na jishi* (Press agreements: The slow death of the Japanese mass media). Tokyo: Daisan Shokan, 1992.

Matsuda Takakazu. *Seiryū kankai 30 pun pointo yomi* (Understanding politics quickly). Tokyo: Asuka Shuppansha, 1994.

Matsudaira. Tadashi et al. *Ta medea o yomu* (Understanding multimedia). Tokyo: Otsuki Shoten, 1992.

Matsuoka Kiichi. *"Jiyū shimbun" o yomu* (Reading the "freedom newspaper"). Tokyo: Unite, 1992.

Matsui Shigenori. *Jōhō kōkai hō* (The freedom of information act). Tokyo: Iwanami Shoten, 1996.

———. *Masu medea hō nyūmon* (Introduction to mass media law). Tokyo: Nihon Hyoronsha, 1994.

Matsuro Moriyoshi, Tokinoya Hiroshi, and Kaneko Isao. *Shakai no jōhōka to komyunikeeshon* (Information-oriented society and communication). Tokyo: Bureen Shuppan, 1995.

Matsuura Sozo. *Jaanarisuto to masukomi* (Journalists and mass communications). Tokyo: Ohtsuki Shoten, 1989.

———. *Masukomi no naka no tennō* (The emperor and the press). Tokyo: Ōtsuki Shoten, 1985.

———. ed. *Bungei shunjū no kenkyū: takaha jaanarizumu no shisō to ronri* (A study of "bungei shunju": The ideology and arguments of hawkish journalism). Tokyo: Banseisha, 1987.

Miliband, Ralph. *The State in Capitalist Society.* London: Weidenfeld & Nicolson, 1969.

Minotani Kazunari. *Hōsō-ron* (Broadcast studies). Tokyo: Gakuyo Shobo, 1992.

———, ed., *Nichijō seikatsu no masu medea* (The mass media in daily life). Tokyo: Chuo Daigaku Shuppanbu, 1991.

Mishima Akio. *Tate, fukutsu no pen* (Rise up, indomitable pen). Tokyo: Joho Centaa Shuppankyoku, 1991.

Mitchell, Richard H. *Censorship in Imperial Japan*. Princeton: Princeton University Press, 1983.

————. *Janus-faced Justice: Political Criminals in Imperial Japan.* University of Hawaii Press, 1992.

Miyagawa Takayoshi. *Senkyo no shikumi* (The election system). Tokyo: Nihon Jitsugyo Shuppansha, 1995.

Mizusawa Kei. *Kunshō seido ga Nihon o dame ni suru* (Imperial award system ruins Japan). Tokyo: Sanichi Shobo, 1996.

Mori Kyozo. *Watashi no Asahi shimbunshi* (My history of Asahi shimbun). Tokyo: Tabata Shoten, 1981.

NHK Hōsō Seron Chosasho, ed. *Seikatsu no naka no hōsō* (Broadcast in life). Tokyo: Nippon Hoso Shuppan Kyokai, 1992.

Najita, Tetsuo, and J. Victor Koschmann, ed. *Conflict in Modern Japanese History.* Princeton: Princeton University Press, 1982.

Nakayama Toshiaki. *Kikohi no migite* (Princess Kiko's right hand). Tokyo: Joho Centaa Shuppankyoku, 1992.

Namiki Nobuyoshi. *Nihon shakai no yuchaku kōzō* (Structure of cozy relationships in Japanese society). Tokyo: Sandoke Shuppankyoku, 1995.

Naminorisha, ed. *Yajiuma masu komi koza* (Yajiuma mass media seminar). Tokyo: Kōshobo, 1987.

Nanjo Takehiko. *Medea no shikumi: shimbun ni seiatsu sareru chihō terebi kyoku* (Structure of media: Local TV stations suppressed by the press). Tokyo: Akashi Shoten, 1996.

Nestor, William. "Japan's Mainstream Press: Freedom to Conform?" *Pacific Affairs* 62, 1 (Spring 1989): 29–39.

Nihon Jaanarisuto Kaigi, ed. *Masu komi no rekishi sekinin to mirai sekinin* (The mass media's responsibility for the past and the future). Tokyo: Kobunken, 1995.

Nihon Janarisuto Kaigi Shuppanshibu, ed.. *Me de miru shuppan janarizumu shoshi* (Visual history of the press journalism). Tokyo: Kobunken, 1989.

Nihon Kyosanto Chuoiinkai. *Hōsō no kōsei to shinjitsu o tō* (Pursuing fairness and truth in broadcasting). Tokyo: Nihon Kyosanto Chuoiinkai Shuppankyoku, 1994.

Nihon Seiji Gakkai, ed. *Gojūgo nen taisei no hōkai.* (The collapse of the 1955 system). Tokyo: Iwanami Shoten, 1996.

Nihon Shimbun Kyōkai. *Heisei 2-nendo Nihon Shimbun Kyōkai no katsudō* (The activities of the Japan Newspaper and Editors Association). Tokyo: Nihon Shimbun Kyōkai, 1990.

————. *The Japanese Press: 1990.* Tokyo: Nihon Shimbun Kyōkai, 1990.

————. *Nihon Shimbun Kyōkai Kenkyūjo nenpō,* No. 12, 1994. Tokyo: Nihon Shimbun Kyōkai Kenkyūjo, 1994.

————. ed. *Nihon Shimbun Kyōkai 10-nen shi* (A ten-year history of the NSK). Tokyo: Nihon Shimbun Kyōkai, 1955.

————. *Nihon Shimbun Kyōkai 50-nen shi* (A fifty-year history of the NSK). Tokyo: Nihon Shimbun Kyōkai, 1996.

————. *Shimbun kenkyū* (April 1965).

Nihon Shimbun Kyōkai. *Shimbun no shuzai* (Newspaper reporting), vol. 2. Tokyo: Nihon Shimbun Kyōkai, 1968.

Nihon Shimbun Kyōkai Kenkyūjo. *2000-nen no Shimbun: Shimbun medea no chū-chōki bijyon sōgo kenkyū hōkokushō* (Newspapers in the year 2000: The final report on the mid- to long-term vision for the newspaper media). Tokyo: Nihon Shimbun Kyōkai Kenkyujo, 1989.

————, ed., *Shimbun to chosakuken* (Newspaper and copyrights). Tokyo: Nihon Shimbun Kyōkai, 1993.

Nihon Shimbun Rodo Kumiai Shimbun Kenkyubu. *Shimbun ga abunai!* (Newspapers are dangerous). Tokyo: Banseisha, 1977.

Nihon Zasshi Kishakai. *Nihon Zasshi Kishakai 25-nenshi* (Twenty-five-year history of the Japan Magazine Publishers Association). Tokyo: Nihon Zasshi Kishakai, 1985.

————. *Kaiinsha hakkō zasshi ichiran* (Magazines issued by member companies). Tokyo: Nihon Zasshi Kyokai, 1993.

Nirasawa Tadao. *Masu komi shinkō no hatan* (The destruction of the mass media). Tokyo: Shiraishi Shoten, 1991.

Nishibe Susumu. *Masu komi bōkokuron: Nihon wa naze "iyashii kuni" ni natta no ka* (A theory on the national ruin of the media). Tokyo: Kobunsha, 1990.

————. *Masu medea o ute* (Attacking the Mass Media) Tokyo: PHP Kenkyūjō, 1991.

Nishiyama Takesuke. *Za riiku: Shimbun hōdō no ura-omote* (Both sides of news report leaks). Tokyo: Kodansha, 1992.

Nomura Hidekazu. *Nihon Terebi-Asahi Hōsō* (Nihon Terebi and Asahi Hōsō). Tokyo: Ohtsuki Shoten, 1990.

Norman, Herbert E. *Japan's Emergence as a Modern State: Political and Economic Problems of the Meiji Period.* New York: Institute of Pacific Relations, 1940.

Odagiri Makoto. *Terebi gyōkai no butai ura* (The behind scenes of the TV trade). Tokyo: Sanichi Shobo, 1994.

Odahashi Hiroyuki. *Kisha wa shindaka* (Is the reporter dead?). Tokyo: Banseisha, 1996.

Ogasawara Nobuyuki. *Shokugyō toshite no furii jaanarisuto* (Freelance journalism as a profession). Tokyo: Banseisha, 1996.

Oikawa Shoichi, ed. *Yasashii kokkai no hanashi* (A simple guide to the Diet). Tokyo: Hogaku Shoin, 1996.

————. *Yasashii senkyo no hanashi* (A simple guide to elections). Tokyo: Hogaku Shoin, 1996.

Okimoto, Daniel I. *Between MITI and the Market: Japanese Industrial Policy for High Technology.* Stanford: Stanford University Press, 1989.

Okuhara Toshiharu. *"Akahata" wa shōgyō shimbun to dō chigau ka* (What is the difference between "Akahata" and commercial newspapers?). Tokyo: Shin Nippon Shuppansha, 1992.

Oshita Eiji. *Hōdō sensō* (The broadcast war). Tokyo: Kodansha, 1995.

Ōtani Akihiro. *Shimbun kisha ga abunai* (Newspaper journalists are in danger). Tokyo: Asahi Sonorama, 1987.

Oyama Ryosuke (pseudonym for a journalist in the judicial club). "Bunya 'deiri kinshi' no fushigi." In *Za shimbun* (The newspaper). Edited by Ishii Masao. Tokyo: JICC Shuppankyoku, 1989.

Passin, Herbert. "Writer and Journalist in the Transitional Society." In *Communications and Political Development*. Edited by Lucian W. Pye. Princeton: Princeton University Press, 1963.

Pharr, Susan J., and Ellis Krauss, eds. *Media and Politics in Japan*. Honolulu: University of Hawaii Press, 1996.

Pierson, John D. *Tokutomi Sohō, 1863–1957: A Journalist for Modern Japan*. Princeton: Princeton University Press, 1980.

Powe, Lucas A. *The Fourth Estate and the Constitution: Freedom of the Press in America*. Berkeley: University of California Press, 1991.

Powell, Walter W., and Paul J. DiMaggio, eds. *The New Institutionalism in Organizational Analysis*. Chicago: University of Chicago Press, 1991.

Protess, David L., et al. *The Journalism of Outrage: Investigative Reporting and Agenda Building in America*. New York: Guilford Press, 1991.

Puresu nettowaaku 94. *Shimbun no ura mo omote mo wakaru hon* (A book about the ins and outs of newspapers). Tokyo: Kanki Shuppan, 1994.

Putnam, Robert D. *Making Democracy Work: Civic Traditions in Modern Italy*. Princeton: Princeton University Press, 1993.

Rakugakusha, ed. *Seifu kokkai kankōchō no shikumi* (The structure of the government, the Diet, and the bureaucracy). Tokyo: PHP Kenkyusho, 1996.

Regulations for Kitami Judicial Club, September 1987.

Reich, Michael R. "Crisis and Routine: Pollution Reporting by the Japanese Press." In *Institutions for Change in Japanese Society*. Edited by George DeVos. Berkeley: Institute of East Asian Studies, 1984.

Ritchie, Donald A. *Press Gallery: Congress and the Washington Correspondents*. London: Harvard University Press, 1991.

Ronsō (November 1996). Tokyo: Toyokeizai, 1996.

Ronsō (January 1997). Tokyo: Toyokeizai, 1997.

Roy, Elizabeth. *Look Japan* (September 1991).

Sabato, Larry J. *Feeding Frenzy: How attack Journalism Has Transformed American Politics*. New York: Free Press, 1991.

Samuels, Richard J. *The Business of the Japanese State: Energy Markets in Comparative and Historical Perspective*. Ithaca: Cornell University Press, 1987.

Sarada Shuhei. *Kutabare! Kabushikigaisha Asahi Shimbun* (Go to Hell! Asahi Shimbun). Fukuoka: Insaido, 1995.

Sato Takeshi. *Nihon no medea to shakai shinri* (Japanese mass media and social psychology). Tokyo: Shinyosha, 1995.

Sato Tomoyuki. *Kyokō no hōdō: hanzai hōdō no jittai* (Fabricated news: The real state of criminal reporting). Tokyo: Sanichi Shobo, 1990.

Sato Tsugio. *Terebi medea to Nihon jin* (TV media and the Japanese). Tokyo: Suzusawa Shoten, 1994.

Scalapino, Robert A. *Democracy and the Party Movement in Prewar Japan: The Failure of the First Attempt*. Berkeley: University of California Press, 1967.

Scherer, F. M. *Industrial Market Structure and Economic Performance*. Chicago: Rand McNally, 1970.

Schudson, Michael *Discovering the News: A Social History of American Newspapers*. New York: Basic Books, 1978.

Schwartz, Frank. "Of Fairy Cloaks and Familiar Talks: The Politics of Consultation in Japan," unpublished paper, Japan Society, 1991.

Scott, Richard W. *Organizations: Rational, Natural and Open Systems.* New Jersey: Prentice-Hall, 1987.

Seaton, Jean, and Ben Pimlott, eds. *The Media in British Politics.* Aldershot: Avebury, 1987.

Sendenkaigi. *Masukomi denwachō 1994-han* (Mass media telephone directory, 1994 edition). Tokyo: Sendenkaigi Shinsha, 1993.

Seymour-Ure, Colin. *The Press, Politics and the Public: An Essay on the Role of the National Press in the British Political System.* London: Methuen, 1968).

Shibuya Shigemitsu. *Jaanarizumu no ishiki* (Journalism awareness). Tokyo: Bureen Shuppan, 1989.

Shibuya Shigemitsu. *Taishū sōsa no keifu* (The origins of mass control). Tokyo: Keiso Shobo, 1991.

Shima Nobuhiko. *Medea kage no kenryokusha tachi* (The hidden powers behind the mass media). Tokyo: Kodansha, 1995.

Shimbun Hōdō Kenkyōkai. *Ima Shimbun o kangaeru* (Studying the press today). Tokyo: Nihon Shimbun Kyokai Kenkyujo, 1995.

Shimbun Kenkyū Dōjinkai. *Shimbun handobukku* (Newspaper handbook). Tokyo: Dabiddosha, 1990.

Shimbun Roren, ed. *Shimbunkisha o kangaeru* (Studying newspaper reporters). Tokyo: Banseisha, 1994.

Shimbun Roren Shimbun Kenkyūbu, ed. *Shimbun ga abunai!* (Newspapers are in danger!). Tokyo: Banseisha, 1977.

Shimizu Hideo. *Masu media no jiyū to sekinin* (The freedom and responsibilities of the mass media). Tokyo: Sanseido, 1993.

———. *Terebi to kenryoku* (TV and power). Tokyo: Sanshodo, 1995.

Shimizu Hideo et al., eds. *Seiji rinri to shiru kenri* (Political ethics and the right to know). Tokyo: Sanshodo, 1992.

Shimizu Katabumi, *Shimbun no himitsu* [Newspaper Secrets] (Tokyo: Nihon Hyoronsha, 1982).

Sigal, Leon V. *Reporters and Officials: The Organization and Politics of Newsmaking.* Lexington, Mass.: D. C. Heath, 1973.

Skocpol, Theda. "Bringing the State Back In: Strategies of Analysis in Current Research." In *Bringing the State Back In.* Edited by Peter B. Evans, Dietrich Rueschemeyer, and Theda Skocpol. Cambridge: Cambridge University Press, 1985.

Smith, Adam. *The Wealth of Nations.* Middlesex: Penguin Books, 1985.

Smith, Anthony, ed. *Newspapers and Democracy: International Essays on a Changing Medium.* Cambridge: MIT Press, 1980.

———. *Television: An International History,* 2d ed. New York: Oxford University Press, 1998.

Smith, Hedrick, ed. *The Media and the Gulf War: The Press and Democracy in Wartime.* Washington, D.C.: Seven Locks Press, 1992.

Sōgō janarizumu kenkyū, no. 116, special edition: "Kisha kurabu no kōzai" The merits and demerits of the press clubs). Tokyo: Tokyosha, 1986.

Sōgō janarizumu kenkyū, no. 158. Tokyo: Tokyosha, Autumn 1996.

Somucho. *Shingikai sōran* (A survey of Shingikai). Tokyo: Okurasho Shuppan-kyoku, 1986.

Squires, James D. *Read All About It: The Corporate Takeover of America's Newspapers.* New York: Times Books, 1993.

Steinmo, Sven, Kathlen Thelen, and Frank Longstreth, eds. *Structuring Politics: Historical Institutionalism in Comparative Analysis.* Cambridge: Cambridge University Press, 1992.

Stepan, Alfred C. *The State and Society: Peru in Comparative Perspective.* Princeton: Princeton University Press, 1978.

Summers, Mark Wahlgren. *The Press Gang: Newspapers and Politics: 1865–1878.* Chapel Hill: University of North Carolina Press, 1994.

Suzuki Kazue. "The Press Club System in Japan." M.S. thesis, Iowa State University, 1982.

Suzuki Kenji. *Nichibei kiki to hōdō* (News coverage and the U.S.–Japan crisis). Tokyo: Iwanami Shoten, 1992.

———. "Nihon no shimbun: Aimai hyōgen jijō" (Japanese newspapers: A case of vague phrasing). *Shimbun kenkyū* (May 1990).

Tachio Ryoji. *Ozawa wachingu* (Ozawa watching). Tokyo: Tokyo Shimbun Shup-pankyoku, 1995.

Tahara Soichiro. *Boku dake no shuzai nōto* (My personal interview notes). Tokyo: Chuo Koron, 1985.

Takasaki Ryuji. *Senjika no janarizumu* (Wartime journalism). Tokyo: Shinnippon Shuppansha, 1987.

———. *Zasshi medea no sensō sekinin* (The wartime responsibility of magazine journalism). Tokyo: Daisan Bumeisha, 1995.

Tamaki Akira. *Nyūsu hōdō no gengoron* (The linguistics of newspaper reporting). Tokyo: Yosensha, 1996.

Tamura Norio and Hayashi Toshitaka, eds. *Jaanarizumu o manabu hito no tameni* (For those who study journalism). Tokyo: Sekaishisosha, 1996.

Tanaka Hiroshi. *Hasegawa Nyōzekan kenkyū josetsu* (An introduction to research on Hasegawa Nyōzekan). Tokyo: Miraisha, 1991.

Taniguchi Akio. *Shimbun ga kieta!* (A newspaper disappears). Tokyo: Fubaisha, 1989.

Tase Yasuhiro. *Seiji jaanarizumu no tsumi to batsu* (The crime and punishments of political journalism). Tokyo: Shinchosha, 1994.

Tatesawa Koji. *Terebi no "yarase" o tsuku* (Opposing television deception). Tokyo: Nisshin hodo, 1993.

Terebi Asahi Shuppanbu, ed. *Gekiron: masu komi & jaanarizumu* (Debate: Mass communications and journalism). Tokyo: Terebi Asahi, 1989.

Thayer, Nathaniel B. "Competition and Conformity: An Inquiry into the Structure of the Japanese Newspapers." In *Modern Japanese Organization and Decision-making.* Edited by Ezra F. Vogel. Berkeley: University of California Press, 1975.

Tilton, Mark. *Restrained Trade: Cartels in Japan's Basic Materials Industries.* Ithaca: Cornell University Press, 1996.

Tokyo Bengoshikai, ed. *Shuzai sareru gawa no kenri.* The human rights of those covered by the press). Tokyo: Nihon Hyoronsha, 1991.

Tokyo News Service Ltd. *Political Handbook of Japan: 1949.* Tokyo: Tokyo News Service, 1949.

Tsuchiya Michio. *Hōdō wa shinjitsu ka?* (Is press coverage truthful?). Tokyo: Kokushohan Gyokai, 1994.

Tunstall, Jeremy. *The Westminster Lobby Correspondents: A Sociological Study of National Political Journalism.* London: Routledge & Kegan Paul, 1970.

Uchikawa Yoshimi and Naoyuki Arai. *Nihon no jaanarizumu* (Japanese journalism). Tokyo: Yubikaku, 1983.

Uchikawa Yoshimi and Yanai Michio, eds. *Masu medea to kokusai kankei: Nihon Kankoku Chugoku no kokusai hikaku* (The mass media and international relations: Japan, Korea, and China). Tokyo: Gakubunsha, 1994.

Upham, Frank K. *Law and Social Change in Postwar Japan.* Cambridge: Harvard University Press, 1987.

van Wolferen, Karel. *The Enigma of Japanese Power: People and Politics in a Stateless Nation.* London: Macmillan, 1989.

Verba, Sidney, et al. *Elites and the Idea of Equality: A Comparison of Japan, Sweden and the United States.* Cambridge: Harvard University Press, 1987.

Wada Chitose. *Terebi wa nani o tsutaete iruka* (What does TV report?). Tokyo: Shinchosha, 1996.

Watanabe Shigeo. *Toshokan no jiyū o kangaeru* (Researching library freedom). Tokyo: Seikyusha, 1996.

Watanabe Takesato. *Medea riterashii* (Media literacy). Tokyo: Daiamondosha, 1997.

Weaver, Paul. "The New Journalism and the Old—Thoughts after Watergate." *Public Interest* (Spring 1974): 67–88.

Weber, Max. *The Theory of Social and Economic Organization.* Translated by A. M. Henderson and Talcott Parsons, edited by Talcott Parsons. New York: Free Press, 1964.

Wellman, Barry. "Structural Analysis: From Method and Metaphor to Theory and Substance." In *Social Structures: A Network Approach.* Edited by Barry Wellman and S. D. Berkowitz. Cambridge: Cambridge University Press, 1988.

Westney, D. Eleanor. *Imitation and Innovation: The Transfer of Western Organizational Patterns to Meiji Japan.* Cambridge: Harvard University Press, 1987.

Wildes, Harry Emerson. "Press Freedom in Japan." *American Journal of Sociology* 32, 4 (January 1927): 601–13.

———. *Social Currents in Japan, with Special Reference to the Press.* Chicago: University of Chicago Press, 1927.

Xhao, Yuezhi. *Media, Market and Democracy in China: Between the Party Line and the Bottom Line.* Chicago: University of Illinois Press, 1998.

Yamaguchi Jiro, Ishikawa Masumi, and Jibo Tetsuo. *Masu komi to seji wa shimin ni manabe* (The mass media and politicians should learn from the people). Tokyo: Honnoki, 1995.

Yamakawa Tsutomu. *Shimbun no jiko kisei* (Newspaper self-censorship). Tokyo: Miraisha, 1984.

Yamamoto Fumio. *Nihon masu komyunikēshyonshi* (A history of Japanese mass communications). Tokyo: Tokai Daigaku Shuppankai, 1989.

Yamamoto Hiroshi. *Taiken-teki chōsa hōdō* (Personal experience in investigative reporting). Tokyo: Yubi-sha, 1990.

Yamamoto Jiro. *Seiji kaikaku* (Political reform). Tokyo: Iwanami Shinsho, 1993.

Yamamoto Taketoshi. *Kindai Nihon no shimbun dokushasō* (The newspaper readership of modern Japan). Tokyo: Hosei Daigaku Shuppankyoku, 1989.

———. "The Press Clubs of Japan." *Journal of Japanese Studies* 15, 2 (Summer 1989): 371–88.

———. *Shimbun kisha no tanjō: Nihon no medea o tsukutta hitobito* (The birth of newspaper journalists: The people who created the Japanese media). Tokyo: Shinyosha, 1991.

———. *Shimbun to minshū* (Newspapers and democracy). Tokyo: Kinokuniya Shinsho, 1994.

Yamashita Kunitsugu. *Nihongata jaanarizumu* (Japanese-style journalism). Fukuoka: Kyushu Daigaku Shuppankai, 1996.

Yayama, Tarō. "The Newspapers Conduct a Mad Rhapsody over the Textbook Issue." *Journal of Japanese Studies* 9, 2 (Spring 1983).

Yokota Hajime. *Terebi to seiji* (TV and politics). Tokyo: Suzusawa Shoten, 1996.

Yonehara Ken and Doi Mitsuo, eds. *Seiji to shimin no genzai* (Politics and the citizenship today). Tokyo: Horitsu Bunkasha, 1995.

Yomiuri Shimbunsha Seijibu, ed. *Matsurigoto* (Politics). Tokyo: Yomiuri Shimbunsha, 1996.

Index